THE MODERN NOVEL
Volume 1

Modern Languages and Literature

Literature Editor
J. M. COHEN

THE MODERN NOVEL

Volume 1
ENGLAND AND FRANCE

Paul West

HUTCHINSON UNIVERSITY LIBRARY
LONDON

HUTCHINSON & CO (*Publishers*) LTD
178–202 Great Portland Street, London W1

London Melbourne Sydney
Auckland Bombay Toronto
Johannesburg New York

First published 1963
Second edition 1965
Reprinted 1967

This book has been set in Times, printed in Great Britain
on Smooth Wove paper by Anchor Press, and
bound by Wm. Brendon, both of Tiptree, Essex

To

Jan and Freddy Bateson

Acknowledgments

I gratefully make acknowledgments to the editors of the following, in which portions of this book have appeared in rather different form: the Canadian Broadcasting Corporation's series 'University of the Air'; the *Hibbert Journal*, the *Kenyon Review*, the *London Magazine*, *New World Writing*, *The Times Literary Supplement* and the *Weekly Post*. I owe a special debt of gratitude to Walter Allen and Janet Adam Smith for letting me write about novels for the *New Statesman*. I am hoping now to find the time to write a volume about the Commonwealth novel, for which there was unfortunately no room here.

For permission to use copyright material I am indebted to the following: Mr James Baldwin for an extract from *Nobody Knows My Name* to be published by Michael Joseph Ltd next year; The Owner of the Copyright for an extract from *The Journals of Arnold Bennett*; The Bodley Head Ltd for an extract from *Ulysses* by James Joyce; Chatto & Windus Ltd for extracts from *Intruder in the Dust* and *The Mansion* by William Faulkner, and C. K. Scott Moncrieff's translation of *Swann's Way* by Marcel Proust; Mr Lawrence Durrell and Faber & Faber Ltd for extracts from *The Alexandria Quartet*; Hamish Hamilton Ltd for an extract from *Resistance, Rebellion and Death* by Albert Camus; Mr L. P. Hartley and Hamish Hamilton Ltd for an extract from *A Perfect Woman*; The Harvill Press Ltd for extracts from *The Trial Begins* by 'Abram Tertz'; The Executors of the Ernest Hemingway Estate and Jonathan Cape Ltd for extracts from *A Farewell to Arms*, *For Whom the Bell Tolls* and 'The Killers'; Mr Hans Hofman and Harper & Row Publishers Inc. for an extract from *Religion and Mental Health*; Mr Aldous Huxley and Chatto & Windus Ltd for extracts from *Crome Yellow*; Mr John O'Hara and The Cresset Press for an extract from *From the Terrace*; Mr John Osborne and David Higham Associates Ltd for an extract from an article in *The Observer*, October 30, 1960; Mr Alan Sillitoe for an extract from *The Loneliness of the Long Distance Runner*; The Society of Authors for an extract from *Finnegans Wake* by James Joyce; Mr Leonard Woolf for extracts from *Modern Fiction* and *The Waves* by Virginia Woolf.

I wish to thank the many people who have discussed with and read for me various sections of the book, especially George Story and Basil Kingstone and, not least because he gave me a free hand, J. M. Cohen, who asked me to write this book. Judith Layman deciphered ingeniously and typed valiantly and the library staff of the Memorial University of Newfoundland, as well as the students of English 220, helped enormously. I am grateful too to Alastair Macdonald for the loan of his typewriter and to him again, as to Bryan Reardon and J. M. Cohen, for the use of books. While I was preparing the manuscript for press, Charles Mann and Allan Landry made contributions, of knowledge and time and effort, well beyond any call of friendship, and I thank them deeply once again here. Any errors and shortcomings are mine, not in any sense theirs.

Finally, I wish to acknowledge the assistance and encouragement given so generously by the John Simon Guggenheim Foundation while I was working on the second draft. Such a book as this necessarily becomes a strenuous co-operative effort, and I am grateful to all those people, known to me by name or not, who have contributed to the book's eventual making.

P.W.

Contents

PART FOUR: OTHER COUNTRIES

Preface

As Sir Desmond McCarthy remarked, the novel is usually thought of as satisfying our curiosity rather than our craving for beauty, meaning or significance. And curiosity, as we know, demands information. The great novelists of the past had therefore to supply a convincingly selective kind of information—simply to show that they knew what they were talking about. Not surprisingly, they resented falling short of, or having to go beyond, immediate social actualities. But the novel of social manners satisfies us only so long as our curiosity remains social; once we begin to look at society with other kinds of curiosity, we need a completer type of novel. I do not say: 'We need the poem or the philosophical system', although of course it is true that the poem specializes in inwardness and the philosophical system in man's cosmic place. No: when we need inwardness and cosmic place *related to man-in-society* we still have to go to the novel or to what 'the novel' has now become; for the novelist has been quicker than the poet or the philosopher to borrow *their* specialities than they have to borrow his.

The novel of manners gave us social man; and when some experimental writers introduced the stream of consciousness into the novel of manners they began to satisfy a second curiosity and, indeed, to create a new type of hero: self-absorbed and rather ineffectual. A third curiosity remained—not social, not subjective, but in the widest sense religious: 'What is man's place in Nature?'

This study sketches the fortunes of these three types of curiosity. I am primarily concerned with the novelist's effort to bring psychology back into proportion with manners, and to augment these two with a view of man in the abstract. The effort has

xi

varied in resoluteness and success according to national and
personal circumstances; but it is, I think, generally true that
novelists cannot escape the stream of consciousness. Either they
ostentatiously ignore it or they introduce it under the auspices of
some theory of 'identity'. It is there, like society: there for all of
us; and it is there in an additional way, for some novelists,
because it is the stock-in-trade of the anti-hero who now typifies
powerless, anti-social man. In other words, the stream was not
(as certain ways of recording it were) a fad; it was a discovery
which has been renewed in significance by novelists who have
lost faith in society and therefore also in the novel as social
portraiture. And the anti-hero—both unsocial and introverted—
tends to brood on his cosmic predicament. The anti-novel, so-
called, reflects the novelist's sympathy with his own anti-heroes.

So there are new forms, new concerns, some of them as old as
the hills. On the one hand there is the novel as an instrument
of metaphysical defiance; on the other, as an old-fashioned
chronicle. The one loses itself in surface minutiae or 'pre-thought';
the other tries to express faith in society by watching manners.
One type, so near to poetry and self-indulgence, looks effete; the
other, extroverted and unphilosophical and unreligious, looks
narrowly robust. The first is common in France and Spain, the
second in England, Italy and Russia. The German and American
novel have something of both, perhaps because bewilderment
is extreme in those countries. When the novelist has to choose
between the absurd universe and the absurd society, or between
those and the absurdity of being wholly inward, he might well be
excused for playing ingenious little games of texture. We are
eventually reminded that the world of art is a substitute world,
devised out of impatience with the 'real' world. And that world of
art is valuable to us only because its limitations are *not* those of
the 'real' one.

I open with a general section which bears equally on most of
the ensuing matter. This means that, to some extent, I save myself
repetition, but also that, to make the book really useful, I ought
to supply a postscript volume of 200 pages or so. All I can do is to
ask the reader who reads to the end to re-read Part One and to
resist thinking of all the names and novels I have decided or
forgotten to include. Rather than pretend to any encyclopaedic

sophistication, I want to communicate something of the adventure of comparing one national tradition with another. I have juxtaposed the English and the French novel in Part Two because they began the century by mutually interacting to some purpose. For the rest, I have discussed what to me seems most worth while. In the chapter on Soviet Russia I have transliterated the titles and, where possible, supplied an accepted translation of them (unless that translation seemed unduly imaginative). In the latter instance I have tried to be literal while still remaining within English. The dates in parentheses refer to the original date of Russian publication although it may look as if they refer to the dates of translations. It seemed to me that the reader, after looking at a transliteration of the Russian, would need the reassurance of a meaning of sorts rather than a date, and that is why the dates follow the English versions. For the rest, reasons of space beyond my own control have kept out translation of titles. The enterprising reader will, I hope, forgive me if he has to use his dictionaries as much as I did.

P.W.

The ancient hero was one who confronted death; the modern hero is one who accepts life.

(*Ardengo Soffici*)

A novel will be all the higher and nobler in kind, in direct proportion to how much it presents inner and how little outer life. . . .

(*Schopenhauer*)

. . . the modern novel seems less and less to analyse its characters in their moments of crisis. . . .

(*André Malraux*)

PART ONE

Flux

I

The limits

Two main themes, neither clearly separable from the other, run through the debate about flux. First: is it possible to give anything like a *full* account of human experience? Second: what *is* it that has experience? The first inquiry tempts the novelist into ambitious realism—necessarily a hopeless quest because no novelist undertaking it would have time to lead his own life. Albert Camus, asking whether complete realism is possible, put this neatly in *Resistance, Rebellion and Death*:

> What is there more real, for instance, in our universe than a man's life, and how can we hope to preserve it better than in a realistic film? But under what conditions is such a film possible? Under purely imaginary conditions. We should have to presuppose, in fact, an ideal camera focused on the man day and night and constantly registering his every move. The very projection of such a film would last a lifetime and could be seen only by an audience of people willing to waste their lives in watching someone else's life in great detail.

The only realistic artist, he concludes, is God: a metaphysical guess no wilder than the quest for complete realism. Obviously, art of any kind has sooner or later to admit its limitations. But it is extraordinary how resolutely several experimental novelists tried to dodge that fact, pretending that art is not a pretence. And when a full catalogue proved impracticable they still cherished their ambitions for realism, but this time in terms of the self.

Where the catalogue is impossible the epitome might be managed: the typical self of a man, the loose formula of his mental habits, could suggest both the nature of experience and

3

the distorting role of the perceiving mind. Hence the relentless realist was obliged to turn his attention upon the mind, upon mental privacy. And it has taken a long time for novelists to realize that even the interior flux and a fictional account of how one person experiences his own flux conflict with the nature of art. Just as C. P. Snow cannot possibly give an exhaustive account of Lewis Eliot's life, so the stream of consciousness cannot possibly be set down in words: it can only be mimicked, symbolized, hinted at. And it is no defence to say that the stream of a fictional character cannot be anything but what his creator intends; for fiction's main claim to our interest is that it refers to our own lives. There must therefore be some correspondence between the simulations of the novel and our own knowledge of ourselves. The novelist is obliged to copy; where he cannot copy accurately he must suggest and constantly refer his readers to experience held in common. It is no use the novelist's claiming: 'Your criticism of character X is unfair; I created him; I know exactly what his stream of consciousness is like; the fact that you find his stream unlike what you know of your own is irrelevant. I *know*; you are merely seeking information from me.' It is no use because we shall only care about X if he has something in common with ourselves; and to object to the improbability of the interior flux is not the same as objecting to the novelist's devices for simulating it.

The novelist who would argue as above is the one who eventually uses the stream as an excuse for extravaganza in its own right. But the stream is not a *carte blanche*; rather, it is a phenomenon which reminds us of art's essential make-believe; and, as such, it ought to make the novelist discipline himself all the more rather than let himself go. Art, after all, is not a letting-go but a search for what is fitting. Unless it is undertaken merely as a private venture, like sleep or physical exercise, it will have to be double in nature, with imitation always curbing self-indulgence.

So there was, even in a novel as mildly experimental as George Moore's *The Brook Kerith* (1916), an obvious interaction between the quest for realism and the limits of art. Moore washes his matter along in style's fluid; inner and outer are made to merge, much as in Pater's *Marius the Epicurean*. The indefinite self, absorbing and transmuting events in the outside world, is the subject; but it is a subject which, more than any other, must suffer from art's double nature; an absolute imitation of this subject is impossible without excessive self-indulgence on the part of the artist. We find, in fact, that to attempt to present reality as an inward thing, personal to each one of us, is to get lost in oneself; and the resulting confusion, between subjectivity as subject-matter and subjectivity as method, wrecks the discipline essential to art. The farther the novelist gets from make-believe (which is really a selective account of reality), the less can he expect readers to regard his offering as a work of art. For art is strain, forcing, distortion, shorthand, symbolism; it is worth having, precisely because it is not life; and to pretend that what one is inventing is not make-believe is simply to fall short of life and to throw away one of the most enjoyable human pastimes.

These objections probably sound middlebrow and dull. One feels like a referee, offering rules during a muddled game in the dark. The players ought to blow their own whistles; after all, the nature of art is fixed in terms of impossibility. If art could be made indistinguishable from life, then art would not be worth creating anyway. One of the most seductive features of the novel is that no matter how vividly we may experience a fiction we can always withdraw from it. We are not committed to the fiction in the same way as we are committed to our jobs, our temperaments and sinuses. All very well to speak of being held or gripped by what we are reading: that experience is delicious because we know we can, if we wish, opt out of it at once. We may not be able to efface the impact of what we have been reading; but, then, it has come to us in the form of 'safe' experience. To be harrowed by a novel is not the same as being harrowed by life. If I read a ghost story and feel scared I can do much more about that kind of scare than I can about the kind I get when I actually do see, or think I see, a ghost. Fiction always, and even on the lowest level, presents experience as an idea: something reaching us primarily through a mind; something already controlled mentally. In life we tend to say that things happen, and that we then start thinking about them. It is fiction's nature to offer us the vicarious and the already-experienced; if it tries to evade its nature it slips down the slope leading into the Valley of the Shadow of Charade in which lies the last and worst no-novel: open the book and it becomes a 'feelie'-serial. When the hero yawns you can smell his breath: an electronic device in the book's spine arranges all this. When the hero swims he splashes the reader. When he has indigestion we too have to reach for our tablets. And so on. This way lies the meta-novel, not a book at all, but a vast structure many times more complicated than a cyclotron and no more portable. To what end? Why not admit that art is the savouring of limitation? Why not accept the novel as a simulated excerpt? If we refuse to do these things we are throwing away a whole human heritage in a mad quest for pointless ingenuity.

So the nature of human awareness is, as anyone can see, the very theme which tempts the novelist to ignore what he knows of art's limitations. And it is not fanciful to see in the experiments of those writers concerned with the flux a weird hope that, with the theme fully explored and stated, the right technique finally emerges. But the limitations of art do not disappear as our knowledge increases; art may be subjected to different limitations, but it will always have limitations of a sort. It is always a deliberate construction and it is essentially parasitical. It can refer as much as it likes; it can allude, mention and suggest. But for obvious reasons it cannot achieve underivedness, whereas that quality is universal in life. Life is derived from nothing else; fiction, although a part of the life we lead, is essentially derivative.

These remarks apply not only to those who pioneered the stream-novel but also to the philosophers and thinkers who first explored the new terrain. William James, writing on 'The Stream of Thought' in his *Principles of Psychology* (1890), tried to establish some kind of formula; instead he found only a mercurial flux and a 'teeming multiplicity of objects and relations'. So he proposed the terms 'river' and 'stream': the human consciousness defies the formula-maker, just as the human personality refuses to become more than a permutation or fusion of many selves. And to read James on these matters is to sense his irritation as well as his awe. The systematic mind is baffled; well, if it is, then surely here is an important fact about experience and about our ways of describing it. Everything threatens to dissolve, and man's precious ability to control becomes merely the capacity to undergo. Coherence, like art, is an illusion, and so art itself is likely to be regarded as either necessarily bogus (which it is) or necessarily chaotic (which it should be only limitedly). One can see why C. P. Snow has stressed the importance of chapter-titles: the reader must know what is going on. Art is meant to enlighten us, not to increase the chances of chaos.

But the picture has another side; it takes us back to the double nature of art. If the novelist is going to copy life he must copy it as accurately as he can; if, at the same time, he is going to indulge himself (and his readers) he must indulge himself as satisfyingly as he can. The two aims are compatible; but so often in the novels of those pioneers Dorothy Richardson, Joyce, Virginia Woolf and Ford Madox Ford the copier assumes too much chaos and the self-indulgence makes the chaos too personal. E. M. Forster's emphasis on the 'fertile muddle', Dos Passos's miscellanies in montage and Lawrence Durrell's relativistic universe are milder versions, all of them manipulated with knowing art. What tempted the first flux novelists and intoxicated Bergson and intrigued William James was the dominance of chaos. Man's appetite for order seemed a puny thing by comparison with a vast, teeming universe of inexhaustible supply. It is odd to read James and Bergson, giving up the formula habit, in conjunction with thinkers who have had the chance to digest all the new views of chaos. Hans Hofman, for instance, of the Harvard Divinity School, writes in his *Religion and Mental Health*:

It was only natural that Sigmund Freud should at the beginning of his career have thought of the irrational aspects of the human personality as chaotic and potentially dangerous powers. . . . It did not occur to him that chaos itself may represent a very positive and fertile current of life. For the people of the Old Testament, especially in the creation story, the question was not: 'Why is there chaos?' but rather 'Why is there order?' For them, order was the outgrowth of daily living. . . . The unique function of man, in their view, is to live in close, creative touch with chaos, and thereby experience the birth of order . . . Surprisingly enough, modern psychotherapists share this ancient knowledge.

James and Bergson overstress the streamingness of life; 'duration' is held in the memory, it is true, but so are clear and abiding axioms. They both undervalue not the efficacy of the analytical intellect but its value as a comforter. Their theories celebrate impotence and passivity; here, perhaps, is the beginning of the unheroic hero who is no more than a full consciousness. And for fear we have to look to Freud; to him chaos is dangerous, whereas, in fact, it is a ferment which surprisingly enough creates possibilities of order. We have only to consider the number of things that can go wrong between the conception and birth of a child, and to compare the possibilities of chaos there with the number of people who 'live in close, creative touch with chaos' through having babies, and we can guess at the average man's estimate of chaos. That a process of such appalling complication so rarely goes wrong is a miracle, but a commonplace one. And the novelist who ignores such a fact, stressing the complexity more than the eventual order, is betraying his trust. He is not copying accurately. Order sometimes just happens; at other times men create it. Either way, the novelist cannot afford to ignore it.

It is only too easy to create a character who has no identity beyond what happens to him or who has no experience save what he projects from his own head. These are exaggerated accounts of recognizable aspects of our human condition. To repudiate both is not, however, to ignore the nature of consciousness or the personal nature of experience. Neither the wholly inchoate nor the wholly conceptualized tallies with what we know of life; the trouble was that at the turn of the nineteenth century the inchoate had not had a run for its money in either abstract thought or the novel. No wonder the flux flooded over everything. No wonder everything soon became a blur.

But neither William James nor Bergson was the first to hit on the stream idea. Chekhov had mastered the art of articulating deliquescent moods; he based his stories not on what Bergson repudiated as 'concepts' but on emotional transitions, sea-changes and upheavals. Dostoevsky, having plunged into the abyss of himself, had emerged with a profound sense of the mind's complexity, of its demoralizing arbitrariness and of the role of accident in human affairs. All these—complexity, arbitrariness and accident—helped him to a view of man as a fusion of pawn, *poseur* and chameleon. What we find in Dostoevsky is not so much the flux as the (literally) infernal complexity of every human condition. He makes special studies of schizophrenia and bewilderment, demonstrating how deliberate an effort we have to make in order to relate the mercurial and the intricate to any code. Some codes he finds impracticable, but he does stress the need to try for order. Where Dostoevsky plunges in, Chekhov tracks and traces. Turgenev, however, evolves a system of notation in which to convey the mental flux; and a few words about him will not be out of place here, for he has never been given much credit for his innovation.

Henry James called him 'the novelist's novelist', and that label, seeming to relegate the Russian to a status of exquisite debility—to a perfection more illustrious than this world can stomach—has done its damage. Critics have accepted it and handed it on. And Turgenev, having called one of his books *A Sportman's Sketches*, is generally taken for a lightweight. Even his concern with politics has been eased out of the *persona* with which the critics have fitted him: that is, the master-miniaturist, the minor poet of the minor idyll, the chef of classical froth, the anti-Tolstoy. In fact, none of this is true. Turgenev was a pioneer and an experimenter who supplied foundations for both Tolstoy and Dostoevsky. He cared very much about 'delicacy of proportion', but his scrutiny of life was direct and unflinching.

Here, from *Smoke* (1867), is Litvinov, deep in a Chekhovian reverie in which the recurring 'smoke-motif' strengthens our sense of his mind's caducity. This is the kind of vision we find time and again in the works of Nathalie Sarraute (*Le Planétarium*, say) and Michel Butor (whose *La Modification* gives us a twenty-four-hour train journey). Turgenev conducts it all, however, in the manner we associate with Proust; there are no verbal alchemies here:

He gazed and gazed, and suddenly a strange reflection came into his mind. . . . He was alone in the compartment; there was no one to disturb him. 'Smoke, smoke,' he repeated several times: and it suddenly occurred to him that everything was smoke: everything—his own life, Russian life, everything human, especially everything Russian. 'All is vapour and smoke,' he thought; 'all seems to change continually, everywhere new forms appear, events follow upon events, but at bottom all is the same; everything hurries, hastens somewhere—and everything disappears without a trace, attaining nothing; the wind changes—and everything rushes in the opposite direction, and there the same unceasing, restless, and futile game begins again.' He recalled much that had happened with clamour and commotion before his eyes of late years. . . . 'Smoke,' he whispered, 'smoke.' He recalled the heated arguments, shouts, and discussions at Gubaryov's and at other people's, young and old, humble and highly placed, advanced and reactionary. . . . 'Smoke,' he repeated, 'vapour and smoke.' He recalled at last the memorable picnic, recalled other speeches and pronouncements of other would-be statesmen—and even all that Potugin had preached . . . smoke, smoke, and nothing more. And what of his own strivings and feelings and endeavours and dreams? He merely made a gesture of despair.

And meanwhile the train ran on and on. . . .

(Chapter 26)

This version of isolated, brooding man is significant in two ways: it does, of course, give an early version of the stream-device; but it also reminds us that Turgenev was particularly concerned with the nature of experience polarized between exile and immersion. In his *Literary Reminiscences* he burned to prove himself both native son and justified exile. He tried not to think in French, found his homeland painfully exotic and was distressed by the obloquy with which it greeted *Fathers and Sons* and *Smoke*. He excelled at, and suffered for, being neutral.

In *Smoke* he poked fun at both factions; he could assume almost any allegiance, and laugh at it. Surely he is the most agile of his own 'superfluous' men, belonging with Rudin and Lavretsky. Primarily a devoted artist, he creates a great deal of landscape: he is not quite sure who he is; he feels that his own identity is not inevitable enough. He can be too many things to be just one consistently, and he finds the landscape, the weather, as variable as his multiple self. Essentially he is *déraciné*, too much so to be a steady political thinker. For him the civilized melancholy of a doomed social class was but another instance of the universe's blind shuffling of human destinies. We have for too long been misled by the sheer order he created in the Russian novel; for that

order was his not entirely effectual protest against the human
condition—not a means of shirking. His protest included a
carpe diem; seize the day before Saturn gobbles it up. It was only
natural that, before William James and Bergson, he should have
created means of expressing inwardness and, before Tolstoy and
Dostoevsky, a model of the novel as a craftly document. No
wonder that, torn as he was, he often wrote melodramatically
when at his most fluent. The sense of the abyss, of life streaming on
and away while his characters thought about it, bursts into such
wildly associative passages as the following, again from *Smoke*:

> He had dismissed without a thought all his reasonable,
> well-ordered, respectable future; he knew that he was flinging
> himself headlong into a whirlpool which was not safe even to
> look at . . . but it was not this that troubled him. That was
> settled and done with, but how was he to appear before his
> judge? And if he really were to meet a judge—an angel with a
> flaming sword—it would be easier for the guilty heart . . . but it
> was he himself who would have to plunge the knife in. . . .
> Hideous! But to go back, to renounce the other, to take advan-
> tage of the freedom that was promised to him and recognized
> as his due. . . . No, he'd rather die! No, he didn't want that
> hateful freedom . . . but he'd gladly sink into the dust if only
> those eyes would look down with love.
>
>   (Chapter 19)

That appeared in 1867. The method of it is not new to us. We
have, of course, to distinguish carefully between soliloquy and
written musing, between what is said to an interlocutor and what
is supposedly overheard by a theatre audience, between the flow
that is coherent and the flow that is not, between the flow that is
logical and the flow that is not, between the flow that is gram-
matical and the flow that is an impasto of neologism and defies
all the procedures of grammar. Obviously, however, when the
flow is used as a notation, it is made to assume countless forms;
there is no point in trying to categorize them. What we can do is to
establish what the novelists of the early twentieth century did
with an old human habit that has also turned up regularly as a
literary device.

The stream of consciousness as such is, presumably, as old as the mind of man; and only a fact-fetichist would want to know when it was first used as a literary device. It must always have found the favour of rambling conversationalists and undeliberate thinkers. One of the characteristics of consciousness is to stream, with thoughts and images now overlapping, now flowing discreetly one after another, and in both instances often bewildering the listener. But to simulate the stream in words is often to substitute a manipulative, creative intention for the passivity of the private brooder, and to force it into being the stream of articulateness. It becomes technique rather than behaviour, and can therefore be regarded as a distortion.

The point to be made, then, is that the attempt to articulate the stream of consciousness was nothing new, even in Dujardin's *Les Lauriers sont coupés* (1888). What was new was the attempt, made by Virginia Woolf, Proust and Joyce, to base entire novels on it. And its eventual inadequacy as a structural device means merely that the stream of consciousness, like the exterior of our bodies, is only one part of us, and that artifice can transform neither it nor our exterior into the whole. This is the argument I wish to pursue here, moving from the incompleteness of the stream to the equally incomplete anti-psychological novels of Robbe-Grillet. The novel, I believe, must fuse as many views of man as possible; and such a fusion is most feasible in the manner of the *roman-fleuve* as handled (although not with constant success) by Proust and Lawrence Durrell.

Men's minds habitually submit to the flux for short spells. There is no need to quote Heraclitus or to explore the Many and the One. Implicit in the fitful streaming of the human consciousness are two possibilities: allowing the various phenomenal world to make its full impact, thus endowing the conscious but relaxing mind with a comprehensive awareness; or (as one can manage by relaxing one's eye-muscles) seeing without looking, in such a way that nothing particular is in focus although one has a blurred *sense* of things.

It is only too easy to submit to the stream within and around us. Problems arise when we try to articulate (in words in the mind or on paper) its make-up: not just its mixed quality, but its items. This is to mimic inconsistently in words an activity often inchoate; and it is almost impossible to appraise the 'accuracy' of such mimicry. All we can do is to point to lacunae, apparent associations, *non sequiturs* linked by spurious conjunctions or misleading adverbs, and random extravagances. When what each of us acknowledges as habit appears as a literary device, each of us is obliged to rely, for criteria, on ineffable experience of his own. After all, what is the point of 'checking' the 'accuracy' of A's written version by comparing it with B's account, also in words, of his own similar experiences? If I am attempting to assess completely the degree of 'likeness to life' of A's version the kind of information I most require is precisely that which has no place and no significance in words. For the stream of consciousness is not identical with the activity of concept-forming; nor is it clearly separable from that activity. So the main difficulty is to admit that the device may resemble the stream only vaguely, and merely suggests an illogical experience much harder to mimic in words than to describe. And the critic, armed with his knowledge of the different ways in which writers have exploited the device, can make literary comparisons only. The main question (How accurate is the device's mimicry?) is unanswerable. Which is one reason, of course, for the device's becoming over-exploited in its own right; we are apt to become impatient with a device that would persuade us where we cannot verify rather than let us appraise for ourselves a distorted account of the obvious and imitable.

2

Flux abounding

I

IT IS worth noting that Edouard Dujardin went so far as to incorporate snatches of music in the interior monologue of his main character in *Les Lauriers*. The one form of notation, fitted into the other, surprises the reader and may baffle him, especially if he cannot read music. But at least the notation of music is a fixed thing, whereas the personally evolved notation of a Joyce is erratic. The artist can endanger his work by forgetting that he works in artifice, not in a ready-given reality; he can also damage his work by making too much of artifice—by glorying in it. The odd thing is that those novelists who want to disclaim artifice are the ones who resort to it most.

Les Lauriers first appeared in *La Revue Indépendante* in 1887, and created little stir. But when Valéry Larbaud talked with Joyce in 1920 (when Joyce was finishing *Ulysses*) Joyce supposedly acknowledged his debt to Dujardin who had used the interior monologue *'d'une manière continue'*.[1] It is true that Dujardin is just as interested in tricks of technique as in his hero's worryings about Léa d'Arsay; Dujardin was an incorrigible experimenter in poetry and the theatre as well as in prose. And Larbaud's eulogy, coming from the globe-trotting creator of the pseudo-fictional 'A. O. Barnabooth', catches Dujardin's habit of gloating self-repetition: Larbaud commends the interior monologue for 'its novelty, its audacity, and the possibilities it offers for the forceful and rapid expression of the most intimate thoughts in all their spontaneity; those thoughts which seem to develop without our

1. *Les Lauriers sont coupés*, Introduction by Valéry Larbaud (Paris, 1924), p. 7.

14

knowing it and which seem to precede deliberate statement'.[1]
The interior monologue, he continues, is 'a form which lets one
catch, deep down in the Self, the very first spurting of thought'.[2]
But the self is memory; more is forgotten than ever reaches the
light. Dujardin's hero sits wondering which person he shall be;
which Léa is going to be; which he wishes she were; which he
thinks she wishes he wished she were. . . . Deep down, all is fluid,
and the personality comes out like protoplasm. Relativism takes
over and all that remains is a vague sense of the outside world
and an over-precise sense of every person's many selves. The
main point, which none of the stream novelists makes, is that
self-definition is a crude feat, bound to crush and mutilate whatever does not fit the self we have decided to be. And those who
cannot choose, the hoverers and floaters, are always consulting
the catalogue of themselves. Gertrude Stein's Teresa has an
indoor self and an outdoor one; Dostoevsky's Versilov in *A Raw
Youth* says 'I feel as though I were split into two'; Dr Jekyll
matches Mr Hyde. The trouble is that, in fiction, if the characters
have a weak sense of identity, they cannot be shown making
meaningful or articulate contact with other lives. But the new
method, or lack of method, caught on, stunting the work of some
writers (for example, May Sinclair's *Audrey Craven*, 1897) and
usefully intoxicating others with what seemed a new vision of
man.

II

George Moore (1852–1933), having read his Dujardin, composed *The Lake* (1950) as an experiment in self-feeding flow: all
boundaries—between self and not-self, between theme and style,
between author and reader—melt into long-winded, rather
cloying euphony. The prose reads like a defiant prank undertaken to prove that Heraclitus's *enantiodromia* (the process by
which a thing becomes its opposite) is compatible with Pater's
Anderstreben—an art's 'partial alienation from its own limitations,
through which the arts are able, not indeed to supply the place
of each other, but reciprocally to lend each other new forces'. At

1. *Lauriers*, p. 6.
2. idem.

the back of it all is the ambition to merge everything as in the
primal darkness; as if one could reach a point at which the con-
trivance on the page would appear to have issued from no human
hand or head, but just to *be*. It is here that all limitations are
left behind and the notion of an art that somehow, suddenly,
has become not-art begins. Because definition is the sign of
human manipulation, the novelist cultivates the vague—which
he can do best by plunging into the flux of self. No wonder, then,
that nearly all the fiction that pretends it is life is chaotic. No
wonder the C. P. Snows have attacked the stream device: they
are also attacking the shallow notion that all reality is inward
and that chaos is somehow more 'real' than order. Moore, like
Pater, trying for 'an expansion and refinement of the power of
reception', merely helped to make fashionable a prose solvent.
And the free association of his autobiographical writings is a
rejection of the organizing mind, just as the interior flux is of a
fixed identity.

Where Moore is expert at dissolving limits and boundaries,
Henry James (1843–1916) excels in creating them where they do
not need to exist. This is as true of his prose style as of his narrative method. The narrators in *The Beast in the Jungle* (1901)
and *The Sacred Fount* (1901) speculate intensively; we are shown
in how many subtle ways human conduct can be interpreted or
subdivided. But often the subtlety seems gratuitous—a cerebral
showing-off. The more James hindered his chosen observer, the
more he could display himself, obliquely commenting on the
distorting mirror. In the preface to *What Maisie Knew* (1897) he
explained the title: 'The one presented register of the whole complexity would be the play of the child's confused and obscure
notation of it.' Because Maisie did not know enough, James
could excel at intervening. By creating occlusions he forced into
being an art of optometry and so justified his own presence in
the novel. James, one is sure, could not have left the Lewis Eliot
of C. P. Snow's *The Masters* to fend for himself: Lewis Eliot, a
fairly reliable but also wound-licking intelligence, would have
tempted James into cunning glosses and ironic twists. If there
is any irony in Snow's novels it is in the overall structure, never
in the texture; in James, however, irony is almost all. Snow lets
the reader make an absolute choice: to infer that the whole is

ironic or that it is not. James constantly jogs the reader into noticing ironies of all kinds. There is a world of difference between creating a fiction which can be taken as ironic or not, and creating the incomplete so that the omniscient author can supply the remainder as an irony.

Of course it is not surprising that James disliked being matter-of-fact: he was too concerned with the shifting sands of identity in an alien land; he was acutely aware of 'the disrespect of chance, the insolence of accident'; too many things were relative to one another; not enough was fixed—not even life in palaces or country houses was as virtuous as gracious; Maule's curse haunted him whenever he compared artistic devotion with moral fervour. The 'point-of-view' method was a means of self-protection as well as a hindrance deliberately created and brilliantly circumvented. James's simultaneity—his curious ability to seem to be telling much less than he is saying—is really the fruit of being tentative. He shied and evaded, as well as prying and speculating. We must not neglect his romantic-mythical heritage; he did not really, as Van Wyck Brooks suggested, produce 'a rootless art'. A convert to gentility and a native son of intelligence, James defined himself by creating, in his fiction, the various stages of truth: exterior, part-understood, glossed into completeness. In this way he conferred upon himself the persona of discoverer; and a self-discoverer, a self-suppressor, he always remained, deploying his private occlusions in impersonal terms. The fact is that subtle truths are no truer than humdrum ones; and James, the disciple of Turgenev, always wanted the truth to be subtler than it was. Where Turgenev could leave the plain alone, James kept refining.

Joseph Conrad (1857–1924) illustrates the imperfections of *any* kind of telling. He traces the progress through minds of what might be called a fact. The minds make the reality which the fact becomes; and Conrad does not do a James: he does not gloss. In *his* book, that is merely to add yet another imperfect version to the others. In other words, he pretends that his fiction is life. Where James takes pleasure in being ultimately in full control, admits that he can or cannot complete the picture, Conrad behaves as if he has not created his own fiction. It is an effective way of making a point, but it also makes fiction as baffling as life—which it should not be. Surely, if we care about understanding at all, we want to know more about Kurtz than Marlow passes on in *Heart of Darkness* (1902). Marlow, obstinately it seems, keeps getting himself between Kurtz and the reader. What a fascinating man Kurtz is. What about the regal native woman who makes only a fleeting appearance? Wouldn't even a Marlow have tried to find out something about her? The pity is that our interest perishes on the altar of Conrad's device. Jim in *Lord Jim* (1900) is deep, too deep for Marlow—and he is deeply symbolic too. Conrad probes into the metaphysical region, which is dark simply because it happens to be a projection and extension of the inner darkness Marlow cannot fathom. Haunted Conrad, with his exotic laboratory, swarming adjectives and parallel clauses, knows his Flaubert but remains a cosmic rather than a social inquirer. He just inquires. His is the lyrical anguish of shifting about: he quizzes the source of being but fails even to understand why men do what they do; pretends that even his characters are unfathomable. It is noteworthy that Conrad, evasive and detached, cherished order and 'fidelity' in the self as in society; yet he had an incorrigible regard for the outlaw. He turned a psychic necessity into a rhetorical device: things are always being shunted off—minds or reports. He is aloof and luxuriant. If his theme is the centre of a circle, he drops various exotic rings, untidily showing where the centre might be. But we are never given the point. James over-defines; Conrad under-explains; and in each instance the cause is the self-effacement of the unfixed personality.

Marcel Proust (1871–1922) came of a family that was wealthy enough to permit him a life of social leisure. He circulated in both bourgeois and aristocratic society and did a good deal of entertaining on his own account. He was far from being a recluse. But soon after his mother's death in 1905 he retreated to the flat where, between 1909 and 1919, he composed the larger part of *À la Recherche du temps perdu*; and his bedroom, lined with cork, has come to typify for us the inbred, shut-in quality of his novel. *À la Recherche* is enormous; to some an enormity, adding as it does dimensions of time and memory to basic narrative in much the same way as Tolstoy added history (or at least what he thought was history). Proust depicts French society from the

1880s to just after the First World War: a society in decay and upset, with the aristocracy failing and the bourgeoisie ascendant. He also gives a finicking and highly personal dissection of love: to him it was a subjective thing, a feat of the imagination. (Other novelists were to stress the subjectivity of 'reality' itself.) Love could thrive only in the absence of the loved object. Consummation killed it, but jealousy, a refusal to yield or to respond, absence and impotence, all fanned it on. In other words, thought Proust, we wander about, with love or the loving attitude ready-made in our heads; and then we deposit it on the nearest appropriate object.

The most important and most baffling aspect of Proust's theory is that of memory. In each of us there is a fathomless pool in which there are many things we have long forgotten. But a chance perfume, a combination of sounds or things, a casual word can evoke one of these forgotten experiences in such a way as to make the evoked experience more vivid than the original itself. This involuntary memory, like the love that is ready-made, dwells in the mind: it enables us to take possession a more complete possession of our lives. And some of the recollections in Proust come through with all the power of religious vision. But, in order to recollect, and in order to sympathize with the recollections in the novel, we have to be attentive and in a suitable frame of mind. To this end Proust works his prose indefatigably: the sentences are complex and long; the imagery is clustered and often bewildering. And, quite often, what is present has suddenly become what is past: a change takes place without its disrupting either our mood or the rhythm of the prose.

The novel is told in the first person by the central character Marcel, who is very much like Proust himself. Marcel is both the main figure and the middle-aged narrator. In a sense, Marcel has his time all over again: he sees everything double. First there is Marcel saying 'I am doing this'; then there is the older Marcel saying 'I recall how it was'. Each mode of statement enriches and informs the other. And the climax to all this occurs when, in the concluding volume, Marcel realizes his calling is to be that of writer. He has, as it were, caught up with himself; for it is obviously the middle-aged Marcel who is writing the book. He is showing the slow realization of his chosen way—how he came to be writing the book we have already been reading.

Yet he does not squeeze the moment in terms of an incomprehensible notation. He is long-winded, fastidiously analytical, both dreamy and acute; but he does write in words we recognize and he does keep clear of chaos. It is wrong, as Pamela Hansford Johnson pointed out in the *New Statesman* (9 August 1958), to lump him together with Joyce and Virginia Woolf. 'The important experiments of Proust,' she says, 'are not verbal at all, or even "aesthetic", in the narrow sense. They are human and metaphysical. Proust's only real *technical* experiment is the extended use of discursion: under the surface of *À la Recherche du Temps Perdu* is a framework as hard and classical as that of *War and Peace*. It had to be so, since he was writing about man in society, not simply about man locked into himself.' This is true, except that *Ulysses* too has a 'hard and classical' framework, and that Proust's framework is really a *jeu* of subjectivity. The main thing about Proust is that he is always explaining; he ties all his meanings together with a very long steel wire. To read him is sometimes like trying to unwind a rheostat, but we do know that the rheostat is intended to do something specific in words that already exist. Proust is always expounding, being accurate; if we have read him attentively, without trying to superimpose on him a label that also covers Joyce and Virginia Woolf, he inevitably sends us back to Balzac. He (who knew, imitated and extolled his Balzac) gorged on people as on illicit sweets. He specialized in self-regarding emotions. Where Balzac's bluff humanism is quick to exhaust itself and move on, Proust sucks dry. Both, over a decade, pursued their *travaux d'architecte*; Balzac repeats characters, Proust different impressions of the same thing. What Balzac does for the Restoration and the July Monarchy, Proust does for the first chunk of the Third Republic. Both are social and historical novelists; they cannot afford to indulge linguistic innovations or pretend that prose is not primarily expository.

The fascination of *À la Recherche* depends on *longueurs*, on the gradual implanting in our minds of event and evocation while the narrator's daedal, transposing memory unfurls. A careful reader can relish the mental snakes-and-ladders without getting lost. He always has the syntax to fall back on. Private associations Proust reveals; the logical inference of obverse, inverse, reverse and converse (which obsess him) is left to the reader. Proust is the breaker of his own images. Because there is a dreamer in him, disenchantment is his only reality. Yet he always strives to incorporate his disenchantment into his dream—to take full possession of his world.

The wonder of his achievement is that, bookish and subjective as he was, he experimented very little with texture and kept a firm eye on the world of objects. He does prolong the scrutiny of feeling, but he is always drawing out the essential vitality and subtlety of the feeling, not stretching it to fit some irrelevance. It may sound odd to praise Proust's care for relevance; but that is what he practises. He seems to know exactly how much attention a feeling merits. He can be brisk: 'And so, when the pianist had finished, Swann crossed the room and thanked him with a vivacity which delighted Mme Verdurin.' He can also extend himself in order to attend minutely to a phenomenon which is affecting a group and, by suppressing the responses of the various characters to it, set the reader to work. In this way the reader is too busy exerting himself to spot how otiose the writing is:

But tonight, at Mme Verdurin's, scarcely had the little pianist begun to play when, suddenly, after a high note *held on* through two whole bars, Swann saw it *approaching, stealing forth* from underneath that resonance, which was *prolonged* and *stretched out* over it, like a *curtain* of sound, to *veil* the *mystery* of its birth—and recognized, *secret, whispering*, articulate, the *airy* and fragrant phrase that he had loved. And it was so *peculiarly itself*, it had *so personal* a charm, which nothing else could have replaced, that Swann felt as though he had met, in a friend's drawing-room, a woman whom he had seen and admired, once, in the street, and had despaired of ever seeing again. Finally the phrase *withdrew* and *vanished*, *pointing, directing*, diligent among the wandering currents of its fragrance, leaving upon Swann's features a reflexion of its smile. But now, at last, he could ask the name of his fair unknown (and was told that it was the andante movement of Vinteuil's sonata for the piano and violin), he *held it safe*, could

have it again to himself, at home, as often as he would, could
study its language and acquire its secret.[1] (My italics)

Because attention is on Swann, we have to work out for ourselves
what the rest of the company are feeling about the music. Proust
says what the music is like generally; although he is at this point
concentrating on Swann, he gives an account as little idiosyncratic as that given by E. M. Forster, in *Howards End*, of Beethoven's Fifth Symphony. In addition, the woman-in-the-street
image stops the sensibility from becoming too exquisite.

There is another way of regarding this passage. Proust overdoes
the relevance. If we are not trying to work out how the other
characters are responding, we may notice and find irritating
certain repetitions. Are we to conclude that Proust is just demonstrating Swann's monotonous habits of mind? Is Swann doing
the rapt savouring, or is Proust? Some of the repetitions add a
subtle distinction, a new shade; but most of them blunt and blur
the effect. It is almost as if matter (although relevant matter) is
manufactured in order to fill in the elaborate sentence patterns.
Ice-hockey crowds sometimes throw rubbish on to the ice in
order to protract the game; and Proust himself seems reluctant
to let things go forward: just like Swann.

But this is not the best way of showing how Swann feels;
Proust's prose need not linger just because Swann does. This is
an instance of the mimetic fallacy: Proust is letting a character
dictate the nature of the prose; is, in fact, abdicating from his role

1. Or, quelques minutes à peine après que le petit pianiste avait commencé
de jouer chez Mme Verdurin, tout d'un coup après une note *longuement
tendue* pendant deux mesures, il vit *approcher, s'échappant* de sous cette
sonorité *prolongée et tendue* comme un *rideau* sonore pour *cacher le mystère*
de son incubation, il reconnut, *secrète, bruissante* et divisée, la phrase *aérienne*
et odorante qu'il aimait. Et elle était *si particulière,* elle avait un charme *si
individuel* et qu'aucun autre n'aurait pu remplacer, que ce fut pour Swann
comme s'il eût rencontré dans un salon ami une personne qu'il avait admirée
dans la rue et désespérait de jamais retrouver. À la fin, elle *s'éloigna, indica-
trice, diligente,* parmi les ramifications de son parfum, laissant sur le visage
de Swann le reflet de son sourire. Mais maintenant il pouvait demander le
nom de son inconnue (on lui dit que c'était l'andante de la sonate pour piano
et violon de Vinteuil), il la *tenait,* il *pourrait l'avoir chez lui* aussi souvent
qu'il voudrait, essayer d'apprendre son langage et son secret. (My italics again)
Du Côté de chez Swann, Gallimard (Paris, 1919), pp. 285–6.

as manipulator. Swann did not write those lines, but Proust seems to let him take over. What is gained in apparent first-handedness is lost in a diffuseness which, ultimately, we have to attribute to Proust. And Proust, as narrator, as Marcel, cannot afford to ignore his professional responsibilities or the aesthetic standards he has established already. To write so mimetically is like saying the theory of gravitation is heavy or that the chemical formula for water is wet. Writing is notation in verbal equivalents. The equivalents are verbal; but even when a writer tries to communicate verbally a verbal peculiarity of one of his characters, he must surely acknowledge that he, the creator, has to be in evidence: the written prose is there on the page; therefore the creator cannot do a vanishing trick. And whichever way he chooses to convey verbal (or other) peculiarities, that way must finally be imputed to him. To the same extent as it is a version of a character, it is also an emblem of the author's presence. He is there, and it is up to him to clarify the exact purpose and limits of the devices he uses. I do not think Proust, for all his passionate regard for truth, always knew the extent to which the pursuit of truth made him misrepresent himself. The truth expressed in art is necessarily a contrived truth: there is no 'real-life' Swann for us to scrutinize; and the actual Proust is always being tempted into the region which Swann inhabits. Swann is fictional, Proust was real, and Proust sometimes forgot both of those facts, letting the passion for mimicry prevail over his analytical intelligence.

It is all a matter of theory, but theory which a novelist cannot do without. For this is the theory of the truth about art, not a theory of the untried possibilities of that activity. When personal pleasure wins, as it often does in Proust, the art of communication suffers. It is even worse that Proust took acute self-regarding pleasure in pushing imitation beyond its usual limits; for such imitation both defies the imperfect nature of all mimetic art and denies the reader the guide he is accustomed to. It is no joke to have to accept an absolute realism without the apparent guidance of the creator himself. Words refer to concepts, but we do not have a blue word to refer to a blue bird. And even such devices as onomatopoeia are inaccurate; they rely on a supplement from our willing imaginations. A distortion is inevitable. The only accurate way of discovering what it is like to be shot is, not to read a book, but to be shot. A book may give us clues and hints, but it cannot by its nature do more. So, in fact, the stream device is tolerable only so long as it is not offered as reality; so long as it remains simply a more ingenious mode of reference. Auguste Bailly has put this well:

> . . . though the analytic method may give a partly false or artificial presentation of the stream of consciousness, the silent monologue is just as artificial and just as false. The necessity of recording the flow of consciousness by means of words and phrases compels the writer to depict it as a continuous horizontal line, like a line of melody. But even a casual examination of our inner consciousness shows us that this presentation is essentially false.[1]

Essentially false: yes, but evocative all the same. Proust is all evocation and his massive evocation is centripetal. Marcel holds things together; so does the syntax.

The same is true of the much less varied, less luxuriant world of Dorothy Richardson (1882–1957). Miriam Henderson is not just a static sensitivity wallowing in nuances and extremes: she develops and, if we have the patience to look hard, can be seen to be doing so. The Newlands Miriam is maturer and more eloquent than the Hanover Miriam; in *Pointed Roofs* she is coyly afraid of men, but in *Honeycomb* she disapproves of them for much more articulate and analytical reasons. And, if we read *The Tunnel* and *Interim* we can see her gradually learning to eschew sweeping interpretations of the world. She discovers how much sense we can gain from puzzling things out, and how much satisfaction we can gain from reaching a banal conclusion. Miriam herself ends her 'pilgrimage' as a Quaker novice.

Pilgrimage, like the *Clarissa* of the other Richardson, takes as its subject an experiencing and developing mind. In the Foreword to the 1938 edition, Dorothy Richardson quotes Goethe on the 'thought processes of the principal figure': she is ferreting out a tradition into which her vast kaleidoscope will fit. But she does not go on to invoke Samuel Richardson, whom in fact Goethe is citing as an example. She is looking for a tradition of theory

1. Quoted in Herbert Read, *English Prose Style* (1952), p. 156.

rather than of practice; although pleading for the world of feminine impulse and feminine intuition, she invades the male world of prescriptive formulas in order to justify her pleading.

It is possible to identify the events which Miriam's mind offers so obliquely. She teaches in a German girls' school and afterwards at another school, Wordsworth House, in London. Next she becomes governess to the Corries, leaves them so that she can attend her dying mother, goes back to London, works for a combination of Wimpole Street dentists, gradually widens her range of friends and acquaintances, dabbles in socialism, falls in love but refuses marriage. Eventually, having rejected yet another proposal of marriage, Miriam starts to write book reviews, becomes the mistress of an eminent writer, has a nervous collapse and goes away to recover. Her recovery leads her towards the Quaker faith. It is a very obvious progress of a soul: summarized baldly, it sounds humdrum and ordinary. But to Dorothy Richardson the outline was of the merest importance; what counted was Miriam's emotional and mental development. One can see why readers grew irritable with Miriam: *Pointed Roofs* appeared in 1915, and the sequence dragged on until 1938, covering Miriam from seventeen to almost thirty. Readers were living Miriam's life at less than Miriam's pace, and living it in spasms and blanks. No wonder those who cared wanted a framework, some basis for selection, some key to significance.

They eventually got one. Before the final volume appeared, John Cowper Powys proposed the novel as 'a sort of Quest of the Holy Grail . . . the divine object of the ecstatic contemplative life, nothing less than the Beatific Vision; and not merely that alone, for she is looking for this as it manifests itself, in diffused glory, throughout the whole inflowing and outflowing tide of phenomena'.[1] Some years earlier, Constance Rourke had defined the novel's method as purposive indirection: 'more than a centralization of narrative within a single point of view. . . . Even more positively than in the novels with which James deals, the material seems transposed from life itself, with all the inevitable irregularity of shape, without the creative arrangement which James demands.'[2] Such perspicacity did not, however, secure Miriam a wide

1. *The Adelphi*, II (1924), p. 514.
2. *The New Republic*, XX (November 1919), Part II, p. 14.

audience. What most readers boggled at was Dorothy Richardson's ruthless exemplification of her own precept that 'The only satisfactory definition of a man's consciousness is his life. And this, superficially regarded, does exhibit a sort of stream-line. But the consciousness sits stiller than a tree.'[1] She stresses stability and primal awareness, throwing a line forward to Colette and Nathalie Sarraute. The power and charm of all literature, she says, resides in its ability 'to rouse and to concentrate the reader's contemplative consciousness'.[2] And in the Foreword to the 1938 version of her novel she picked out Balzac and Arnold Bennett as 'realists by nature and unawares'. She went on: 'They believe themselves to be substituting, for the telescopes of the writers of romance whose lenses they condemn as both rose-coloured and distorting, mirrors of plain glass.'

Reality, in fact, is a subjective thing, and character is response. She began her long novel as a 'feminine equivalent' to the 'current masculine realism', determined to illustrate the power and scope of 'contingency'—the very thing which the orthodox novel had to ignore in favour of plot, structure and coherence. She obviously felt acutely the gulf between the purposive activity that writing a novel is, and the haphazard indirection of human life.

Yet her mistake is clear. Although objecting to 'the vast discrepancy between the actuality of life as experienced and the dramatic fatalism, shared in spite of its relative freedom from the time-limit, by the orthodox novel with the stage',[3] she could still envisage a complete realism. It is not imitation she objects to; only a kind of imitation not her own. After setting up the chimera of a highly systematic realism—so tightly constructed that excerpts cannot fairly be made—she proposes an absolute of her own. In *Life and Letters Today* (July 1939) she explained the difference between the orthodox realism and the new; the new was fluid:

> Opening, just anywhere, its pages, the reader is immediately engrossed. Time and place, and the identity of characters, if any happen to appear, are relatively immaterial. Something

1. *Authors Today and Yesterday*, ed. Stanley J. Kunitz (New York, 1933), p. 562.
2. idem.
3. *Life and Letters*, LVI (March 1948), p. 191.

may be missed. Incidents may fail of their full effect through ignorance of what has gone before. . . . He finds himself within a medium whose close texture, like that of poetry, is everywhere significant. . . .[1]

This is life-tasting; and, although the remark about poetry is true of *The Waste Land*, *The Cantos*, and St-John Perse's *Anabase*, it would not be true at all of, say, *Four Quartets*, Rilke's *Duino Elegies* and Valéry's *Cimetière Marin*. The aesthetic outlined is that of the imagination's logic, of the art that not only expresses chaos but also enacts it. This is a long way from even so ambitious a formula as Henry James advanced in his essay 'The Art of Fiction' (1884):

A Novel is in its broadest definition a personal, a direct impression of life: that, to begin with, constitutes its value, which is greater or less according to the intensity of the impressions.

It seemed that the new novel, the novel of subjective sensibility, could be almost anything; formal convention was essentially secondary to the splurge of response. Oddly enough, Dorothy Richardson complained that Henry James and Conrad showed 'self-satisfied, complacent, know-all condescendingness'; or at least that is what Miriam says. She goes on: 'The torment of *all* novels is what is left out.' It is almost as if Miriam-Richardson identifies torment with being systematic. Or does she mean that what torments is the impossibility of being completely realistic? James, says Miriam, creates an 'enclosed resounding chamber where no plant grows and no mystery pours in from the unheeded stars'. Obviously, James had to miss things out; other things he preferred to leave out. But when we read Miriam's gibe at 'a charmed and charming high priest of nearly all the orthodoxies, inhabiting a softly lit enclosure he mistook, until 1914, for the universe', we cannot help feeling that all this talk of absolute realism is just another genteel, subtle game played by poseurs. James's enclosure is not as softly lit as all that, and Miriam is not as wide-minded as she thinks she is.

The few critics who take Gertrude Stein (1874–1946) seriously as

1. p. 47.

a novelist invariably over-attend to her theories. All very well to discuss her affinities with, and her borrowings from, the science of William James and the distortions of Cézanne; to note how she fused the methods of the Harvard psychology laboratories with the domineering style of the French painter. In her theories Einstein and *Clarissa Harlowe* come together. There is no doubt that she advanced from an 'all-at-once' revelation to a stylist's delight in incantation. Analysis of one moment led her to attempt a catalogue of simultaneity; synthesis led her to concentrate more on a moment's quality than on its relationship to experiences simultaneous with it. *Tender Buttons* (1915) marks her first confident transition from cataloguing to expatiation.

Yet it is hard not to conclude that she was deluded. For words are not brush-strokes or notes: they have inescapable connotations and denotations; they have to be used in accordance with arbitrary rules with which we are familiar (often unthinkingly so) and which we expect to see heeded. The reading eye takes its English from left to right, expects guidance from punctuation, steadies itself at stops and keeps on the lookout for those sentences whose total pattern is predictable from the arrangement of the first few words. We hate to skid through whole paragraphs; but that is just what Gertrude Stein makes us do.

The reader has to come to terms not with her theory but with what it entails. She was right to suggest that each individual speaker has his own rhythms; but spoken language is rhythmical in a different way when mimicked on paper, and the span as well as the speed of our attention is not the same for the one as for the other. It is points such as these, humdrum and indicative of the strength of mere habit, that Gertrude Stein in all her Aristotelian theorizings ignored.

But then, she was besotted with the impossible and she thought she was a genius—not a sterile, morbidly self-critical one like her brother Leo, but a literary Einstein of ripe prolificity. 'I have destroyed', she declared, 'sentences and rhythm and literary overtones and all the rest of that nonsense. . . .' She meant, of course, that such things did not find a place in her own prose; and it was T. S. Eliot who discerned the true nature of her utterances: they had, he observed, 'a kinship with the saxophone'. Her prose stutters and blurts, keeps going over the same phrases again and again until a general effect has been produced within the restrictions of a method that is designedly imprecise. There is no exposition; at her most specific she never achieves a greater exactitude than, say, such a piece as Moussorgsky's *Pictures at an Exhibition*. At her vaguest she lacks even the rhythms, the rapidly built and easily followed transitions, of the jazz drummer.

But she did at least give a lead to Ernest Hemingway, who sensibly stopped short of her own dead end of anaphora; and she enlarged Sherwood Anderson's notion of the possible by demonstrating where the impossible began. Gertrude Stein begins, in fact, a good deal farther from the language of daily discourse than we tend to think. She has to be gulped; her art is one of time-lag and after-effect; her texture cannot be discussed except in terms of general outline. This would seem to be implied in her theory that 'passion' in writers must precede what the vulgar assume to be its cause. Details, for her, like 'the woman or the idea', are mere incidents in a surging emotion that survives them. It is hard to reconcile what she called 'the inside of things', and her cult of that, with her experiments in word-collage. Of the psychic interior of Melanctha, the negro girl in the third story of *Three Lives* (1908), we get an accurate and vivid idea; and Gertrude Stein manages this without resorting to verbal dabbling. In fact, the style which brings Melanctha to us has something in common with the pungent bits of Dorothy Richardson: Gertrude Stein's dialogue here is deftly constructed, a staccato within flow, while Dorothy Richardson's prose (especially when she resorts to marks of ellipsis) reminds one of a mass of crystals, coruscating into a dazzle: sharpness within flow. (It is worth noting that Babette Deutsch, in *The Nation*, CVI, 1918, p. 656, drew attention to the imagism in Dorothy Richardson's style.) But where Gertrude Stein suppresses nouns, Dorothy Richardson suppresses verbs; the one creates the cult of energy—an automatic, compulsive free-for-all; the other is principally concerned with the static, the stable: nothing is more stable than the consciousness of Miriam, nothing more static than a noun. Stein bustles on, her wheels moving rapidly to get nowhere; Richardson sustains pauses, damming up the mind until it spills over. How odd it is that William Carlos Williams, who himself brought out in Paris in 1923 a book called *The Great American Novel*, written as an

interior monologue on the lines of *Ulysses*, should then proceed
to write the poem *Paterson* and declare that the Novel is inferior
to the Poem, for the novel cannot penetrate to 'the underlying
nudity'. If anyone found the nudity and the vacancy it was
Gertrude Stein. If anyone exposed human awareness in all its
nakedness, its pre-verbal nakedness rendered in words, it was
Dorothy Richardson. It would be difficult to see how such a
poem as *Paterson* could have done more, or how such a work as
Pilgrimage or *The Autobiography of Alice B. Toklas* (with Gertrude
Stein supposedly seen through the eyes of Miss Toklas) could have
been turned into a poem without losing a considerable amount
of 'underlying nudity'. Carlos Williams is really saying that it is
hard to take account of the stream without turning your novel
into a poem. He is rationalizing his own practice. But the novel
can, carefully managed, *set* 'underlying nudity' in a context,
which is more thought-provoking than (and more than is achieved
by) such ambitious poems as *Aurora Leigh*, *The Ring and the
Book* and *Paterson* itself, for all its eponymous hero-who-is-
a-city.

Of course, 'underlying nudity' implies the mind at its least
disciplined; no logic, no clear divisions, no system, no care, no
syntax, perhaps no sense. What we often find is spiritually nude
man playing with civilized counters and letting his mind free-
wheel. In this way, experience is often presented from several
points of view, although always imperfectly, on the principle that
what is lost in exactness may be regained in overlap. It is the
agglutinative method, not the precisian's; all things become inter-
dependent and relative.

It is his theory of relativity which makes Proust an obvious
precursor of Virginia Woolf (1882–1941): both wish to see an
experience from all possible points of view. The result is an im-
position upon one another of different impressions: the trick is
to be able to see them all simultaneously. And this trick of seeing
the many as the one relates Proust's structure to the texture of
Joyce (1882–1941). But Joyce mutilates the language too: in
writing one word, which he has constructed from three others,
he creates new relationships. A less high-falutin version of Joyce's
verbal alchemy has emerged in the United States under the name
'scrabbledegook'. For instance, we understand what is meant by

'a philanthrobber', or the verb 'to reno-vate', or 'teetotalitarian-ism', or, on a perhaps lower level, 'mirthquake', 'disastrophy' and 'slimousine'. The essence is a new view, a synoptic view, in double-quick time.

Ulysses often aims at the same sort of thing. Here is an attempt to suggest a hearse going quickly by with a baby's coffin inside; the vocabulary itself is orthodox:

> White horses with white frontlet plumes came round the Rotunda corner, galloping. A tiny coffin flashed by. In a hurry to bury. A mourning coach. Unmarried. Black for the married. Piebald for bachelors. Dun for a nun.
> —Sad, Martin Cunningham said. A child.
> A dwarf's face mauve and wrinkled like little Rudy's was. Dwarf's body, weak as putty, in a white-lined deal box. Burial friendly society pays. Penny a week for a sod of turf. Our. Little. Beggar. Baby. Meant nothing. Mistake of nature.

Notice his impatience with the usual means of expression: Joyce wants to show how half-formed thoughts enter and leave our consciousness with almost impossible rapidity. If you look in-wards you find so much more to notice; and the fleeting impression must be seized instantly, even if inadequately. The mind keeps racing on; and if you stop to stare you will miss an enormous amount.

Proust is long; Joyce is short. Proust builds up a composite picture slowly with thousands of touches. Joyce dashes off the key phrases or words. Fill in for yourself, he says. But both Proust and Joyce want to show the essential relatedness of things. Joyce's language in *Ulysses* is usually simple. His urge for a highbrow 'scrabbledegook' shows in full force only in *Finnegans Wake*. For instance:

> She was just a young thin pale soft shy slim slip of a thing then, sauntering, by silvamoonlake and he was a heavy trudging lurching lieabroad of a Curraghman, making his hay for whose sun to shine on, as tough as the oaktrees (peats be with them!) used to rustle that time down by the dykes of killing Kildare, for forstfellfoss with a plash across her.

We get the dominant impression: the contrast between the frail and the ponderous, between the fearful and the aggressive. A little further on Joyce uses the phrase 'give her the tigris eye' which perhaps sends running through our minds the notions of— give the eye, tiger's eye, Tigris the river, the lithe tiger and the tiger's eye burning bright, the tiger's spring, the sudden assault or onset of sex as the tiger leaps or the Tigris fills and flows. At any rate, Joyce is using an associative shorthand of his own in an attempt, not always successful, to suggest associations made in his own mind. This is the flood of consciousness; and in reading the jerky, laconic Joyce, or the languid Proust, we have to succumb and see what is washed into our own minds. In reading *Ulysses* we find the language little problem; what is often baffling is the spaces between the ideas: Joyce gives us two polarities and expects us to provide our own connecting spark.

Ulysses is the story of a single day, 16 June 1904, in the lives of several people in Dublin. The principal characters are Leopold Bloom, a converted Jew, timid and tentative, lecherous and kindly: his view of life, in so far as he has one at all, is physical. He is perhaps the *homme moyen sensuel*. This is modern Odysseus in his diurnal journey from morning to midnight and so into dreams. His Penelope is his wife, Marion, a Dublin soprano. And a third personage is Stephen Dedalus, who—rather like Raskolnikov in *Crime and Punishment*—tries to study life in the abstract. He and Bloom meet in the place or condition called Night Town, which is a version of Hell or the Palace of Circe.

What happens, then, in these 400,000 words? There is a journey—much like that in *The Odyssey* itself; a journey into spiritual night. It begins with getting up and is pursued through the tedious chores of everyday; it takes in a funeral, a newspaper office, a library, a bar, the lavatory, a maternity hospital, a stroll on the beach, a brothel, a coffee stall, and so—as children's books and Pepys used to say—to bed. There are numerous parallels with Homer; but that is a dimension we can take or leave as we prefer. *Ulysses* is a very down-to-earth novel: it puts brilliantly the muddle and mediocrity which afflict us all daily. Stephen, just back from Paris, lives with two students in a tower overlooking Dublin Bay. He teaches history at a boys' school. At eight o'clock

Mr Bloom goes out to buy some kidney; he prepares breakfast
for his wife. She is unfaithful—a lush, sensual mixture of Irish,
Spanish and Jewish. In her morning mail is a letter from her
current lover; Mr Bloom knows this, but passes no comment.
Two hours later, he picks up a love-letter all of his own, from a
girl-friend; but he stops at a chemist's shop to buy his wife some
face-lotion. Then he goes to a Turkish bath to relax. Joyce has an
unflagging eye for the squalid and pathetic. But, because he is
constantly switching from lyrical to dramatic, from these to
straightforward—or nearly straightforward—prose narration,
the matter is transfigured.

The same is true of the typically rarefied world of Virginia
Woolf's *The Waves*: these are the waves of consciousness, followed from inception to dispersal with tremendous acuteness and
subtlety. *The Waves* appeared in 1931, and reveals the influence
of both Joyce and Proust. Six friends, all at different stages between birth and death, are made to soliloquize against the backcloth of the Sea, which is Time. They all speak alike, in an intense,
delicate, fluid language that quite blots out the distinction between
characters. The novel is, in fact, a hymn to the fertility and
variety of human awareness. The sun is life, and it shines on the
sea of time: so there are incessant changes, countless effects of
shimmer and illusion. Each long section is preceded by a prose
poem:

The waves massed themselves, curved their backs and
crashed. Up spurted stones and shingle. They swept round the
rocks, and the spray, leaping high, spattered the walls of a cave
that had been dry before, and left pools inland, where some
fish, stranded, lashed its tail as the wave drew back.
'I have signed my name,' said Louis, 'already twenty times.
I, and again I, and again I. Clear, firm, unequivocal, there it
stands, my name. Clear-cut and unequivocal am I too. . . . The
sun shines from a clear sky. But twelve o'clock brings neither
rain nor sunshine. It is the hour when Miss Johnson brings me
my letters in a wire tray. . . . I am half in love with the typewriter
and the telephone. With letters and cables and brief but cour-
teous commands on the telephone to Paris, Berlin, New York
I have fused my many lives into one. . . .'

We have arrived at realism and gone beyond it. In this genteel but factual soliloquizing, we watch a fine sensibility extend the fertile muddle of the realists into the recesses, the undusted corners, of the faltering mind. What is real is certainly in those places; but it is in others too; and neither represents the whole of experience. The difference between the two emerges at its clearest only when we watch the novelist's efforts to reconcile imitation with symbolism. As arguments about the flux of consciousness have shown, human experience must be presented both imitatively and symbolically. No one method is absolutely adequate.

When we read the early Joyce, we can see what is coming. The story 'An Encounter', in *Dubliners* (1914), uses the device of the imperfectly realizing but frankly observing child, while *A Portrait of the Artist as a Young Man* (1916) gives a more adult version of the flux in a notation that does not baffle us or bore. *Ulysses* (1922), defining the Blooms and Stephen by catalogued indirection, is ventriloquistic but still meant to be read conventionally, even when punctuation vanishes. *Ulysses* is packed with point-of-view devices, and it is not hard for us to sense the presence of the supervising artist: parody, operatic devices, stretches of Socratic elenchus, stories-within-stories and even fugal logic all remind us he is there. Oddly enough *Ulysses* does not quite do what Virginia Woolf said it did: its offering is more robust than those 'flickerings of that innermost flame which flashes its messages through the brain'. Such terminology is too delicate—and too delicate-minded. What Joyce gives constantly, and in paralysing abundance in *Finnegans Wake*, and what Samuel Beckett (*More Pricks than Kicks*, 1934; *Murphy*, 1938; *Molloy*, 1951) and 'Flann O'Brien' (*At Swim-Two Birds*, 1939) achieve under his influence, is a version of robust inarticulateness. The characters' minds are almost too full to notice that 'flickering', whereas Virginia Woolf's characters are so anxious to see the flame that they miss a great deal of what is going on around them.

But there is this to be said for Dorothy Richardson, Joyce and Virginia Woolf: they evolved a complex form evocative of the complexity of life. In presenting, they all mimicked, and the difficult question is not 'Are their respective methods apt?' but, 'Cannot the same account of life be given just as well in another way which, at the same time, does not weary the reader with

longueurs, disintegrating vocabulary and excessive self-analysis?'
To put it in another way: if we presuppose an intelligent reader,
is it not more meaningful to give him a novel which *discusses,* say,
solipsism, rather than a novel which merely exemplifies that
state? Much of the attractiveness of Jane Austen consists in her
oblique little commentaries on the behaviour of the characters.
She interprets and is willing to be thought opinionated. Not that
Richardson, Joyce and Woolf do not interpret: they do, but their
effort is mostly towards showing the mind interpreting itself.
And the result of that is lost objectivity: they deal in *personae,*
not in assessment. They deploy the various aspects of themselves
rather than devise instances of behaviour; and even the individual-
ized monologues of Joyce and the complementary-characters
device of Virginia Woolf cannot disguise their supreme self-
indulgences. Gush is gush, however carefully adjusted, and it
suggests both presumption and self-engrossment.

We have already noticed that what Virginia Woolf said about
Joyce applied better to herself. In fact it is in complete accord
with her often-quoted manifesto in *Modern Fiction*:

> Life is not a series of gig lamps symmetrically arranged; but a
> luminous halo, a semi-transparent envelope surrounding us
> from the beginning of consciousness to the end. Is it not the
> task of the novelist to convey this varying, this unknown and
> uncircumscribed spirit, whatever aberration or complexity it
> may display, with as little mixture of the alien and external
> possible?

To Joyce, the external was not alien; nothing was alien to him.
He was a tremendous analyst as well as a complete master of the
synthesizing impulse. Virginia Woolf, on the other hand, thought
the novel should generalize, not analyse; and her art is much more
evasive than that of Joyce. Not only that: her aesthetic is essentially a social thing, prescribing decorums and proscribing crudi-
ties. Her characters are always breaking off at the point where
Joyce begins. The streaming reverie she creates in the story
'The Mark on the Wall' (1919) is technically deft—as deft as
anything she did; but what she makes of the mark (a snail) is
worlds away from what Joyce would have produced. (Alain

Robbe-Grillet's narrator in *Jealousy*, meditating on and recurring to the stain of a squashed centipede, is much nearer to the Woolf method.) Compare Mrs Ramsay with Molly Bloom and we have, primarily, a social difference: Joyce is concerned to create Molly's streaming consciousness, whereas Virginia Woolf is concerned to refine something *from* an imagined Mrs Ramsay. No sooner has Virginia Woolf established the flow than she is turning it into something else, more Woolf than character.

Mrs Dalloway (1925) shows the influence of Joyce especially in its recourse to techniques of synthesizing several minds. If minds can be united, then, Virginia Woolf seems to think, they are united only by being irrational. The flow is the inner highest common factor; reason is the inner obstacle. The flow relates us to eternity, reason only to clocks. *Orlando* (1928) is a fugue on this theme: Orlando is both 36 and 336 years old, although the concept 'old' is meaningless in spiritual terms. It is a tract with a key, a pastiche of Sackville family history, an extravaganza on the life and genealogy of Vita Sackville-West, to whom it is dedicated. Is it a novel? What is Orlando? We cannot say; we come away from the book feeling, like Bernard in *The Waves*, that all identity is illusion, that all persons are really the same. And we soon begin to wonder whether, to float on the stream, we need to strip ourselves of so much. As long as we regard Virginia Woolf's characteristic novels as bouts of immersion, we shall profit a great deal: the profit of increased awareness, of presumptuous intellect called to order, of arid systems shown to be too Procrustean for *human* beings.

But if we read Mrs Woolf for Proustian documentary, then that is like looking to Shelley for what we find in Pope. She let one device obsess her; and it is a pity that it did so. No doubt every idiosyncratic life-view pre-empts some methods more than it does others. Even so, one cannot help thinking that Virginia Woolf's best efforts went into an exposition which would have gained immensely from being contrasted with other sides of life expounded in a contrasting technique. She never synthesized in one book the Forsterian method of *The Voyage Out* (1915), or the deep psychological (but non-streaming) method of *Night and Day* (1919), with her instinctive preference for waves. For her, the tide was always coming in.

III

Eventually we have to regard the stream as the least disciplined form of romantic poetry. We can ask nothing of it; it supplies a *carte blanche*; and whatever the version we select—from Dujardin's rambling lists to the massive (and under-esteemed) Tietjens trilogy of Ford Madox Ford—we sooner or later have to admit that it is not the one and only method open to the sensitive writer. There is a dangerous assumption that the stream is the stream of sensibility: C. P. Snow, for example, attacks the stream by calling it sensibility. The fact is that the novel of sensibility cannot be written without a full exploitation of all notational devices or with one technique only. The novels of Elizabeth Bowen and the stories of Katharine Mansfield demonstrate that sensibility is compatible with shrewd analysis and remind us that we spend less of our time 'streaming' than a Joyce or a Woolf would suggest. The stream, like deliberate thought, is intermittent: the two sometimes coincide. It is therefore not honest (if we are trying to be honest at all) to present life as either all stream or all intellect. Perhaps only Dostoevsky got the proportions right; Lawrence and James indulge themselves too much; Proust, coining a brilliant excuse in his narrator device, still gives more stream than we can credit or stomach; his sentences create too many ox-bow lakes as they flow forwards.

The solution is surely not to be found in experimental novels. Not now. Experiment is for a purpose: its discoveries have to be related to what existed previously. And sensibility, set in a vacuum, is a fraud, for it belongs among the world of things, weather, rheumatism, prices, technology and politics. That is why such ingenious experiments as Djuna Barnes's *Nightwood* (1936), Philip Toynbee's *Tea with Mrs Goodman* (1947), *The Garden to the Sea* (1954) and *Pantaloon* (1961) attempt more than they can attain. True, the only canon, and a limited one, is what has been previously written. The novel is whatever the novel does. But it weakens itself if it trespasses too far into the territory of the poem; for the poem generalizes through abstraction, whereas the novel's special excellence is that it can generalize through depiction. We must face the fact that between preciosity and the kitchen sink there is a vast area, of both subject-matter and style, which can best be dealt with in prose of no great intensity. If the world were as intense as a sonnet, then perhaps we would need sonnets only; if life were as dull as a catalogue, then we would need catalogues only.

But life is neither; and in trying to articulate it, and that fact, we have to be sensible about our means: in other words, not use the howitzer in hand-to-hand combat or the bayonet from a mile away. If we care about being comprehensive, we should waste nothing—no method, no device, no point of view. If we stop trying to be comprehensive, then we are letting self-gratification oust the intention to report. And it is the poet who has always proclaimed his right to do that; not the novelist. This is not a matter of professional ethics: it is simply that the notion of a genre helps the reader to know where he is. The novel evolved as the soup-spoon did, and the notion of the genre 'novel' is one of the conveniences of communication, just as the soup-spoon is one of the conveniences of consumption. One cannot be didactic about the form of the novel; but one can afford to be about the tradition of its use. The sensible course is surely to throw away nothing useful while incorporating the fruits, if any, of all experiments. If we do that, then the experimental novel itself will not be criticized for inapt reasons.

3

The novel in retreat

STREAM technique, then, forced into being some of the wildest as well as some of the sanest conceptions of the novel as an art form. The debate about the stream had to consider such anomalies as the plotless novel, the novel without apparent structure, the missing story, the character who is no more than a succession of instants, the instant which endures for pages and pages, the outside world as a reflection of the perceiving mind, and the self-regarding identities which lose themselves in introspection. It was not just a dispute about a new method; it was an inevitable investigation of the novel's essence and boundaries. The upshot of the debate was the undefined novel, giving scope for everything, giving the novel all the possibilities of the movie and yet, even from the beginning of the debate, accidentally making plain the essential artificiality of art and revealing the stream device as a deluded quest for greater realism; deluded because art and complete realism are incompatible. I say a greater realism, which may seem to imply that the stream innovators were not aiming at an absolute but only at a degree. It is clear, however, that those innovators thought a complete realism possible and that a greater realism would lead to it. It has taken a long time—from the twenties to the mid-fifties—for the intoxications released by the stream to wear off. The best novelists of our time now know it for what it is, and seem to have it in proportion.

In 1914 Henry James objected to Arnold Bennett's addiction to data in much the same terms as modern critics have objected to the dossier methods of John O'Hara. James's objections, in *Notes on Novelists*, simply renewed Flaubert's objections to the naturalism of Zola; both of them fastidious and self-conscious practitioners of a high art, they wanted art separated from the

39

mundane world—not in subject-matter but in procedure. Flaubert knew that art had to make something new of its material, and that no matter what degree of realism might be achieved, there was nothing else in the world identical in its nature with that 'something new'. In other words, art, once created, was unique; and Arnold Bennett seemed to be forgetting the nature of the things he created. Not that Bennett was deficient in aesthetic sense; far from it, he was a painstaking artificer. But, as James saw it, Bennett appeared to think that enough realism would conceal the contrivedness of art. Unfortunately the principle is double: no amount of realism will disguise the artfulness of art, any more than much art will conceal the essential incompleteness of realism.

It was Virginia Woolf, in *Mr Bennett and Mrs Brown* (1924), who pointed out that Bennett's meticulous documentary missed out the important things: the drama of the spirit and the maelstrom of personality. Galsworthy and Wells she found similarly deficient. Not that she was demanding a pageant of sensitive souls; she just thought that art could excel itself in articulating the results of spiritual investigation. She was arguing more for the Dostoevskian novel than for her own socially restricted type of meditation. It has not often enough been observed that, although Virginia Woolf failed to realize the narrowness of her vision, she wrote broad-mindedly about other writers. It is not the first time that a writer has preached better sense than his practice embodies.

In some ways she was entirely alone: out on a limb with subtlety, impressionism, aura and spirit. No wonder she over-stated her position; other critics were pleading for old virtues which she appeared to scorn. Herbert Read, in *Reason and Romanticism* (1926), maintained that the novels of Conrad, Joyce and Proust all displayed a 'terrible fluidity' based on tem-peramental self-indulgence and lack of consideration for the reader. Only Henry James was virtuous; only he had the mastery of the stream. Wyndham Lewis, offering himself as rational and classicalist, beat away at Bergson and Joyce in *Time and Western Man* (1927). What, he asked, was happening to the mainstream of mind? Mind's power to organize no longer seemed respect-worthy: the cult was all sloppiness, diffuseness, dream, incoher-ence, inchoateness, mess. What had happened to topple logic, order, nomenclature and limpidity? Why were there no sharp outlines? Most of all, he hammered away at the Bergsonian cult of the timeless duration: in *The Childermass* (1928) he set Gertrude Stein and James Joyce meandering in the fluid, protean world of their own devising. Derision became creative here, and one sees his point as well as relishing his scorn. I. A. Richards put forward in *Coleridge on the Imagination* (1935) the idea of form-as-proceeding rather than shape superinduced; even so, he was not satisfied with mere flux, any more than Coleridge had been. In Richards's terms (and Coleridge's) the poems of D. H. Lawrence can show the novelist the way. And eventually, of course, Eliot's fragmentary epic of a wasteland can be seen as another version of a Browning monologue and *Ulysses* as structurally clever as *Four Quartets*. As Richards saw, it was no good refusing to countenance experiment; what was important was to extend the genre of 'the novel' without blurring it. Of the other contestants in this early debate, Yeats (of all people) composed *Fighting the Waves* (1934) to protest against a spiritual superplus 'breaking over us and within us, melting limits whether of line or tint'. One would have expected more sympathy from Yeats; but he was really protesting against a kind of writing which almost wilfully denied the requirements of art. Joyce and Virginia Woolf were Yeats's villains; and it took Richards, the critic and philosophical writer, to spot the true value of what he called 'a self-dissolving introspection' and to commend the intricacy of the flux in which images are made to 'shift and flow and merge'.

In 1918 Julien Benda, a highly emotional rationalist, attacked the Bergson cult, dismissing it in *Belphégor* as a feminine prank unworthy of anyone with serious intellectual pretensions. Just as astringently F. R. Leavis and C. P. Snow, here at one, brand the stream as a dead end, both of them—despite their humanity and intelligence—inclined to let the novel be dull if only it will be comprehensible and moral. Joy they seem to equate with otiose emotionalism. They know what the novel is for and, although Leavis has more sensibility to style, they both dislike seeing temperament at work on literature—especially when an idiosyncratic prose style results. Their most engaging appeal is for the novel of worldly discussion, their least engaging for something scientifically exact and morally elevating. Surely the *Bildungsroman*

is not the best the novel can achieve; life's abundance is a
more exciting theme than society's codes. What we want from
the novel is the sense of life, of human complexity; and such a
sense educates more than overt moralizing. This seems to be what
Sir Charles Snow is arguing for. The odd thing, however, is that
he, like Virginia Woolf, theorizes persuasively without practising
thoroughly. I mean that in his novels Snow often suppresses an
obvious lyrical bent as well as avoiding irony and occasional
bravura. Either we sympathize with his life-view or we do not.
Life as a grim, daunting transaction redeemed only by self-knowledge and humility is accurate except for one thing: Snow keeps
subduing an old-fashioned fact which might be called the response
to beauty; hardly a businesslike response, it is true, but one every
bit as sustaining as humility and just as productive of it.

While many critics have been pontificating about the defunct
and the dying novel, Snow has addressed himself to a definition
of the novel's limits and possibilities. What Snow has said is
worth examining in some detail because it puts the case for the
novel with both a professional insight and a degree of worldly
wisdom rare among academic critics. At the time of writing this,
Snow's various essays on the novel remain uncollected—which is a
pity, for in a small volume they might manage such a fillip to
public awareness as *The Two Cultures* achieved in a different but
related sphere.

Snow clears up the muddle in terms of two kinds of novel: that
which loses little in translation and that which loses almost
everything; say, *War and Peace* and *Ulysses*, to put things extremely. Less extremely we might select, say, *Madame Bovary* and
The Waves. To Snow, there is the novel that can engage the non-
academic reader because it embodies the reflective intelligence,
and the novel that suits only the literary specialist. Snow tries to
set the novel in the world at large, seeing the ideal novel as a
disciplined exercise of the intellect. Style and texture get rather a
raw deal from him, but other aspects of the novel (plot, causal
psychology, social analysis, exemplified philosophizing) are made
to seem attractive and indispensable.

In an article in *The New York Times Book Review* (30 January
1955) he contends that the novelist must face today's world and
link us informatively to it. The novel, he says, has been going

underground, 'and it is the influence of science which has driven it there'. He means science in its technological consequences since the first years of the century, and assumes, perhaps glibly, that the novelist has shrunk from those consequences. He goes on to outline 'a particularly English response' to the scientific hegemony: it is

> to take refuge in a trivial kind of belles-lettres, made up of snobbery and nostalgia, nostalgia for the near past as though it were an Old South, full of yearning of a way of life that never existed and that would have been dislikable if it had.

This is a bit overstated but largely true. Aestheticism offends him, especially when it takes the form of shiftless literary experiments which, in fact, are not experiments at all but merely off-shoots of 'a kind of novel-writing which fundamentally has not budged for thirty-five years'. From Dorothy Richardson through Joyce and Virginia Woolf to Carson McCullers, what he calls the novel of sensibility has stood still; and, oddly enough, because it has favoured the stream device. Such writing, he argues, is an attempt to find a specialization commensurate with the specialization of science; but all it has produced is a disorganized form of sensation seeking. All the same, he says, 'from about 1925-45 the sensibility novel was taken for granted, not only as the best kind of novel art but the only one'. In consequence, the novel became marginal and criticism came out on top.

This account is not quite fair. The stream device, it is true, gives its practitioner a great deal of scope for self-caressing, and no reader who is not a fanatical enthusiast can stand much of that. But to equate the stream novel with the novel of sensibility, or stream with sensibility, or even to regard the stream as an important part of any sensibility, is going too far. It is not sensibility that is wrong, but one particularly extreme method of appearing to communicate it. Snow dismisses what he calls 'wodges of moment-by-moment sensation' and the so-called 'experimental' novel; the latter is 'as dead as cold potatoes'. He is right: the novel never needs to be as 'experimental' as it often has been. But sensibility and the stream have always been with us; the stream device has not; and it is hard on sensibility to dismiss it for the company it has been made to keep. That company, obviously, has been composed of esoteric stylists who owe a great deal to the aesthetes of the nineties: the motives and drives have been both social and rebellious. Torn between popular success and private self-esteem, persons of sensibility have turned inwards. Finally, as Snow points out, the novelist (or any creative person) manages to convince himself that he must choose between art and an audience. Cultural suicide then follows.

But, Snow says, the situation is not yet as extreme as that. Endorsing Wyndham Lewis's onslaught (in *The Demon of Progress in the Arts*) on the extremes of abstract painting, he declares that 'the fatuous extreme . . . is the theoretical discovery of the decade'. Because we can go to extremes, that does not mean that extremes are worth having. (And, of course, that applies also to Snow's own dismissal of the 'sensibility' novel.) Snow then cites several English novelists who show no 'interest in the sensibility novel or the *avant garde* of ten or twenty years ago': Doris Lessing, William Cooper, Emyr Humphreys, Francis King, Kingsley Amis, J. D. Scott, Brigid Brophy and John Wyllie. These novelists, he says, do not shrink from society: 'their attitude to their art is much tougher than that of their immediate predecessors'. But is their attitude 'tougher' than that expounded in *The Common Reader* or in Dorothy Richardson's essays? More relevant is the artist's attitude to himself: how much self-indulgence combined with how much 'imitation'? Virginia Woolf and Dorothy Richardson indulged themselves exceedingly in terms of a restricted social milieu. It is not that they faced life less but that, in describing life, they allowed their own temperaments almost unlimited scope. So we find their imitation of life too idiosyncratic; and we can do that without denying the novelist a right to his own kind of texture and a distinctive prose style. The trouble starts when the novelist (or artist of any kind) identifies himself with Art rather than Society or with Society rather than with Art: either course is wrong, and there is no prescribed, clear middle way. The art we best understand usually flourishes in the tension between these two attitudes, and it usually has a bit of each in it. It is a matter of what the artist is 'tough' about. Virginia Woolf is tough enough to face the truth but not to deny herself some stylistic indulgences. Snow, on the other hand, is tough enough to deny himself stylistic indulgences but not to risk sustained lyricism or irony. No wonder, then, he is so severe on *To the Lighthouse* and stream writing in general. What is really exacting is to work at one extreme without assuming that it is just as right as its opposite seems wrong.

Both in their criticism and their novels, Virginia Woolf and Snow have more in common than their extremest formulations of principle would suggest. This much is evident from the conclusion to the essay I have been quoting. Differences of social background and of literary methods apart, Snow's plea for the novel of ecology evokes Virginia Woolf's own concern with a sector of the social world. In their respective endeavours, these two novelists limit themselves about equally; their methods differ considerably, but neither is writing about kinds of life he or she is not familiar with. Snow has a clear idea of his own theme, and he is well qualified to tackle it:

> . . . the novel only breathes freely when it has its roots in society. That is another lesson we have learned from the aesthetic cul de sac. Sensibility is not enough; the novels of the near future, the novels of the atomic age will make a new attack on the relations of men to their environment. The environment will be the labyrinthine and highly articulated complex of our technological society, but the problem is the constant one, the problem of what has been called the ecology of man.

After all, society is not to be defined as just the life outside groups of intimates. We are all involved in society whether we are stay-at-homes or not. In our lives, as in our creative efforts, we are bound to select: no one can root himself everywhere. Virginia Woolf was rooted and stayed so; Snow transplanted himself, but I do not think his area of knowledgeable reference is much wider than Virginia Woolf's. In psychological insight they are about level: Snow parades his sensibility less than she does but captures just as well many complex states of mind. She imitates them; he defines them. Between his 'labyrinthine and highly articulated complex' and her 'pattern, however disconnected and incoherent in appearance' there is a similarity: complicated states of mind result from both; both writers are concerned with impact, with the impact of environment.

Sensibility is not enough; but neither is information. What we need most is the well-informed sensibility not too quirky in its style of utterance. This is not an impossible dream, for we find it realized in Dostoevsky at least, and sufficiently often in a dozen other novelists to encourage an aspirant majority into falling short of standards which, at any rate, are right and attainable. Add Snow to Woolf and we have something along the lines of Tschaikowsky's conception, expressed in a letter to Nadedja von Meck, of life as 'a persistent alternation of hard reality with evanescent dreams and clutchings of happiness'. That conception, which Tschaikowsky contrived as a 'programme' for the first movement of his Fourth Symphony, makes one wish that Snow's characteristic concern with the hard facts of power-seeking included also the 'evanescent' experiences which Virginia Woolf conveys with such articulate fidelity.

Resuming the inquiry in *The Times Literary Supplement* (15 August 1958) Snow, in kinder mood, declared: 'I do not believe that, within the foreseeable future, the novel in particular, or literature in general, need become alienated from the intellectual life of the time.' Sensible novelists would avoid the self-indulgent, sensuous texture which 'is often, though not always, a singular mixture of invented colloquialism and inflated "poetic" mandarin, delivered in a tone as near as possible to an alcoholic's mumble'. Notice the disdainful moral tone; he wants the novel free from the bizarre verbiage which texture-fondling critics cherish and which he summarizes in his own words:

The novel is an arrangement of words. The value of this arrangement is to be judged by nothing but an aesthetic criterion. There is only one aesthetic criterion. The arrangement of words either does or does not exist as the correlative of a 'personalist' vision; if the words are arranged so as to be the exact correlative, the novel is good. It is irrelevant what the vision is, or whether it tells us anything about the external 'objective' world, or whether what it tells us has any correspondence with objective truth.

Here, says Snow, is the anti-novel prognosticated in Flaubert's letters, envisioned by Joyce and Italo Svevo in Trieste before 1914, and condemned by Raymond Radiguet as artistic suicide. Style and technique created for their own sake strike him as absurd: 'The basis . . . is, of course, a naïve comparison with non-representational graphic art.' This is the point he made in the 1955 essay: 'the fatuous extreme . . . [as] the theoretical discovery of the decade'. The anti-novel is anti-social: 'It bears all the signs, not of a primarily intellectual or artistic response, but of a social one.' He goes further, for the 'anti-novel'—which is really an attempt to get poetic satisfactions from a primarily expository activity—comes out of a response we find in the nineties. Yeats was careful to distinguish 'popular' from 'sincere' poetry; the public lacked taste; the newly literate were just as vulgar as the unlettered. The true man of taste kept apart and kept his *hauteur* well polished. Here is Snow's version:

> There is a syndrome of attitudes in literature, nearly all quite modern, apparently unconnected, which spring from the same root—the romantic conception of the artist, the alienation of the intellectual, the aesthetic of the anti-novel, the abdication of the generalizing intellect, the hatred of the scientific-industrial revolution, the prizing of verbal innovation, the desire to contract out of society. This syndrome is seen at its most complete in writers like T. E. Hulme, Joyce or Pound. It has been visible in a considerable sector of advanced literature all through the first half of the century.

He goes on to discuss the retreat into art of temperaments which have found 'complexity of social organization' too much for them. But, of course (and he does not say this), the fugitive impulse is nothing new; nowadays there is simply more to flee from and to revile. The mass-media have filled in the air around us, and the rarest commodity is silence. These phenomena bear considerably upon the essential loneliness of the creative artist: when he retires to compose, he is necessarily aware of the vast amount of life going on outside his room. And, if he feels—as Snow suggests he might—that so much of the modern world has been created according to lumpish and debased precepts, he tries to create his own world of words, shapes or notes. It is the urge for the uncontaminated which tempts many writers into esoteric innovation. Sociology trespasses upon the novel's old purlieus, and literary criticism tries to make itself scientific. The resentful creative person feels he is being displaced; his *sense* of fact seems no longer valid in a world of factuality.

But such a view is unnecessarily gloomy. As Snow says, literature and the novel in particular can always find itself something worth doing, something which only it can do satisfactorily:

> There is a particular fusion of the investigatory, reflective and moral intelligences that specially fits the novel, and which is still the only way open to us of exploring certain aspects, including the most important aspects, of the individual and social condition.

I think Snow should have made more of this: the full implications of that assertion include the novel of sensibility: the subtle states of mind that no sociologist or psychiatrist can track. It is literature's job to record sensibility and the novel's to explore the sensibility of man in society. The method cannot always be as systematic as some critics would like nor, for that matter, can it often be idiosyncratic. Snow stresses the importance to the novel of thinking about experience: not just *presenting* it but being discursive about it. That is what Proust attempted, and Proust is the antithesis of Joyce. Only Anthony Powell, Snow says, has taken Proust's practice to heart; but English novelists of recent decades have at least not taken heartily to naturalism or symbolism. Instead, and Snow applauds, Doris Lessing has tried the *Bildungsroman*; Graham Greene 'has shown that the Stevensonian romance can be given different meanings'; Evelyn Waugh, William Cooper and Kingsley Amis have explored the pert comic novel evolved by William Gerhardi from Chekhov; Joyce Cary has tackled the novel of 'multiple viewpoint'. It is all fairly robust, extroverted stuff, quicker to knockabout and mockery than to the analysis of sensibility. Obviously this kind of writing selfconsciously repudiates the self-conscious exquisiteness of aestheticism. Like the so-called anti-novel, it is a social response and prompts us to look back to the end of the nineteenth century. We cannot fully interpret the modern novel without recalling the nineteenth-century provenance of the attitudes which it eschews and Snow deplores.

4

The novel narrowed

THE novel of sensibility is not confined to the stream device, or to the stream itself, any more than it is confined to the social or abstract view. The novel of full sensibility demands mainly three views: the deep and thorough psychological; the social; and the abstract-religious-universal; and when one of these views is underplayed, the result may be a thought-provoking novel but will necessarily be inadequate. If we are going to use the word 'sensibility' at all, we have to see that it is treated fairly and not defined too narrowly. The novelist himself, if he is going to save sensibility from becoming effete, crude or incomprehensible, must give as complete an account of humanity as he can. In other words, not just refinement of the spirit in self-regarding ecstasy, not just the modification of manners towards gentility and courtesy, not just the resumption of all sensibility under the heading of *Angst* or religious awe, but all of these. Sensibility is not the monopoly of a social group, of the religious fanatic or the recluse; it is the sum of emotional possibility, and can be illustrated endlessly according to the novelist's power of creating characters. Sensibility does not entail the stream device any more than it entails the novel of manners; but it has appeared substantially in these and, unless the novel stultifies itself, will continue to appear in their modified versions.

The main point is that the novel of sensibility is the novel of the novelist's own sensibility: if he is narrow, then so is his novel. I do not think any novelist can afford to devote a whole novel or a whole novel-cycle to redressing a balance. But this is what Snow, Anthony Powell and Lawrence Durrell, in their respective ways, have done. Because the subjective has predominated over the social is not a good reason for making the social predominate over the subjective or for pretending that the universe is bounded by social codes. The great danger is that such English novelists as Snow, Powell, Amis, Cooper, Doris Lessing and Nancy Mitford not only exclude the subjective but also stop short of the universally mythical as distinct from the socially mythical. After all, the human condition is man's place in Nature, and man's place is to be defined as much in spiritual as in social terms. Camus, in *The Plague*, defines our condition in terms both abstract and allegorical; yet one is not convinced that the characters are people. Scott Fitzgerald's *The Great Gatsby* offers a fragment of social mythology; yet we never quite get to grips with Gatsby's inmost self. Naturally, since art cannot be comprehensive, it has to select specimens and generalize from them only. But to amass all the necessary data is not the same as conveying the essence of a character's mind and spirit. A great novelist like Dostoevsky amply suggests the complete vision he cannot state.

We need a synthesis of all the ways of writing novels. No honest novelist could clearly separate the novel of human ecology from the mythic novel: the biology of an organism's habits in relation to his surroundings is bound to be intimately linked with large magnetic images which confer meaning on the facts of ordinary lives. Myth-making is part of ecology and part of the habits ecology studies. Ecology itself establishes new summary images: there is something in common between Snow's concept of 'the new men' and the Zulu notion that rain is the rain-god weeping for a dead bird. To label is to explain; to sum up in a category is to achieve partial mastery. When the modern novelist rejects unsystematic inwardness and the devices associated with it, he attempts a social myth-making which stops short of the cosmic inquiry that may lead him back into inwardness.

Snow is not the only practising novelist who has held out for old-fashioned virtues. Angus Wilson, writing in *The Times Literary Supplement* (15 August 1958) on 'Diversity and Depth', carefully separates such a novel as *Wuthering Heights* from the work and tradition of Jane Austen, Thackeray, George Eliot and Trollope, all of whom 'could command the serious attention of men and women of affairs, of people who had tasted responsibility in government, law, industry, social service and so on'. No doubt the novel can fairly be regarded as a kind of public service, even when it is attacking the existing state of things. But, equally, the novel cannot be tailored to suit 'men and women of affairs'. What a pompous phrase that is. One has an appalling foretaste here of the committee-man's novel: no romanticism, no introversion, no flourish of style, no quirks, no mysticism, not much ecstasy and even less ingenuity. Everybody is saying that the novel must be serious; the prima donna has to become a fifth-form prefect. Only 'social' themes will do; the *Wuthering Heights* type of novel is regarded as an aberration, and individualism is deplored. This is not a surprising attitude to come out of our present-day society in which everyone is told what to think, to buy, to enjoy. If people will only, the collectivist argument goes, do as they are told, they will do better than by thinking for themselves. Big Brother knows best. So does Science: for it has evolved recipes for success and can prescribe for the good life. Out of such ideas comes the idea of the unexceptionable mediocrity. Literature, that risky and erratic business, is going to be cleaned up. The neurotics ought not to be allowed to write it at all; and the novel has got to be plain, sane and didactic. Out of the window with the awkward side of art—its play-element; art must be responsible, must pay its tribute to the established order, must give necessary vicarious instruction to 'men and women of affairs'. Away with the urge to self-expression; in with the mimetic. Not that high-sounding proposals for art are new; what is new is the role of acknowledged legislator for the novel and the guilt that now seems to accompany self-expression.

All kinds of modern writers insist on taking themselves seriously as social orderlies. Sartre speaks of 'the responsibility of the writer'; Brecht fussed away about instruction that delights and delight that instructs; Camus toiled away at the idea of justice; Snow wants fiction that is not irresponsible. It looks as if the social concern to prevent people from becoming automatons has lapsed into a conformism all of its own. When you write to quicken minds lulled by mass-media, but end up prescribing a cure just as rigid as the ailment, where have you got? Surely play is the ultimate expression of one's individuality; and if, as writer, you are too earnest to play a little in your own work, then how much good can that work do for others? Such is the liberty of statues. How can the novel that the novelist does not enjoy writing give enjoyment to others? One can *enjoy* expressing a tragic view: that is why literature comes about. But just to express a tragic (or comic) view because that is the socially approved thing—what a mockery of art.

The trouble is that literature is having to exist alongside science and in the possession of pedagogues. All writers know this. Aestheticism, pure form, innovation, privacy, aloofness and un-didactic entertainment tempt them; but the spectres of morality, duty, exoteric clarity and humble homily tug them back. These are the worries of an age of literary criticism in which codified irrelevances and dullard historicism have ousted the pleasure-principle (i.e. fun). Literature, fitted out with suitable rationales, is fitted into the university curriculum. In America, especially, the critics have art by the short hairs and the sciolists, pushing possibly useful methods too far, evolve New Criticism, Myth Criticism, Literature as Psychometry, as Logogriph, as Logology, as *literae inhumaniores*—for nothing does more harm to literary study than the feeling that an artefact came out of the untidy, self-indulgent head of a chap. Pirandello knew what was going on; in his lecture-essay 'The Theatre New and Old', in *Saggi* (Milan, 1952), he supplied a complete answer to the prescribers:

> It ... appears clear to me that in the field of art every polemic, every critical attitude, every theory, if postulated and developed systematically and abstractly, *a priori* or *a posteriori*, whether discussed according to intellectual or moral criteria, or even from a purely aesthetic point of view, risks continually being disarranged and turned topsy-turvy or remaining bewildered at the disconcerting appearance of the created work. ...

That long, potent sentence ought to be written into the statutes of every Arts Faculty. Art pleases itself; its only rules are its limita-tions; and no amount of social conscience is going to change either fact. It is vain to propose an agenda for art, for there is no com-mittee-art. Old methods (plot, sub-plot, suspense, straightforward chronology) reassert themselves from time to time because art's nature is fixed and its possibilities are limited; such methods cannot be *decreed* back because they are 'sensible' or because they embody a long tradition. For the same reasons, the novel will occasionally become bad poetry or bad sociology and it cannot be told to do differently.

Also, because art is art—and not civic documentary or public archives—it will fail in spite of having the worthiest purposes thrust upon it. Snow's Lewis Eliot, like Faulkner's Gavin Stevens and Doris Lessing's Martha Quest, are good ideas that do not quite turn into credible characters. All three are blurred, although for different reasons. The idea of setting them in the *Bildungsroman* is obviously right; we need a prism that does not refract too much. But, for all their justifiability as presences, they have to exist in the fake world of art; and somehow they are diffused, echoing and self-parodying. They tell us the kind of thing their authors think the novel should tell us, but that does not justify them aesthetically. If the novelist is a moralist, he should always remember that his honest homilies have to flourish in a world of the contrived and may themselves be taken as no more than exercises in a mode. How much we take in, and how much we take seriously, depends on the power of the novel's illusion; and this point brings me back to myth.

For myth, odd and fantastic as it may be, is often more convincing than so-called realism or attempted documentary. If it is going to 'make points', moral or otherwise, it will often make them the more forcefully by avoiding 'imitation' in favour of a captivating structural metaphor. It is significant that the reaction against flux has prompted novelists to attempt a not very ambitious realism rather than to generalize about life in terms of images born in their imaginations and temperaments. It is foolish of novelists to eschew style and idiosyncratic texture simply because some critics have made a cult of textural savouring. The story is not the only thing to the novel: C. P. Snow, arguing in the *Kenyon Review* (Winter 1961) for the novel in which 'at one and the same time one sees oneself with total intimacy and at the same moment as though one were someone else', is really making the case for a subtle, supple style capable of sustained irony. The stream device hinders such an attempt; but the thick, wordy style of a Faulkner (which presumably incurs Snow's strictures against elaborate texture) does not. Snow goes on to define one of his major interests as 'the power-relations of men in organized society': 'you've got to understand how the world ticks, if you're going to have any chance of making it tick better'. So what he writes is really under the heading of documentary; it takes us back to Balzac and Disraeli as well as to Godwin's *Caleb Williams* and Trollope's *Phineas Finn*. A stern, worthy project indeed; but surely one calling for analysis of high-placed men during their acutest dilemmas and for careful annotation of their uncontrolled thoughts both on and off duty. One would have thought that to such an enterprise the subtlest methods were more pertinent than those of Galsworthy and Arnold Bennett, with both of whom Snow has much in common.

It is not a matter of maintaining a strict, unpoetic analysis; it is a matter of utilizing all methods in order to communicate as much as possible of the fiction's facts. To ignore sensibility, the stream, and the uses of irony, is surely to underequip the fiction which purports to make general statements about 'power-relations'. My own feeling is that Snow's Lewis Eliot is too much of a property and not enough of a person. He is the predominating filter, and yet we are always left to our own resources in establishing his degree of self-consciousness. Lewis Eliot theorizes about other men but never seems to test himself according to his assertions. They do apply to him, however, and we have to *guess* whether or not he knows that fact. Is Snow deliberately exposing him without comment or simply not disposed to pursue his theme that far? Henry James would have anticipated that question and so, I, think, would Virginia Woolf. Once again we have to admit that the novel *à thèse* too often demonstrates in the manner of mythology, leaving psychology far behind. Snow is nearer to allegory than he suspects. For allegory effaces the very thing that Snow praises in Proust: 'tireless commenting intelligence'. Allegory and myth explain themselves, need no commentary, and confer special facilities for being convincing about man in society.

PART TWO

Reflux

England

(a) Fantasies of fact

I

THE child who plays on his own too much usually ends up talking to himself. In a similar way, the writer who looks inward too much, perhaps in pursuit of his true self or his 'essence', may waste an enormous number of words. He will probably lose himself altogether. Many of us have no identity apart from our routines, our context: we are only ourselves because we are familiar with our own patterns of conduct, with those quite arbitrary but settled arrangements we make in order to survive and not feel bored. And in this sense the novelists who attempt to swim down the stream of consciousness take chances. First, they explore too much for too long; and so risk losing a clear sense of themselves, their characters and their plot. Second, they take the daily flux home with them and, sooner or later, try to draw it all into their own minds. Their aim is laudable: it is to tackle more of life than other writers in order to emerge with an even bigger coherence. But as often as not, these probers of the soul end up with a narrower view than anyone else. The human mind is too imperfect to perform such prodigies of assimilation and synthesis. Appearing to offer everything, they in fact select; and their selection is often much more limited than that made by novelists who rely on the standard traditions which say: a novel must tell a story; must keep us in suspense; must show outside appearances as well as psychology—and do this clearly; must keep the characters sharply differentiated; must, in fact, not become too personal, too private or too idiosyncratic.

I turn now to conventional novels. I am not suggesting that any of these lacks insight into people's minds; that would be preposterously untrue. But they show us the mental landscape without bewildering us too much. We know how erratic the human consciousness can be; and if we feel that the erratic quality needs to be stressed, then we have only to read ourselves into the characters given; there is room for us to do that. Indeed, there is often a clear sign from the author that, if we do not involve ourselves, we shall be wasting our time.

Unless he has a sense of humour and intends to be partly humorous, the mythologizing novelist usually attains comprehensiveness through solemnity. Myth tends to be vague and high-sounding, so the novelist has to gain his summary effect without slipping too far into the region of the sermon. In the English novel especially, there has developed a mythology of fact noteworthy for its combination of an overall pattern, usually ironic, with a wealth of detail. In this way E. M. Forster, Aldous Huxley and Evelyn Waugh have managed to play off the particular's oddities and lack of dignity against the general's pomposity. Why the English are good at this it is hard to say. Certainly such myth-minded novelists as Hesse, Bernanos and Pavese do not seem able to achieve the same doubleness. This is not just a matter of some putative English bent for satire or of a certain novelist's aims being 'serious' rather than comic. It is rather that a self-conscious novelist, as distinguished from one who works compulsively, will stand back from his page and consider his activity for what it is: a devoted manipulation of the contrived. Art is no more artificial than *mores*, no more arbitrary. And the farther you stand back from *mores*, whether or not you happen to be writing about them, the weirder they seem. Familiarity breeds acceptance; a self-imposed estrangement from things long familiar confers not only opportunities for generalization but also a chance to laugh at the homuncule. Everyone knows that we have an affectionate regard for things at hand, or an affectionate disdain, and that we become more callous the further away we go from the immediate. With the opportunity to generalize into myth comes an opportunity to indulge in sharp, derisive laughter.

Aldous Huxley (1894–1963) shows this; he is the distant observer

watching the antics of ants. Like Forster and Waugh, he creates
parables but without quite achieving their richness and reverbera-
tion. Huxley's novels remain in the mind as equations carefully
worked out—although in the most bizarrely expressed symbols,
whereas theirs have more panache and make more capital out of
human awkwardness. Huxley is the most clinical perhaps because
he has the strongest sense of overall pattern. But it is true of
all three that not only human pomposity but also the pomposity
of the mythologizing habit itself is proved ridiculous.

'So Philip Quarles is going to settle in the country and be a
mixture of Mrs Gaskell and Knut Hamsun. Well, well. . . . But
it's good that somebody should have illusions. At any rate he
can't be more bored in his village than I am here.' That is Lucy
writing from the Quai Voltaire. A little farther on in *Point Counter
Point* (1928) we find this note from Philip's notebook: 'Found
Rampion gloomy and exasperated, I don't know what about
and consequently pessimistic—lyrically and violently so. "I give
the present dispensation ten years," he said, after cataloguing the
horrors of the modern world.' These quotations cover a great
deal of Huxley's world: secession, illusions, disillusion, boredom,
pessimism, modern manias—and of course the recalcitrant hope-
fulness that has made him write at all. Huxley shows only too
well that the detached, impartial intellect runs considerable risk
of boring itself: it has to eliminate so much, either on rational
grounds or because a mystical habit dispenses not only with
horror and boredom but also with life's fulness, exuberance and
viscosity. For most of his novel-writing career he has needed a
framework within which to relax the trigger-happy intellect that
fired endlessly at the monsters and monstrosities of our times.
Yet his diatribes were life-enhancing: it was a triumph of im-
aginativeness, although not of utter originality, to have sent Mrs
Viveash's taxi, Mr Hutton thinking of sea-cucumbers while he
kisses his mistress, Burlap's tub, 'the gorgeous buttocks of the
ape', infantile geniuses, *The Rabbit-Fancier's Gazette* and clever
bombs toppling back into eternity. We have never had a more
thorough and elaborate cleaning-up of what, in pompous moments,
we might call the Western heritage.

But, one asked, reading one Swiftian indictment after another,
where did the rubbish end? And the scourging? What is not, in

some measure, daft or despicable? Go far enough away and anything will look petty. All we know is that the unbiased intellect,
excoriating social man, cannot answer such questions; not to the
heart's satisfaction, anyway. The heart is relevant because Huxley
admitted it in the company of vegetable diet, yoga, enemas, Mr
Propter's greenhouse, deep breathing, cows and Swami Prabhava-
nanda's Hollywood Ramakrishna Mission. One says 'heart' not
because these items have to do with compassionate fraternity or
any such worldly nonsense, but because that is a convenient way
of referring to the world of the spirit—into which Huxley himself
penetrated by way of D. H. Lawrence, Gerald Heard and Zen.
How far daily charity and the practice of meditation mutually
interact we cannot know; but certainly their divorce is bad for
literature and bad for living. For a long time it lost to obscurantism
the most adept cynic, the most articulate Diogenes we have had.
Huxley, it seemed, had substituted one absurdity for another.
Always the master of paraphernalia, he seemed only to be en-
cumbering himself. Sidney Dolphin, the decadent poet of 'Per-
mutations among the Nightingales', may be the epitome of
nihilism; but not more so than the Huxley who specialized in
disregard. After a whole opera of meaninglessness conducted in
terms of preposterous baroque novels, Huxley did hover about a
compromise. *Point Counter Point* offered a picture not unrelievedly
black. That was the stage of possibility: tempted to throw in his
hand, he could yet discern something worth-while in a world full
of knaves, cranks, monomaniacs and clowns. In 1915 he accepted
Lawrence's invitation to found a utopia in Florida and so evinced
some care for the possibilities of the human animal.

The Huxley of the mid-thirties spoke largely of love; but *Ends
and Means* (1937), stressing spirit as otherworldly rather than
powerful in personal intercourse, marked the decline into mystagogy. Mr Miller in *Eyeless in Gaza* (1936) suggests various cures
for scepticism; in *After Many a Summer Dies the Swan* (1939)
Mr Propter runs a sect of contemplatives. The secession began,
then ended. Not suddenly (for *Brave New World Revisited*, 1958,
showed an astonishing concern for the quality of human societies),
but almost bewilderingly a collection of Huxley's best essays
appeared in 1960 at the same time as he began, at the Massa-
chusetts Institute of Technology, a course of seven lectures on

the theme 'What a piece of work is a man! How noble in reason!' Philip Quarles had begun to wear a developed heart on his sleeve.

Late in 1960 Huxley said he was two-thirds through a new novel which would depict a 'utopian society, opposite from that of *Brave New World*': '. . . it will include', he said, 'all the complexities and richness of human beings along with some realistic ways of coping with the elements'.[1] Not that one expects Huxley ever to relinquish his view of the novel as an opportunity for adapting Peacockian mental games into phantasmagoria: his world is that of people with ideas, people peacefully coexisting with the bogus and being bogus; and he thinks in terms of disquisitions, not of plots. It is possible, however, that his new emphasis on 'awareness' may supplant bizarre fantasies with a solider kind of documentary and so ballast the homilist. Most of his novels read like reports compiled by a tremendous inspector, and respecter, of intellect. The prose is plain and so is the disgust.

What is especially noteworthy is his affinity with writers more dated than he is: Sacheverell Sitwell and Norman Douglas. It was the baroque extolled by the former that helped Huxley to make interesting to himself, and to others, a world he loathed; and the amorphous baroque of *South Wind* (1917)—all catalogues, monologues, digressions, exotica and humours—showed him the kind of plot he could safely undertake. 'We live', he says in the essay 'Variations on a Baroque Tomb' in *Themes and Variations* (1950), 'habitually on at least three levels—the level of strictly individual existence, the level of intellectual abstraction and the level of historical necessity and social convention.' Baroque mortuary sculpture 'has as its basic subject-matter the conflict, on one important front, between the public and the private, between the social and the individual, between the historical and the existential'. These conflicts appear in his fiction and to some extent cripple it. He is more interested in the private exercise of intelligence than in social reportage; in the blunders of individuals than in mass idiocy; in self-definition than in the nature of society. The result is a highly idiosyncratic application of reason, turning the novel into personal parable. His only theme is that the mind has a body, just as skeletons and skulls on baroque tombs temper

1. See *Weekly Post* (24 December 1960); *Island*, a melancholy fable, appeared in 1962.

the lavishness of the monuments. It is all a matter of adjusting oneself to the immutable facts. The grotesqueries of his novels mock the cool intellect which objurgates them endlessly: Huxley is always chastening himself.

Along similar lines, E. M. Forster (1879–), just as scathing although for reasons more humane than rational, contrives instances of vitality, cosmic force or sheer charity bursting through the net of cramped *mores* and rejuvenating, blighting or awakening. Forster's stress on devotion is also stress in another sense. His cult of friendship is the atavism of a man of taste aspiring to the world of animal zest from an almost painfully class-conscious standpoint. When death arrives in a Forster novel, the reader is made to feel lonely in surprise: a facsimile of the very loneliest experience of all. We should not labour Forster's idiosyncratic use of calamity; after all, it rarely announces itself, and Forster's deaths do not ruin his kind of mimesis any more than the long dying of Tolstoy's Ivan Ilyich dissipates the sense of dismay. Fundamentally, too, Forster is reluctant to get his hands sticky. Interviewed in 1952 he admitted that he had had no first-hand experience of the kind of life lived by Leonard and Jacky in *Howards End* (1910): 'I knew nothing about that'; and of the seduction of Helen Schlegel, if such it was, he said: 'I did it like that out of a wish to have surprises. It has to be a surprise for Margaret, and this was best done by making it a surprise for the reader too.'[1] With such statements in mind, and remembering Forster's rather blatant symbolism, his preference for the least sexual of his women characters, his refusal to conceal the mechanics of his storytelling and his persistent recourse to irony, we should not be surprised to find him saying in the same interview: 'In no book have I got down more than the people I like, the person I think I am, and the people who irritate me. This puts me among the large body of authors who are not really novelists, and have to get on as best they can with these three categories. We have not the power of observing the variety of life and describing it dispassionately.'[2] In other words, his novels are demonstrations of a few simple theses; as long as the ideas get through he is not much worried about the suspension of disbelief or the

1. *The Paris Review* (Spring 1953), pp. 33–4.
2. ibid., p. 37.

rupture of fictional illusion. His irony often saves him, and stops us from laughing at him as well as at his characters. It legitimizes his self-consciousness, his perpetual trick of disowning the personage: 'The train reached Charing Cross, and they parted—he to go to a matinée, she to buy petticoats for the corpulent poor.' The alliteration there draws attention to the incongruous image and also to the motives of Caroline. Who thinks thus? Forster, obviously; but he might be offering it as a verbal ricochet from her. Certainly it is not a gratuitous flourish; Forster's flourishes are less ostentatious and make themselves felt through understatement.

Sometimes he goes further and burlesques a character: wilfully, as if to show that he is so unpretentious an artist, so honest an expositor of the world's fatuities, that his point will stand even when we are aesthetically deserted. In *The Longest Journey* (1907) he makes his point in a manner like Huxley's: 'Her face had no expression. . . . Then her lover kissed it.' It's rather callous to evade the colloquialism at that point and write 'it' rather than 'her'. When another pair of lovers kiss, the man's gold *pince-nez* get dislodged and poised between them; while the clinch goes on the glasses do not fall. Worst of all are the quietly noted calamities: 'Gerald died that afternoon. He was broken up in the football match.' It is the choice of phrase that rattles us, suggesting dismemberment, rending, and also, by a deliberate trick, turning the hyperbole customary for injuries into a bizarre accuracy that seems almost a euphemism. Forster plays many such games with idiom and circumstance. He has confessed to liking 'that idea of fantasy, of muddling up the actual and the impossible until the reader isn't quite sure which is which'. And when, in his short stories, the supernatural irrupts into the dull lives of everyday, we are being shown how the poetry of life can connect with its prose. A topsy-turvy world suddenly has virtue, and the ordered world none. Just as Pan is likely (as in 'The Story of a Panic') to invade a picnic party, so is death or beauty likely to ravish the everyday self. Why, then, he argues, get too systematic about life? Life is a mess, as he has said; and the arrival of something wonderful or awful only creates further confusion.

So he aims at no rigid aesthetic. His novels—even the best of them: *Where Angels Fear to Tread* (1905), *Howards End* and *A*

Passage to India (1924)—are contrived demonstrations worked out in terms of many cardboard characters and a few that are life-like. His ideas are fiendishly accurate whilst his portrayal of life is only approximate: rather like the brilliant mathematician who knows he is right and cannot be bothered to write out all his equations. Cyril Connolly thought Forster's unostentatious style gave an impetus to such writers as Virginia Woolf, Katherine Mansfield, David Garnett and Elizabeth Bowen. It is more likely, however, that Forster's handling of the *sense* of fact has chimed in with a general myth-mindedness that derives from the example of Kafka, Lawrence and Hemingway. His quiet voice has few heirs: Snow and Angus Wilson; perhaps L. P. Hartley and P. H. Newby (*The Picnic at Sakkara*, 1955, especially). But his ethic relates him to the tradition of 'charity' that stretches from Tolstoy to Pasternak, and takes in Camus, Malraux, Silone, Faulkner and Snow. This is the tradition expounded in Tolstoy's *Happy Ever After* as: 'All of us . . . must discover for ourselves all the futilities of life in order to come back to life itself.' That is the moral of Forster's fertile muddle and, in a peculiar way, the explanation of his cavalier attitude to the art of the novel. In the last analysis, art which Forster finds the antithesis of mess does not matter half as much as personal relationships. Perhaps that is what his comparative abandonment of the novel means. He was always being tempted to give it up. The predominant tone of even *A Passage to India* is ironic and satirical; the wit is the preservative, keeping the myth from being solemn and the rather thin characterization (of all save Aziz) from being too noticeable. We get Forster's intellectual play between the flat personages and ourselves, and that has to suffice. Anything else we must imagine, but only at the novels' cool bidding.

A similar kind of comic or sardonic myth-making turns up in the work of Evelyn Waugh (1903–) and Ivy Compton-Burnett (1892–). Once again, what we miss in depth of characterization and high-flown apocalyptic is compensated for in intellectual activity and scarifying inventiveness. Waugh is altogether more giddy than Huxley; his touch is more Dickensian, and the gaga gallery of Aimée Thanatogenos, Margot Metroland, Miles Malpractice, Parsnip and Pimpernell, Sebastian with his teddy-bear, Mrs Melrose Ape and Miss Runcible is the perfect demonstration of energy without heart. These appalling marionettes make vain echoes in the sterile chambers called Public School, University and Society. Waugh diligently records the noises they make, the capers they cut. His virtuous people are passive; it is the fatheads who have all the energy and cavort among fake fungi in the air-conditioned nightmare of cultivated society. Waugh refrains from comment: none of Forster's perverse exposure of the people or the machinery. The titles are eloquent enough. *Decline and Fall* (1928) prepares us for *Vile Bodies* (1930): amid the monkey-chatter of the animated soulless, the man of comparative virtue perishes. All that remains is secession, which Waugh anatomizes without homily in *Brideshead Revisited* (1945). His abiding theme is that of immersion in the destructive element —which is fashionable society, Hollywood, totalitarianism, total war and boobydom in general. The only protection is faith. Converted in 1930, Waugh has excelled at the unpropagandizing novel and has come into the open on only a few occasions: in *Brideshead Revisited* making the dilemmas of faith explicit, in *Edmund Campion* (1935), and in *Helena* (1950), his exercise in hagiography. His exposure of inanity is more blistering than Huxley's, more inventive and more callous than Forster's. There is no doubt that the spiritual security he elected has given him extra licence for savagery: almost as if the world did not matter at all.

The End of the Battle (1961) completes his trilogy about World War II, makes much of two gestures of selflessness ('not the normal behaviour of an officer and gentleman') in the context of a very British dream which begins with *Men at Arms* (1952) and continues in *Officers and Gentlemen* (1955): Bellamy's Club, Jumbo, Fido, Chatty, Uncle, oaths on the sword of Roger of Waybroke, Trimmer the ex-hairdresser, and so on. It is not that there is no actuality corresponding to all this: English idiosyncrasy survives all wars and all heroic exploits. One can see Waugh's reason for juxtaposing Guy Crouchback's childish military infatuation and his eventual double amends—remarrying his ex-wife because she is pregnant by Trimmer, and trying to rescue some Jews from Yugoslavia. But 'Trimmer'?—as a name for an ex-barber, in a seriously meant trilogy? It is an example of the parochial, uneasy nature of the English imagination;

not that cosmic facts alter, whether the parochialism is that of Waugh or that of Faulkner. The English are simply too attached to their odd ways, too fond of embellishing these to write novels of general appeal. Not only Waugh but Forster and Huxley have impaired their appeal because of this fetish for whipping up *mores* into creamy fantasy. Waugh's *The Ordeal of Gilbert Pinfold* (1957) presented one kind of hallucination with careful consistency, and the daring experiment worked. But of the hallucinations that beset him when he vows to have fun in his fiction, he seems unaware. It is one thing to admit the impossibility of utter realism; it is quite another to refuse to countenance the convention based on that admission. Only in *The Loved One* (1948), his brilliant farce set in a lavish Hollywood funeral park, does he seem to distort in full knowledge of what he is doing.

Ivy Compton-Burnett is another who makes her puppets fend for themselves; she remains diabolically aloof as if to suggest that the trained animals are out of hand and always will be. This is the deadliest kind of exposure and it calls for immense power to sustain. The creatures must have life of their own in abundance; their creator must possess to an extraordinary degree the power of self-projection—with no explanations allowed. Any attempt at didacticism wrecks the effect: for this is the method of caustic demonstration. Miss Compton-Burnett's paraphernalia vary little: a country house, we might hear her saying in deadly parody of Jane Austen, is the very thing to work upon. Set it in late Victorian time—a world that Strachey apostrophized in terms of gas-lamps, enormous bedpans and terrible disasters in bed—and expose the brutality of the comfortably-off. The creatures hold forth interminably and are crazily articulate. The matriarchs puff and rear; the patriarchs huff and bristle; the small go through all the levels of nursery hell; the retinue of butlers, maids, manservants and maidservants fawns, snoops, whines and leers. Their utterances plague us but we never see the faces: the screen is blank but the sound is always turned on. Words fill the rooms; they all speak as if raised to their highest power; and the result is a demented, revealing symposium of ordinary people caricatured in their very choice of words. They do not get on any better for being so articulate, but the dreadful parade of relationships—men and wives, daughters and sons, elders and betters, mothers and sons—goes on: pointlessly, cruelly; as relentless as the universe itself.

The main subject-matter is the fabric of the family, and those who leave for the outer world do so protestingly. The families hypnotize themselves; their special kind of jungle is centripetal. One can see the power of such a microcosm and its wider applications; but so much of the dialogue is undifferentiated, so much of it like stichomythia as to give the reader a mental St Vitus's Dance. There is no way out once the monstrous conversations have begun: the people never shut up. Insulated from one another and from the outside world, they support a mode of writing so stylized that one's imagination convulses into activity: anything to disrupt the verbal glaze. Compared with the proliferating and vivacious chatter in Virginia Woolf's *Between the Acts* (1941), this is a sinister pageant of clicking nonentities. Each speaker has his own rhythms, but the reader's attention to rhythm flags very quickly. This is what happens when an intelligent novelist resolves to make all the characters intelligent too; not intelligent enough to be virtuous, but intelligent enough in their weakness to supply several mouthpieces. The irony is that Miss Compton-Burnett does not need mouthpieces for her ideas but merely vehicles for the one style she has. The characters enact her points but all in the same idiom; and that, I feel, is a failure of ventriloquism. Between *Men and Wives* (1931) and *A Father and his Fate* (1957) the pellucid accounts of motives, pretence and selfishness have piled up on top of one another like sheets of glass. No doubt this was a feat of considerable energy; it is just as fair to think that the style itself has brought most of the novels into being. Miss Compton-Burnett's gimmick unfortunately insulates us from her vision just as much as it isolates her characters from one another.

As we have seen, Huxley, Forster, Waugh and Ivy Compton-Burnett are highly self-conscious about the properties they deploy. Implicit derision is built into the overt myth. They want us to know that they are falsifying and distorting, are willing to sacrifice everyday texture to universal relevance. The sense of pattern is strong in all four. Self-consciousness becomes vituperative only in the novels of Wyndham Lewis (1886–1957). *Tarr* (1918) and *The Wild Body* (1928) demolish human marionettes by robust hyperbole in tinny prose. *The Apes of God* (1932) derides the Bloomsbury set with verve and deliciously perverse psychology; but then, such a set would give any hyperbolist a good start. After spending the war in Canada, Lewis wrote *Self-Condemned* (1954), a novel that shows his increasing garrulity and decreasing self-criticism. The anti-socialist *Rotting Hill* (1951) is too earnest although it abounds in grotesques and caricatures, as does *The Revenge for Love* (1937). Oddly enough Lewis, the apostle of order and system, needed a good deal of elbow-room before he could create his wildest travesties. His novels became sloppier, looser, although his targets—bohemian phoneys and earnest left-wingers—remained the same. Seeing himself as an 'enemy', he tended to turn satire into circus: he needed spaciousness in which to mythologize himself and his targets. The true Lewis appears in the subtitles for *The Human Age*: Childermass, Monstre Gai and Malign Fiesta. There is as much carnival and burlesque in him as deliberate, economical rationality. Taking himself seriously as the 'enemy', he is not half as persuasive as when swelling into a Falstaff; for his genius was less exiguous than he wanted to admit. The novels show an expansive temperament attacking according to strict principles; but *Self-Condemned* marks the beginning of a solemnity that cloys. Between self-mocking Diogenes and witty buffoon he is nothing, and his right-wing propaganda soon gets tedious. A recent exercise in the Lewis mode, Ronald Duncan's *Saint Spiv* (1961), indicts the same offenders and, curiously enough, in getting too serious about satire, lapses into the same unwitty acerbity.

II

I have already suggested that the abstract view of man amounts really to man in his extremest privacy. When the novelist, aiming at a general pattern (e.g. a version of the 'absurd' universe), hits on this fact he has to run the pattern and the privacy in parallel. After all, it is absurd to be articulating what men hardly ever express to themselves; and it is understandable the novelist should feel that, as well as inventing a fiction comparable to reality, he is also inventing a fiction of what is unobservable. Depending on his

sensitivity to device and artifice, he will dispose of his embarrass-
ment through irony, self-exclusion, self-advertisement ('This is
really only me after all'), and so on. We think of Huxley's homilies, Forster's deliberate unbuttoning of the fabric, Waugh's and
Ivy Compton-Burnett's self-suppression, and Wyndham Lewis's
melodramatic irruptions as the 'enemy'. Rose Macaulay does
something similarly ironic in *Orphan Island* (1924) and so makes
her narrative job more difficult; and even that cumbersome
exponent of rustic cosmography, T. F. Powys (1875–1953), in-
jects a lambent irony into the dark symbolisms of *Mr Weston's
Good Wine* (1928). Powys's novel thus becomes subtler than it
otherwise could have been.

Such irony is all very well when the novelist means to crusade
for common sense. Irony implies the dispassionate intellect, as
does satire. But when a novelist is an enthusiast for something
irrational, what can he do? If he has an acute sense of art's
artifice, he will be torn between sensitivity to the contrived nature
of all he writes and the need to maintain a prophetic tone. This is,
or rather should have been, D. H. Lawrence's problem. Lawrence
(1885–1930) neglected irony, preferred obloquy and, as a gesture
of self-consciousness, devised symbolisms of texture. The artist
occasionally embarrasses the preacher. It is possible to take
Lawrence's novels, exposing in each a pattern of ritual, a regeneration theme expressed in flowers and sexuality, and above all the
emotional form which in Lawrence's work is as ever-present and
inclusive as destiny itself. A man is born at the end of *Sons and
Lovers* (1913); a woman in *The Rainbow* (1915); in *Women in Love*
(1921) there is a marriage; in *Lady Chatterley's Lover* (1928) a
child is conceived; and in *The Man Who Died* (1931) the act of
conception is presented as almost beatific. These are stages in the
growth of a mythology which rebuts bourgeois gentility, the cult
of goodwill, industrialism, Mammon, ratiocination, commercial-
ized or merely purgative sex, and a bankrupt Christianity which
harps on the deathly aspect of the Crucifixion. Lawrence had
no social view: his appeal was to the individual's instinctive and
purposive sides together; and we have to see that appeal in both
'phallic consciousness' and 'the courage of tenderness'. Lawrence's
use of the word 'touch' is multiple and reverential; and so should
be our apprehension of his main themes. In other words, we

should not laugh or yawn; and that is hard because he is both pompous and long-winded.

He relies, in fact, on the suasive power of myth and the hypnotic power of his rapt intensity. But, as I have said, myth through its very nature as well as for aesthetic reasons makes us self-conscious: we are supposed to fit ourselves into the pattern, but not supposed to feel embarrassed because the novelist takes the myth more seriously than we do. If, in fitting ourselves in, we also lose our sense of awkwardness, all is well. If not, we feel only the abstractness and remoteness of the myth, and suspect it of being a merely cerebral exercise by a writer who cannot manage the full complexity of society. This is an important point for both the satirist and the myth-novelist.

Society, with its paraphernalia of technology, manners and morals, will always seem to stifle the primitive within us: that is Lawrence's theme, and Forster's too. We should be prepared to allow ourselves a little submissiveness; we are not as much in control as we think we are. All our systems are inadequate; we should not try to make them perfect. And a thorough scrutiny of man in society leads us back to the general, abstract human condition which, ultimately, is private to each of us. It should be obvious that anyone anxious to avoid the technologically complex society (of which Snow makes so much) can turn either to the inward stream or to the remote myth. A satisfying novel will not result from either kind of avoidance or even from a combination of both. Sooner or later the novelist has to pay his tribute to the stuff of society; what he adds to his tribute is his own affair. There is no bureau of ratios to keep him straight.

It is time now to look at some novelists who have attempted to distil mythology from human situations without, so to speak, presenting their laboratory-books. We, the readers, are supposed to supply whatever data we think apt; the novelist supplies the matrix. Inevitably the result is simplification, a degree of shallowness and of austerity. At the other extreme are the novelists who pile up the facts and the decades and, if they create a myth at all, create one of sheer social arithmetic which, after all, does what myth does: it typifies and interrelates. For example, the myth-writer will deal in journeys into darkness, emergences of the deity, the mechanicality of humans and the feeling for an earth-mother. Utopias, lands of Cockaigne, the Frontier, prisons and mountains all appear in his imagery. He draws on the commonplace and the trite, and he may offer them as the simple outline or basis of a complicated narrative. We can then work out preciser significances in differing contexts. But significance is not everything; guided by the banisters we may still trip over subtlety in the stairs; and, equally, we may manage the transit without using the banisters at all. Myth is wasted on some readers, is essential to others. Usually it evokes in us a primitive or simplified response: James's *Daisy Miller* (1879), for example, gives us the Innocent Abroad but also a subtly written account of *mores*, motives and misunderstanding. And a novel like *Ulysses* (1922) gives us not only myth and society but innermost privacies verbalized. Whether or not we can digest so much at once is a different matter. The main thing is that myth helps the novelist to organize and intensify—and sometimes, also, to achieve a spurious profundity.

(b) Fantasy as actuality

I

In 1913 Lawrence declared war on the Galsworthys, the Shaws and 'the rule and measure mathematical folk'. Once he had finished *Sons and Lovers*, with its unselfconscious Oedipan complexities, he began to mythologize his obsessions in terms almost manichean: mere intellect and mere charity had to go, and the unconscious in its full force had to be helped to prevail. Lawrence's life-force is a more mystical, more magical thing than Shaw's. Seen dispassionately (as his *longueurs* are apt to make us see it) his mythology takes the form of deliberate vagueness. Trances, raptures, ecstatic catalepsy, ecstatic bouts of frenzy, swoonings over flower-beds, dances in the presence of cattle, daisies planted in pubic hair, a continual litany of fruits, crops, horses, figurines, symbolic rods, sterile barons of industry, fertile peasants, milkmen and redskins, horserubbers and scarabs, resurrections and dragons—all this dissolves his heroes and effaces his evil-doers. There is far too much Frazer, Tylor, Frobenius and Jane Harrison, too much Blavatsky and Wagner in his novels. He failed to realize that myth expounds itself and needs little commentary. It communicates before it is explained; but he wanted to be sure. Natural or rural man does not need explaining but making interesting (which he often is not).

Such novels as *St Mawr* (1925), *Kangaroo* (1923) and *The Plumed Serpent* (1926) amply make the point about earth-ecstasies: we know what he is driving at long before he gives up. In the last-named he shows how such myths as Quetzalcoatl can restore the past to us, and the notion is rich; but he too readily loses sight of the kind of people who might want to see themselves implicated in the novel without their having to labour at the basic myth. His *Psychoanalysis and the Unconscious* (1921) and *Fantasia of the Unconscious* (1922) are in some parts more readable than the theorizing sections of his novels. Freud, he said, exaggerated the importance of incest; Jung was wrong about the

74

primitive unconscious; Dostoevsky was too cerebral; Proust and
Gide were arid, too civilized; even Joyce was 'putrid'. The auto-
didact always bites a feeding hand. So we cannot be blamed ourselves if we neglect the hectoring Lawrence and find malicious
pleasure in the irritable traveller in *The Sea and Sardinia* (1921).
People in what we call real life get irritable as often as they get
rapturous, and Lawrence tends to forget the fact. He offers his
own plenty. Those who like myth diluted will turn naturally to
the longer novels. But the novellas wear best: for elegance,
narrative economy, as well as a more than facile suggestiveness,
nothing in the Lawrence canon can quite equal, say, *The Ladybird*
(1923) and *The Fox* (1923). The concise Lawrence, like the concise Thomas Mann, makes one wonder whether the novel, in
asserting itself against the short poem, has not gone too far. For
myth, as well as sustaining a large structure, can also save a waste
of words. It works both ways, making the concise profound and
the lengthy steady; but also tempting the miniaturist into length
and the full-scale artist into being perfunctory.

My main concern at the moment is with myth that seems to
come from, and to be related to, nothing specific in the daily
round. The novels of May Sinclair (1865–1946), for instance,
always seem to be on the edge of revelation, but never quite
fulfil themselves. *Three Sisters* (1914) is every bit as claustrophobic as an Ivy Compton-Burnett recording-room. Set in a
country vicarage that evokes the Brontës and the bitter clerical
ménage of *The Way of All Flesh*, this novel shows how undue
devotion destroys. The vicar continually thwarts his daughters
and, when they rebel, manages to re-tie one of them to his de-
crepit side. She sublimates her sexual instincts while the others
continue into hypocrisy, undiscriminating man-hunger and
marriage. The trouble with May Sinclair's conception of this
promising theme is her coolness: she is analytical almost before
she has described the situation in all its complexity. Between her
calm dissection and the sisters' locked-in frenzy there is not
enough demonstration. Theoretically the novel makes sense; but
the novelist herself seems to have needed a good dose of animal
vigour. After all, lust dissimulated and disappointment wrenched
out into words need more than merely intellectual presentation.
This far, Lawrence was right. Logically enough, *Mary Oliver*

(1919) is her most convincing novel because it employs the stream device: some hot blood gets into the cerebral rivulet and spills over the proprieties. There are some hot thoughts too. The novel reads like a game of Beggar-my-Neighbour played with cards marked Incest, Oedipus, Infantilism, Drink, Rapture and Madness; there is just too much repression and psychosis. Mary is a frost-piece, as well as a stage-property anticipating the heroine of *The Life and Death of Harriet Frean* (1922). Unfortunately May Sinclair never got over the novelty of the new psychological science: unfortunately, because she had the intelligence to write a masterpiece about even the feminist cause.

Oddly enough, nothing is more sterile than some of the myths based on the idea of thwarted vigour. Forster's fertility rites in his short stories, the atavism of Carella in *Where Angels Fear to Tread* and its more cumbersome version in Stephen Wonham in *The Longest Journey*, all seem rather dusty. Forster does not idealize his dionysiacs as Lawrence does, and perhaps for that reason fails to give them much life even on the level of personification. They seem diagrammatic and even as theoretical as a Mary Olivier. We might say the same of Rima, the woman-bird heroine of W. H. Hudson's *Green Mansions* (1904), and Mary Webb's insubstantial Hazel who loves foxes in *Gone to Earth* (1917). Prue, in *Precious Bane* (1924), is not much better, but she at least is backed up by a more thoroughgoing rural necromancy. *Wolf Solent* (1929) by John Cowper Powys does for Dorset what Mary Webb did for Shropshire—but with a redeeming flavour of farce. Somehow, we have to be a little crazy to deal in myth at all; and farce supplies a key to the condition. Solemnity cripples the surreptitious part of myth, the part we absorb without really knowing.

This is evident from the performances of Huxley, Forster and Joyce. There is no doubt that Lawrence's resurrection-story, *The Man Who Died*, aims at the serious reader, as does Conrad's dossier on frustration and sexual abnormality, *Chance*. The outlines are vibrant; but they blur the immediate for the sake of the transcendent. They mean more than they say; and even what is said is said seriously. Such ambitious writings take us continually to the edge of dreams, to what remains of our primitive awareness, to the generalizations of the folk-memory and the whole complex mythologizing of ignorance we call religion. Whether rural or urban, whether sexual or religious, whether heroic or ignominious, the matter of myth always asks of us a mental and imaginative effort. We have to cope with blurred effects as well as with mundane data; with reverberations and with implications. Wit or irony, in disposing of the self-consciousness that myth provokes, makes virtue out of necessity. Myth alone does not make good literature; but good literature of any kind can profit from the presence of a myth—and best of all on a take-it-or-leave-it basis. The meaning is that part of the novel which keeps us busy while the myth works on us more intimately.

Elizabeth Bowen (1899–) is one of the best at making a profound significance sink in while she preoccupies us with carefully marshalled trivia. Weird people in empty hotels work upon us to a Kafka-like conclusion, but without Kafka's overt anxiety for us to understand in full. She excels in the use of hallucination, reverie and the severely rationed stream. Her titles suggest the mythic ambitions she has for her narratives: *The Hotel* (1927), *The Last September* (1929), *To The North* (1932), *The Heat of the Day* (1949). This is the geography of self-regarding, the substantiation of human vacuity. No novelist has expressed hollowness so poignantly, whether that of the Portias (*Death of the Heart*, 1939) who look vainly to the respectable for shows of soul, or of neurotic parents who live through their children (*The House in Paris*, 1935). If Elizabeth Bowen has a fault it is sparseness of evidence: almost as if she could not be further bothered with facts already transmuted into philosophy in her own mind. For her, something is always there—in even the emptiest of situations; her prose is always equal to such situations, but sometimes the patience of her reader is not. Perhaps, all along, she has been too oblique, too exacting.

Of other novelists who have suggested outlines and left main points unmade, Christopher Isherwood (1904–) has done for pre-war Berlin not what Joyce did for Dublin or Mann for Lübeck but has typified the urban microcosm in sexual renegades. Mr Norris of *Mr Norris Changes Trains* (1935) is a masochist and needs to pay for regular flagellation; Sally Bowles in *Goodbye to Berlin* (1939) is a genial nymphomaniac: both epitomize something more than the coming to terms with one's intimate nature.

They do no harm with their aberrations but provide an antithesis to lusts and apathies which, just as personal, will coalesce to form the basis of Naziism. The novels expose a great deal, but not believable people. Isherwood never quite emancipates himself from his fantasy world of Poshocracy, secret watchers, juvenile conspirators, glaciers, goat-tracks, departing trains, self-made misfits, the drama of ineffectuality and the hyperbolic interpretation of his own life as a Test whose worst trial is scruffy lodging-houses. The Search for a Father and Mastication by the Evil Mother recur in Isherwood's novels and his autobiography, *Lions and Shadows* (1938). Philip in *All the Conspirators* (1928) never amounts to more than his feeble self; and the ending, which shows him winning second prize in a poetry competition, is not the final degradation of a sensitive soul but a tedious Q.E.D. Isherwood's main skill is in crisp narrative and cinematic reporting. As long as he can make one scene follow another, he is entertaining; but when he tries to go beyond, into moral significances, he achieves only an inflated pretentiousness. In *Prater Violet* (1945) he goes beyond the photography of the Berlin novels and tries to present Bergmann, the middle-aged, touchy European Jew, as 'the face of a political situation, an epoch. The face of Central Europe.' This is altogether too facile. It would be hard to swallow even if Bergmann seemed a person; as it is, he is no more than a cute marionette.

At his best, Isherwood is Issyvoo, the good listener, the affable unretiring jury; he has something in common with Somerset Maugham. Both compile a boyish, exotic, facilely worldly mythology of spiritual decay in foreign parts; both collect the facts, the fascinating copy, and hinge it all carefully into non-committal albums. Both have turned to oriental religions: Maugham in *Points of View* (1959) enthuses about the life of a Hindu saint; Isherwood edited a *Vedanta for the Western World* (1946) and in 1944 collaborated with Swami Nikhilananda on a translation of the *Bhagavad-Gita*. And Isherwood's *The World in the Evening* (1954) recommends charity and the Quaker way. It seems that only a thorough vision of the trivial, only a complete abdication from judging, pave the way for illumination. To read either Isherwood or Maugham is to undergo some kind of cool, readable *ascêsis*. Certainly, both are as serenely literate in their early lack of faith as in the spiritual repose of their later years. They are interesting more for being (or electing to be) symptomatic than for exposition of any message; and Isherwood's elaborate, wry shedding, in *Down There on A Visit* (1962), of his old selves amounts to regarding himself as a symptom, under the auspices of Huysmans, from the repose of maturity.

Decadence and morbidity have also found exponents who have no allegorical intentions. Denton Welch, an English Truman Capote, managed to produce two novels before his premature death: in *Maiden Voyage* (1943) and *In Youth Is Pleasure* (1945) the young protagonist indulges in masochistic and transvestite fantasies that Isherwood himself, less elaborately, evoked in *Prater Violet*. In 1938 Lawrence Durrell had published *The Black Book*, the story of Lawrence Lucifer, a young man who goes to the Adriatic 'to be a writer'. There is an anticipation here of the Alexandrian tetralogy; but everything is cruder, more garish. A Peruvian voluptuary, a prostitute, a gigolo and a hypochondriac keep Lucifer company but hardly provide him with a local hell. The prose is sluggish and tends to be pretentious. Four-letter words can be found among the *recherché* latinisms, and the general effect is almost coy—as if Durrell had decided to refurbish Firbank.

After Beardsley's *Under the Hill* (1903) Ronald Firbank (1886–1926) had to work hard to force something still more perverse from even his foetid imagination. The topsy-turvy post-war world which Michael Arlen apotheosized in *The Green Hat* (1924) impressed Firbank not at all. A dedicated writer owing much to the example of Henry James, he constructed a world of *malaise* in which perversion was the normal thing. Wars, personal tragedies and the life of the majority happened between chapters. Inside, he created an uneasy Tussaud world of puns, nerves and attenuated grotesques. His characters embody futility; in fact, they are all the same character, giggling and confusedly prattling about sexual policies or their heart's desire. Lechery, boredom and mysticism get them into tangles from which they can extricate themselves only verbally. The novels twitch onwards; nothing is sustained for long. Cardinal Pirelli while naked chases a choirboy round the church, but dies under a fresco of eleven thousand virgins. The blue puppies at the font, the flagellations, the Italian counts, the twisted Catholicism and the offstage lightning are lush emblems of nihilism. Even Firbank's nagging, straining punctuation gives an impression of someone caught between languor and hysterical insistence. He could not resist the grotesque; a gaudy boy himself, he pepped up and enamelled his personages until they projected just that little bit more: enough, anyway, to persuade him that the gulf separating one person from another could be crossed—or at least concealed. The same preoccupation turns up in Dickens and explains his sentimentality. Firbank too is sentimental: he languishes in idiosyncratically witty accounts of the spiritually, the sexually and the socially forlorn. Depravity and pranks are the only anodynes. *The Artificial Princess* (1934), his rococo cushion for Salome, *The Flower Beneath the Foot* (1923), a perverse account of a saint (compare with Waugh's *Helena*), and *Valmouth* (1919), his attempt at a *Brideshead Revisited*, are well worth a careful reader's time. His work deserves to be seen as more than a freak fiesta. He has something in common with both Waugh and Huxley, as well as with analysts of other wastelands.

Fear is Firbank's principal drive: he externalizes what look like nightmares and so has something in common with the surrealists. At the exhibition in the New Burlington Galleries in 1936 Mme André Breton appeared with blue hair; another woman wore a mask of red roses; and Salvador Dali, from within a diving helmet, inaudibly addressed the gathering. That much is in the Firbank and Dada tradition; but the automatic writing of Philippe Soupault and Breton, of course, is not. Sufficient here to recall the Gothic excesses of Monk Lewis, Horace Walpole and Swinburne. The paraphernalia of the unconscious, and of the conscious aping the dream, rarely change. Despair resorts to the same tricks as madness. Breton's *Poisson soluble* lacks the adroitness of both Firbank and Hugh Sykes Davies's *Petron* (1935). Petron is a pilgrim whose preposterous adventures include a man who slices his fingers into hands, those hands' fingers into hands, and so on. He also encounters a self-disembowelling crab and a man whose jaw hangs level with his knees. We have to guess like mad if we want to interpret. The mixture of Swiftian fantasy and Freudian obsession is daunting, but it certainly communicates the sense of futility prompting destructiveness. Some kind of

mythology develops all the same—a barrier against the incomprehensible.

It may be that we save ourselves only with what we create
deliberately: such creation attests to our own power. More probably we feel safer when looking at life in terms of a myth we have
acquired involuntarily: some kind of heritage from the racial
memory. Either way we look to myth for a means of social and
spiritual adjustment. The fund is so vast that everyone should be
satisfied: a Robert Graves sets up his cult of the White Goddess,
but a Lawrence presents woman as the white peacock, 'all vanity,
screech and defilement'. For every bout of dark interiority there
is a craving for external pattern: the surrealism of J. B. Yeats's
The Aramanthers (1936) is at the opposite pole from Rex Warner's
political mythologies in *The Professor* (1938) and *The Aerodrome*
(1941). What we know of our unconscious drives us in fear to the
most arid systems. This, surely, is Orwell's point: *Animal Farm*
(1945) demonstrates the *orgueil* of the bestial, and *1984* (1949)
shows man on the rebound from metallic system to a Lawrentian
reverence for such animal pleasures as sexual intercourse and
cherishing an illicit, dark thought. Orwell, like Lawrence, is a
polemicist: he concocts a pastoral—Lower Binfield in particular
and southern England in general—which reflects his paranoid
hatred of modernism and bizarrely embodies his complex ideal of
rural peace, respect for the past and for any kind of reactionary
humanitarianism which despises money. His early novels, from
Burmese Days (1934) to *Keep the Aspidistra Flying* (1936) and
Coming up for Air (1939), reveal an Orwell who has not quite
thought his beliefs, plots and prejudices carefully through. The
fastidious artist who admired Gissing and George Moore eventually steadied himself by writing a series of critical essays and then,
with unfortunately little time left to him, managed to fit his
pastoral into truly polemical works which required of him not
character-creation but the imaginative effort of fantasy. His
personages remain two-dimensional and Crossgates, the school
in *Such, Such Were the Joys*, reappears with the Head's study
become Room 101 and Bingo, the Head's wife, who had exacted
from the boys 'a sort of guilt-stricken loyalty', enlarged into Big
Brother. Orwell's warp continued; the muck and murk and the
wilful destructiveness persisted. But the main pity is that he took

so long to clarify what he most believed in before candidly
devoting himself to the genre he managed best.

William Golding (1911–), after presenting in *Lord of the Flies*
(1955) a gradual descent into bestiality, switched to a different
kind of epitome in *Free Fall* (1959): it is the introspective vision
here that becomes vital. All apocalypse sends us back into ourselves—to the beast in us or the potential saint. In *Lord of the
Flies*, for example, childhood turns up red in tooth and claw. A
group of English schoolboys are marooned on a tropical, unin-
habited island when their refugee aircraft crashes during an
atomic war. Slowly and horribly, the boys degenerate into
savages: the school code gives way to war-paint, bestiality and
ritual slaughter. The aptest commentary on this is *The Inheritors*
(1955) in which Golding creates his own account of early man and
of the creatures his initiative enabled him to oust. In *Pincher
Martin* (1956) the torpedoed sailor, fending for himself on his
Atlantic rock, reviews his life and finds it poor. Between early man
and that sailor has come a whole series of civilizations, culmin-
ating in the skill that invents torpedoes. Small wonder that
Golding's abiding point—that depravity continually besets us—
leaves him no room for social detail. All the same, one wishes he
would make his tremendous point other than allegorically; after
all, our depravities are as superficial as deep.

The English novelist is especially attuned to the idea of innocence; of spirituality pure and uncorrupted. Such is the basis of
Animal Farm (1945); and Winston Smith's rebelliousness at the
end of *1984* is dispelled by a nursery rhyme. Childhood is the
phase of uncontaminated living; it is also the heyday of the un-
selective sensibility, and it fascinates many English novelists from
L. P. Hartley to Olivia Manning, emerging in the nightmarish
idylls of William Sansom (*Fireman Flower*, 1944) and the weird
Gormenghast novels of Mervyn Peake. Childhood mythologized
is probably the most familiar form of evasion among the English.
Sartre in *Les Temps Modernes* (No. 2) suggested that 'Anglo-
Saxon intellectuals who form a class apart, severed from the rest
of the nation, are always staggered to find French artists and
writers firmly involved in the life and affairs of the nation'. That
is overstated, but the gist is true; and its basis is the English
novelist's addiction to gentility and escape. Class-distinction and

a hankering for the quiet, locked-in pools of an apparently medi-
tative childhood have successfully seduced some English novelists
away from larger responsibilities. The temptations to retreat from
a mostly commercial world are strong for the middle-class author;
and, of course, no matter who prates about the responsibilities of
the novelist, the novelist will please himself. This is not a moral
matter; the widest vision wins in the end anyway.

But what is intriguing is the way in which childhood's animism
and ready mythologizing resembles the methods of the political
fabulists and so mocks a little the ultimate devices of those who
care passionately about society. Henry Green's first novel,
Blindness (1926), traces a blind boy's growth through the images
of caterpillar, chrysalis and butterfly, with insinuations of rose
and bird. Kafka's clerk awakes one day to find he has turned into
a bedlouse. In children's stories the animals always speak and are
usually genial; the adult world either stresses almost manically
our difference from the animal or morbidly insists on the bestial
in us. Children can make free with the world, metamorphosing
things and beings at will. No wonder, then, that Ivy Compton-
Burnett's monster parents live through their offspring. Peter Pan
rejects adult responsibilities in favour of a world both surrealist
and dramatic: pirate, crocodile and inland lake pull at us in the
subtlest way—like Alice in the well. Herbert Read's *The Green
Child* (1935) demonstrates the same point and his 'The Innocent
Eye' in *Annals of Innocence and Experience* (1940) exemplifies in
a much subtler, more Proustian way the nature of 'virgin sensibility' and how to develop its vestiges. Richard Hughes's *A High
Wind in Jamaica* (1929) shows that the child's world is not simply
an earlier version of the adult's, but a different thing entirely.
Innocence defends itself with shifts not available to an adult
world which consoles itself with images that the child's awareness
and the primitive mind have in common. Joyce's earwig, Kafka's
impossible castle and the toad of Toad Hall belong in the same
fable. The wheel of innocence comes full circle. Every adult boy
has wanted at some time or other to reverse the letters in Dylan
Thomas's 'Llareggub' but to leave Butler's 'Erewhon' as it
stands.

A symbolist novel will either use our residual childishness
against us or make it seem our only support. The method is

usually not discursive but suggestive; we have to be in the right state of mind or the devices will seem laborious and insulting. Conrad's *Heart of Darkness* works upon us by evoking a host of images implicit in the title. He resorts to a child's elemental impressions of white and black, studding the novel with close-ups that carry a whole climate of sentiment with them. Similarly elementary but sophisticatedly used images are the silver mine and the drifting ship in *Nostromo* (1904), the city in *The Secret Agent* (1907), the captain's double in *The Secret Sharer* (1912) and, in *Victory* (1915), the island, the volcano and the exile of Heyst. Much of this is the stuff of the boys' adventure story, and Conrad uses it against us in order to awaken a vague sense of insecurity. These images, which we know well, ought not to be in such a context; they suggest to us all kinds of comfortable dangers and yet are obviously meant to deprive us of comfort itself.

Ulysses is packed with images which have both to be responded to mindlessly and yet stored away for an analytical next reading, No one is going to respond to everything; so Joyce's is the blanket method. Sooner or later something in his medley will strike fire from each of us: sublimely fat Buck Mulligan, profaning the Eucharist; the Moses theme; Mr Bloom fussing to buy tea; the brown mackintosh; coffee, ale and cocoa; Plumtree's Potted Meat. Which of these we prefer matters not, for we have soon (childlike) established our own ritual, and we keep looking for our preferred motif to turn up. Before long we have linked another to it, and the symphony of images begins to emerge. We are, as Joyce has it, 'astoneaged'. In *Finnegans Wake* Earwicker develops into Uru-Wukru; Anna and Isabel become the Liffey, a cloud or the sea. Then Earwicker becomes manifest as the hill of Howth, his sons as Shem and Shaun, Napoleon and Wellington, Mutt and Jeff. Earwicker's indiscretion in the park is metamorphosed into various evasions of its true nature. All the same, he is tried in the pub by a boozy jury, and washerwomen make his dirty linen public. Because the texture is more difficult the method is more hit-or-miss than that of *Ulysses*: here we have to catch ricochets from a disrupted vocabulary whereas in *Ulysses* we take our associations from the structure. The structure of *Finnegans Wake* will do for us all; which is to say that, to feel really implicated, we need something much more personal which the puns perhaps fail to provide. One wonders how much help are the Freudian dream-images of Babel, the ladder, the switch-back, falling asleep during sleep, and Lipoleum's hat. The dream is that of all of us and yet it has to be independent of us. Whether or not we can get into it, and then stay with it, depends largely on the extent to which we ourselves might think of Tristan as 'tree-stone' or of Vico because of Vico Road. If we cannot talk ourselves into borrowing these echoes, then we have to pack up the novel altogether or burrow more deeply into the texture. And the depths are unlimited.

But, whether we are making the conscious intellectual effort demanded by the myth of *Ulysses* or trying to swoon into *Finnegan*, we are limited and assisted by what we retain of childhood's arbitrary cosmology. It is all, to the adult, fresh as paint, a symbolism evocative of aboriginal magic and Athenian boys casting tops on the paving of the agora. The quintessence of childhood is a bemused atmospheric awareness which, failing to survive puberty, is sealed in haunting details. Great dreamers, awake or asleep, children adapt all they see to their own bizarre cosmography; sensible almost from babyhood of the Pentecostal wind threatening the dream-edifice, they indulge in a joy at once natural and apocryphal.

That alchemy, whether of demonologies or raptures, cannot come back. Yet it is a part of all that is, and that is sufficient justification for the Henry Greens and the L. P. Hartleys. They apply more intensely the method of the Forster who insists on hay in *Howards End*, the Proust who makes the Duchesse de Guermantes put out a female orchid to be fertilized, the Virginia Woolf who erects a lighthouse before us and the Lawrence who makes Hermione fell Birkin with a paperweight in *Women in Love*. These are the punchings of our return tickets, whether we are on our way back to the cave, childhood, man in the abstract or anthropoid Adam.

Upon the novels of Henry Green (1905–) one critic, Edward Stokes[1] (not an American but a New Zealander), has brought to bear the close analytical technique deplored by C. P. Snow. It may be useful to know the number of sentences of various lengths, how many colour-words Green uses, and so on; it is certainly not

1. *The Novels of Henry Green*, 1959.

necessary. Green's novels are lyrical and symbolist. His main theme is that loneliness can only be overcome by love. (Here is a maturer solution than Firbank's, a subtler one than that of Dickens; but the obsession is common to all three.) The trouble, as Green exposes it, is that people cannot communicate valuably with one another. In a volume of autobiography, *Pack My Bag* (1940), he has himself referred to the 'void of unmentionables' depicted in *Loving* (1945). There is no main structural image, nor any blanket technique, but a selection of wandering hints of different dreams associated with images of castle, peacock, weathervane, lost rings and dovecote. Perhaps symbolism is like punning, there being three principal types: the inadvertent, the impromptu and the deliberate. Green's symbols are mostly deliberate but inadvertent-looking. *Party Going* (1939) presents the claustrophobia of frustration in almost Dickensian tokens: fog, people trapped (surely *Trapped* is *the* Green title?) and a forlorn dead pigeon that one could interpret endlessly. In *Living* (1929) a flock of pigeons wheel over the industrial landscape and counterpoint in a way almost giddy in the context the grim life of the foundryworkers. Everything else is trapped; *Caught*, for instance, shows Londoners hemmed in by the hot air and whirling metal of the blitz. In *Loving* (1945) two housemaids whirl into a waltz in the deserted ballroom. The free, the rapt and the happily partnered are contrasted with the prison of sodality. Not that freedom is any use without someone to whom you can express all of yourself, or that sodality necessarily entails indifference to one another. Green does not deal in absolute states, any more than his bird symbolism is rigid. *Back* (1946) is an intensely poetic evocation of a soldier's return, and the symbolism is roses. *Concluding* (1948) sketches a sensitive's response to the welfare state, but the symbolism is less obvious—indeed, at times, gratuitous. Of two missing girls one is found, but a goose, pig and cat keep on appearing and vanishing without rhyme or reason. *Nothing* (1950) and *Doting* (1952) are less poetic than chattering: the subtlety of the symbolism is transferred to the intonations of speech without, however, the creation of lacunae in place of the symbols' indefiniteness. To get much from Green, you have to work yourself into his mind; guessing and free association help as much as careful ticketing of his symbols. The prose is exquisite but it cannot disguise the principle that emerges: If the reader needs to follow, then either blanket him or give him a central image to chew at. Too often Green does neither and in his latest novels seems to be heading in the direction of colloquial comedy almost too perfect in form.

L. P. Hartley (1895–) tightens up not only form but symbolism. Three of his novels, *The Shrimp and the Anemone* (1944), *The Sixth Heaven* (1946) and *Eustace and Hilda* (1947) deal with the tyranny of sister over younger brother. Eustace and Hilda open things by trying to disentangle a shrimp from the mouth of an anemone; but they pull out the anemone's innards too. Things close with Eustace, now quite subjugated by Hilda, returning to the pool and sticking his finger into the anemone's mouth. Hartley's touch is gentle but relentless; the children are not guinea-pigs but states of apprehension trapped in bodies. The symbols never seem laboured-after; but this most natural terminology disappears with *The Go-Between* (1950). Here all is zodiacal, portentous and con-trived—like ill-digested Lawrence. Another female uses another boy; he gradually senses what is happening but succumbs all the same, involved in an adult triangle that precipitates a tragedy and disillusions him for life. Into the ears of babes indeed; and out of their mouths, in *A Perfect Woman* (1955), comes a daunt-ing chorus on the ineffectual shufflings of Isabel and Harold Eastwood disrupted from their suburban inertia by the arrival of Alec Goodrich, a writer who has not quite fulfilled his promise. Take this:

'I don't know what's wrong with Daddy.'

'What is wrong with me?' asked Harold rashly.

'Don't ask her,' Jeremy said, 'she's sure to say something silly.'

'What is the matter with me?' repeated Harold, ignoring Jeremy.

'You must have fallen in love.'

'Fallen in love, why?'

'Because you're forgetting everything—you forgot to kiss Mummy when you came in, you forgot to say "Hullo, how's tricks?" to us, you forgot to have your tea, and then you sat down in my chair.'

'Thank you, Janice, that's quite enough,' said Harold repressively.

Tragedy follows. The children provide a *danse* unintendedly *macabre*; in a delirium of precocious acquiescence they exemplify once again Hartley's uncanny knack of getting inside the child mind *via* the adult conscience.

In Hartley's world, having a conscience is usually a painful business. But having it does at least ensure that when we meet evil we do not flounder. As *My Fellow Devils* (1951) shows, through the virtuous Margaret Pennefeather and the diabolical film-star whom she marries, conscience and the sharpened awareness it includes are the essential prerequisites for action. Act without conscience to guide, and you create slack havoc. Margaret leaves her flashy husband, and her action has at least the merit of definiteness. But one wonders if she had enough understanding: after all, if conscience is the knife, then it should have an accurate cross-section to its credit. And one cannot help feeling that Hartley himself tends to confuse quietness with silence, receptivity with promiscuity and self-discipline with being hermetic. For once, in *My Fellow Devils*, he deserted his familiar ground, broke out of his Austenish circle, and therefore seemed to be fabricating rather than deriving morality. But *The Go-Between* (1950) returns to the life of country houses, and a lonely middle-aged man excitedly reads through his boyhood diary, while *The Hireling* (1957) extends a hardboiled chauffeur into love for a titled widow. Hartley's scope is widening slowly, but one wonders if his notion of conscience ever will.

The novel of adolescence, like the novel of childhood, concerns itself with a sensitive plant and its surroundings. Precious moments can be recaptured and can even be used as a defence against the adult world in which the novelist has to write his pages. It was only natural that the advent of psychological science should, of all things, rejuvenate the novel of adolescence—a type of writing which flourished in the nineteenth century and has become increasingly popular in our own. (Susanne Howe Nobbe's *Wilhelm Meister and His English Kinsmen*, 1930, and Justin O'Brien's *The Novel of Adolescence in France*, 1937, testify to the vogue.) But the vein that runs from Meredith (*Richard Feverel*,

Evan Harrington and *Harry Richmond*) through Samuel Butler (*The Way of All Flesh*), Arnold Bennett (*Clayhanger*), J. D. Beresford (*The Early History of Jacob Stahl*, 1911–15), Compton Mackenzie (*Sinister Street*, 1913–14) and Forrest Reid (*Peter Waring*, 1937) splits and branches into strange countries of the mind in the work of Dylan Thomas (*Portrait of the Artist as a Young Dog*, 1940) and the novels of Denton Welch, surviving unchanged only in Anthony Powell (*A Question of Upbringing*, 1951, *Buyer's Market*, 1952, *The Acceptance World*, 1955) and C. P. Snow (a sharp light on possessiveness).

Lawrence's *Sons and Lovers* (1913), Maugham's *Of Human Bondage* (1915) and Joyce's *Portrait of the Artist as a Young Man* (1916) show, in their respective ways, signs of a change: a new frankness displacing excessive analysis; a willingness to get off the point (or apparently so) into symbols. Maugham's club-footed Philip is an elementary Baudelaire; Stephen Dedalus has a great deal of Baudelaire's fanatical devotion to art (and, of course, reappears in *Ulysses* to penetrate new reaches of human darkness); and both suffer, although at a different social level from him, the parental incubus so movingly suffered by Paul Morel. The middle-class parental shadow always seems starker than that surrounding the working-class youth; its culture seems thinner, remoter from the young, whereas the working-class attitude to the adolescent is at once chummier and more mercenary.

It is perhaps not peculiar that most of the *romans-fleuve* of our time start no earlier than adolescence; to go fully into childhood, without wasting the possibilities of suggestion conferred by symbolism and by readers accustomed to symbols, is to commit oneself to a style that might become tedious when the subject becomes an adolescent and an adult. The *Bildungsroman* has a more intimate atmosphere in which a consistent method can be sustained: Romain Rolland's *Jean-Christophe* (1904–12) is a triumph of consistent method. But, for the most part, a Hartley does not follow his Eustace and Hilda through into adolescence or adulthood; he prefers to imply extrapolations by contrasting the child's mind with adults in the same novel. Proust is the only novelist who has successfully traced a sensibility right through; and his method runs in reverse. An easier way of relating childhood and its mythologies to adult experience is to set the childhood mythology floating about in the stream of the adult: Joyce does this magnificently; so does Virginia Woolf. Without Freud, Jung and the stream such an endeavour would have been impossible. At the same time, though, the technique of flash-back or unwitting recall creates recurring technical and reading problems. After all, it is much easier to follow a person right through than to try fathoming all the private memories and associations with which the author equips him. The novelist who wants to be thorough has eventually to choose between writing a whole work in a manner best suited to the evocation of childhood and writing it so plainly as to risk over-articulating the child's world of undefined arcana. On the one hand, Proust combines free-association with relentless intelligence; on the other, Hartley and Green change methods according to their subject-matter, while Anthony Powell writes all the volumes of *The Music of Time* in the same 'unpoetic' style.

We must face it: the worlds of childhood fantasy, adolescent self-dramatization, adult daydreaming and primitive man merge together and cannot be separated by any technique known to the novelist or anyone else. If you suggest a child's awareness of the world, then you are probably also half-way into the cave where the dramas of adolescence coincide with the pipe-dreams of maturity. So, quite often, a seriously meant political allegory or myth (*Animal Farm*) seems a child's phantasmagoria, a book of childhood magic (*Lord of the Flies*) slides into shocking allegory, and Nigel Balchin's *The Small Back Room* scores by presenting an adult, scientific theme in a manner readily assimilable to the fears of childhood and the relished thrills of boyhood adventure-reading. All this is deliberate and advantageously performed. But, occasionally, because the novelist is dabbling in mythic matter over which his control is only intermittent, he admits images that destroy the atmosphere he needs. I am thinking of the novels of Charles Williams (1886–1945), in which theosophy gives the thriller a new twist but also deprives the thriller element of the claustrophobia we have to feel in order to be 'thrilled'. If the eternal keeps butting in on the fiercely secular, we cannot feel hemmed in. The magic stone, for instance, in *Many Dimensions* (1931) deprives the novel of the thriller's essential limitedness without transforming it into fantasy. We hover uneasily between the boys'-thriller type of fantasy (which admits anything) and the adult fondness for clear categories. No doubt Williams thus achieves an excellent allegory, pressing a sophisticated message into the most juvenile parts of our minds. But we can take only so much of the medley-novel which, including black magic, the Grail, the Tarot pack and the philosopher's stone, yet seeks to operate at the thriller level. The novel is formal and will sustain medley only through brilliant, innovatory technique. There must be many readers who come away from Williams feeling they have encountered not a man talking to men but a prosy hierophant entombing sincerity and vision in a pastiche of Wilkie Collins.

On a rather different level, Huxley's *Brave New World* prevails upon us as a serious manifesto only because we are always conscious of the intelligence behind the fantastic paraphernalia; Huxley makes his point all the more forcefully for creating images which, on the level of the boys' fantasy, would mean nothing at all and would strike the adult mind as meretricious. Huxley himself should have the last word on this; here it is, from *Crome Yellow*. Scogan is holding forth, as ever:

'Why will you young men continue to write about things that are so entirely uninteresting as the mentality of adolescents and artists? Professional anthropologists might find it interesting to turn sometimes from the beliefs of the Blackfelloe to the philosophical preoccupations of the undergraduate. But you can't expect an ordinary adult man, like myself, to be much moved by the story of his spiritual troubles. And after all, even in England, even in Germany and Russia, there are more adults than adolescents. . . . Jean-Christophe is the stock artist of literature, just as Professor Radium of *Comic Cuts* is its stock man of science.'

No one sees more clearly than the author of *Ape and Essence* (1948) how worlds merge, retrogress and fade. A little farther on, Mary Bracegirdle goes off to bed:

'I hope I shan't dream of falling down wells again tonight,' she added.

'Ladders are worse,' said Anne.

Mary nodded. 'Yes, ladders are much graver.'

And then, of course, we *know*; or at least we are provoked to guess more ironically about these girls than we otherwise would. Huxley is working primeval fear and modern symbolism against them, and the blithe mockery intensifies accordingly.

II

From the evocation of fragile or atavistic states of the spirit to judgments served on the spirit in its relations with the deity. In the nineties those who doted on symbol and the evanescent turned eventually to Roman Catholicism for, as Arthur Symons put it in his essay on Huysmans, 'its venerable age, valuable in such matters as the age of an old wine, its vague excitation of the senses, its mystical picturesqueness'. Over went Henry Harland, Lionel Johnson, Beardsley, Frederick Rolfe (author, as 'Baron Corvo', of *Hadrian the Seventh*, 1904) and Oscar Wilde. It is always hard to separate the 'mystical picturesqueness' of unorthodox religions (say theosophy or Zen) from the same quality in those that are orthodox. Obviously all ritual appeals to something childlike, and perhaps childish, in us: ritual is both tutelary and spellbinding; the symbols and ornaments both reassure and inspire.

We can see both sides of ritual in the novels of Charles Williams and G. K. Chesterton (1874–1936). Both writers try to epitomize guiding and misguiding principles, Williams contrasting the vacuities of the clubland hero with truth too pure to be stated outright, and Chesterton in *The Man Who Was Thursday* (1908) countering modern nihilistic materialism with a vague religiosity which in 1922 he relinquished for the Church of Rome. Tradition, later in Chesterton's career than in Williams's, is implanted through the very symbols that lift the mind to insubstantial things. The fact that, in the novels of Williams and Chesterton, the religious appeal is made at a childlike level is important in two ways. First, because the customary ingenuity of the detective story or the customary claustrophobia of the thriller is belied: the symbol, whether a policeman or black magic, appeals neither cerebrally nor sensually, but captivates the offguard mind. With both his higher and lower responses engrossed by the whodunit or violent element, the reader absorbs trustingly. Second, the oddity of combining theosophy with anthroposophy expresses in crude form the gulf between spiritual and secular. In other words, the reader, if he is going to tackle this kind of novel at all, is both seduced and given a dichotomy. This much achieved (and if at all it is usually achieved early on in the novel), the story then becomes an allegory offered in terms both unusual and exaggerated. In the holy thriller the crook (or materialist) is doubly wrong—in both the social and the spiritual worlds. The reader is worked upon by deliberate obliquities and disciplined by the believer who has chosen his images from the enemy's trophy room.

In the novels and entertainments of Graham Greene (1904–) two kinds of love are set in conflict: it is an old game, in which the lover resorts to the mystic's tropes and the mystic to the lover's. Taken as a whole, Greene's work is one long metaphor: like that of Williams and Chesterton, it argues spirit against the secular not so much to proselytize as to advertise the power of love. Abel uses Cain's mark to draw attention to Cain's opposite. In *Brighton Rock* (1938) Greene chooses an adolescent whose life is twisted because, like an L. P. Hartley child, his boyhood sensibilities encountered the adult world too early. In this instance, Pinkie regularly witnessed the love-making of his parents and thus gained a traumatic glimpse of a violent universe. Once again, the child's precarious world is wrecked by something he cannot mythologize until he is older; by which time Pinkie has developed into a power in the 'protection' racket. He goes on to travesty the norms of society—marrying to save his own skin, then planning to murder his wife. With one murder already to his discredit, however, he is thwarted and disposed of. The world of the novel is as mixed-up as Pinkie himself. Because Pinkie is so many things—stunted teenager, petty crook, lapsed Catholic, slum kid and social detritus—Greene can mingle the genres. The novel is a psychologist's dossier, a thriller, a sociological study, a theological pamphlet and also a structural oxymoron. To borrow the dictionary's example of the last-named, 'faith unfaithful kept him falsely true': the conjunction, as the Greek *mōros* implies, is 'foolish'. Yet, at the last, Pinkie recalls snatches of the liturgy, a vestigial passport. We can understand such a novel only if we read it as a thriller—a 'gangster story'. If we go into it looking for special significances, we lose the impact, the spiritual antithesis which floods over us, when we read it as a thriller. The adolescent wounded violence needs to be taken seriously and, to some extent, without pity. Full understanding comes to us only if we go through the charade of reading the thriller with 'thriller'-type attention: that is, not worrying too much about the psychology but concentrating on the outline, the spasms of violence and the consequences of luck. At the back of our minds is the notion of the evil getting their deserts; the spiritual desert we have witnessed is borne in upon us only towards the end.

The Power and the Glory (1940) gives another kind of paradox. The Mexican priest on the run from the secular force epitomizes all types of unintelligible terror. A good priest would not have been on the run; or—the question is pure Greene—*would* he? The terror here surpasses that in the similar forest-flight in O'Neill's *The Emperor Jones* because it is double: not only physical flight, but also from the spiritual salvation which is, of course, the only remedy for the physical kind of flight. Eventually the priest manages to make his spiritual return and physical revolt a second coming into his own again. Yet Greene is on both sides, the whisky priest's and the police lieutenant's. Both embody a discipline; both present modified extremes. Greene, in fact, the man who rebuked the Cardinal-Archbishop of Paris for refusing Christian burial to Colette, whose life has become (as Malraux's used to be) a series of well-timed sorties to the secular trouble-spots, who is as much a journalist as a Jansenist, is closer to an enraged compassion than to sectarian hebetude. He sees and is appalled. He has trekked across Liberia (*The Lawless Roads*, 1939), delved into Mexico, Sierra Leone, Vietnam, Cuba, Kenya and the Congo, and preserved the memory of continued Russian roulette: the empty chamber always evoked its opposite; the boredom always implied the possibility of spiritual fulness—or busyness at any rate. His main images—of adjacent and opposed worlds, of self-inflicted tests, of spiritual deformity—expose a great deal of his boyhood. In the opening chapters of *The Lawless*

Roads he recalls the door which separated his parents' quarters from the school of which his father was head. On one side security, haven; on the other the jungle. It is a dichotomy he never escapes.

It emerges most of all, and in its most moving form, in his suspicion that the religious sense is hostile to human aspirations. In one sense man's faith is not his own until he has investigated God for himself; but as soon as he rejects lip-service for meditation he imperils the very possibility of faith. That is the paradox of many intellectuals; implicit in it is the essential destructiveness of human thought. Faith is too *a priori* for any but the most inactive or the most desperate mind. And Greene, more intensely than anyone save Bernanos and more operatically than anyone, has illustrated for sceptics the befuddlement of believers. The humanist rigmarole—the absurd universe, secular mystiques, the reverence of human genius, the pseudonyms for a truncated God —appears in his novels minus all metaphorical aura but with, as it were, God's guard-van attached to the train. God appears to Minty who slinks into a Lutheran church in Stockholm; Scobie hides a broken rosary in his desk; Sarah's prayer in *The End of the Affair* (1951) is granted. The epiphanies show God rather than mirror man to himself. But God's general absence is not construed (as it is by Simone Weil) as certain evidence of presence. The dichotomy persists: Scobie loves God, but no one else; the priest in *The Potting Shed* (1957) loves his nephew only to lose faith in God. There is no hedging. Saints, like humanists, create themselves. And their serenity is no greater. Bendrix in *The End of the Affair* gains nothing from the gradual increase of his religious sensibility; and Father Rank, in the epilogue to *The Heart of the Matter* (1948), warns Mrs Scobie: '. . . don't imagine you— or I—know a thing about God's mercy'. It takes a human irrationality to justify a divine irrationality. And it takes scrupulous reason to discern, as Locke does in *The Reasonableness of Christianity*, that 'many are beholden to revelation, who do not acknowledge it'.

The End of the Affair (1951) pushed the average reader's credulity too far; when obsessive jealousy is dispersed by divine subterfuge, even the devout are apt to wonder. And Greene's next novel, *Loser Take All* (1955), reads like a book produced absentmindedly, while he was himself wondering what, on earth anyway, could come next. But *The Quiet American* (1956) saw him back on a less wilful road, getting to grips again with the soul's own resources, and God decently disguised in the machinery, while *Our Man in Havana* (1958) skilfully resumed his preoccupation with surfaces. Obviously he was wondering whether to materialize the mystical and so distort it, or leave us baffled.

A Burnt-Out Case (1961) shows a revulsed man of the world—empty of ambition and love, bored even by his eminence as an architect—voluntarily entering a leper colony on a tributary of the Congo. This is not so much a self-punishment as a recognition of his membership. He adds himself on, just as parts of the lepers' members deaden and fall off. Querry, this chastened Catholic man of the arts, is rather incredible: after all, how much notice does the world take of architects? Rycker, the small-time businessman, tries to see him as a saint in the making but also recognizes him as '*the* Querry'. It is Rycker who sends for Parkinson, the journalist, so that another Schweitzer can be announced to the world with the right degree of slickness. But Querry himself is too far gone to care: like his servant, Deo Gratias, he is a burnt-out case; he has achieved his cure by losing all that can be eaten away. He has no ties; he perhaps seeks a return to innocence. When he spends a night in the jungle comforting Deo Gratias, he listens to ramblings about 'Pendele' and 'a dance at a friend's house, a young man with a shiny simple face, going to Mass on Sunday with the family, falling asleep in a single bed perhaps'. Perhaps, Querry amusedly thinks, this is what he himself wants. The priests of the leproserie are childlike creatures, preoccupied with carpentering and dynamos; when Querry tells Rycker's child-wife about himself he does it in terms of a fairy-story in which he figures as a jeweller. He cannot feel pain or pleasure; the night he spends with Marie Rycker is innocent: she herself is Innocence just as (too obviously) Parkinson is Corruption. And Querry, designing a rudimentary extra hospital, what is he? A little bit the spoiled saint, a great deal the successful failure. Rycker shoots Querry—disappointed, like Father Thomas and the journalist, in the presumptive saint who slipped. But of course Querry knows the truth; truth is the only thing he still respects—so he laughs out loud when Rycker accuses him of impregnating his wife. Rycker *thinks* Querry is laughing at him, and shoots him.

A Burnt-Out Case re-presents the argument of *The Heart of the Matter*: 'Here you could love human beings nearly as God loved them, knowing the worst.' Querry, like Scobie, feels no responsibility to the beautiful, the intelligent and the graceful. Lerophilia is the extremist answer to such a view as Yusef puts forward: 'The way is not to care a damn, Major Scobie....' Everyone in *A Burnt-Out Case* cares his damn; but Querry has eliminated not just his own aesthetic standards but his character, his personality. He may look utterly empty until we realize that there is a great deal of impersonal compassion in him. He becomes aware of others' suffering in a theoretical way; he does not share their pain but (as in the anaesthesia which is a side-effect of leprosy) notes the fact of it. In some ways this is an almost Hemingwayan formula, except that it has this subtlety: in Hemingway, when the person cannot feel a fact, it escapes his mind entirely; in Greene, the unfelt fact still provokes a kind of sleepwalking reflex. Greene, and this puts him head and shoulders above any English novelist writing now, keeps on using his mind—not only about compassion and worldliness but also about the problems the mind can never solve; problems which the mind itself continually creates in order to stay human. Such torture puts Greene close to Dostoevsky and also equips him with the characteristic Dostoevskian fault of repeating, in the same novel, the same point in too many allegorical versions.

Greene's symbolism (leprosy, the hospital being the riverboat's last stop, the road almost but not quite overwhelmed by jungle) simplifies, as does the violence of the thriller. And such simplification gives the reader more opportunity to read himself into the novel; no heavily stressed idiosyncrasies get in the way of his own. But violence not only simplifies the reader's entry; it also figures in Greene's novels and in those of Liam O'Flaherty (1897–) as a despairing attempt to simplify the contorted world. O'Flaherty's *The Black Soul* (1924) shows how an overpowering sense of futility compels a returned soldier to clutch at coherence by murdering the deranged husband of the woman he loves. In order to simplify he has to obliterate. In *Mr Gilhooley* (1926) violence once again becomes the remedy: an antithetical retort to Creation; and it reappears in *The Assassin* (1928) in McDara's anarchism. O'Flaherty's political novels also reflect and allegorize the very human habit of melodramatic simplification. *The Informer* (1925) and *The Martyr* (1933) are noisy in a way that even Greene's 'entertainments', and still less his serious novels, are not. With Greene, experience in the trouble-spots has tended to produce a melodrama almost as theoretical as Forster's, with all the subtlety of life separated from it into confined analyses. With O'Flaherty, the melodrama predominates over the analysis, and violence becomes an almost literary device. Greene's triumph is that he has always tried to make the simplicities of the thriller condemn themselves. For the main agony is in the constructions, not the destructions, which the mind achieves while seeking to answer an examination none can pass. What is disturbing in Greene's work is the increasing efficiency which has brought about, between say *The Power and the Glory* and *A Burnt-Out Case*, an apparent disregard for incidentals of human personality. For it is these which compose half the novel's fascination, whether they exemplify or enact a thesis or not. Over and above despair or metaphysical certainty there is always life's unfailing abundant interest—the fertile muddle, perhaps. Greene seems to have advanced from the thriller-outline to the almost completely metaphysical one. Of course, that is better than confining oneself to the thriller, like O'Flaherty; but there is more personality to the protagonists of *The Quiet American* and *Our Man in Havana* than to anyone in *A Burnt-Out Case*. To create personality is no doubt a celebration of the world; to crowd the void with personifications is a gesture of efficient despair—rejecting the human travesty of the human tragedy while cerebrating brilliantly about both. But to write at all is to care; and Greene's skill conflicts with his seeming proof of its futility. One is glad the paradox is fertile and grateful for Greene's constant airing of it.

Greene's development brings to mind André Malraux's observation that the French novel has become 'a privileged means of expressing the tragedy of man' rather than 'an elucidation of the individual'. *A Burnt-Out Case*, like Malraux's *Le Temps du mépris*, is an instance of the novel of *situations* rather than of psychology: it demonstrates how the novel, in becoming too metaphysical, in trying to be too comprehensive and too universal, can end up as painstakingly transposed philosophy. Farther on I shall consider how the French and Spanish novel have suffered from the elimination of psychology, and the German novel from an obsession with universality. For the moment I shall suggest how three English novelists in particular (Cary, Snow and Durrell) have found themselves in a dilemma entailed by the previous vogue for flux: in other words, tempted to overdo structure at the expense of psychology and the social at the expense of the metaphysical.

III

The resulting expedients reveal something old-fashioned: preferring character to metaphysics and structure to stream, these writers have created loose, capacious forms which give plenty of scope for character in the round and for a framework so extensive in time and variety as to give an illusion of universality. The main characters are made to generalize themselves through sheer documentation: they add up, are added up over the years and made representative. After so much data, with so little apparent selection, the human condition seems to have been defined by catalogue. This is a peculiarly English empirical way of avoiding the fable's abstractness and the stream's disorder while yet suggesting, over several generations, general statements about life's untidiness. Joyce Cary is, if anything, too much inside his characters; Snow not enough or at least not enough inside them at their most emotional moments; and Durrell too willing to use them as an occasion for a flourish of his own rhetoric. But, imperfect as any *romans-fleuve* have to be, their chronicle-novels achieve something which both the stream and the fabulistic eliminate from the novel: 'likeness' (to life as we know it) which also reminds us of the illusion's artificiality. If we are going to look to the novel for social man but with his other sides vigorously implied, we should look to Cary, Snow and Durrell, as well as to Anthony Powell, Doris Lessing and Henry Williamson's *A Chronicle of Ancient Sunlight*. In their attempt to flesh the skeleton of the abstract and to force the self-analyst into action, all these novelists have become long-winded. They expect us to relate ourselves not to myth but to the facts of life fictionally and voluminously compiled. To them symbol, like myth, is a 'throwing together', and so is their concept of ecology. They are reviving the epic idea (with all its clutter of social data) but with economic rather than heroic man in view. Imagination—not in the sense in which it creates fiction but in which it creates the unusual—tends to be missing from all but Durrell. But that, surely, is a natural consequence of the stream—novelists' over-indulgence in private phantasmagoria. Eventually man's imaginative activity must once again be restored to its place even in imagined, fictional accounts. Until then—until a Durrell is not regarded as a dabbler in stained glass whose main interest is not in his characters at all—the English *roman-fleuve* is there to tell us what people create involuntarily, with repercussions down the years, in every moment of their mundane existences. The mechanics of society make a refreshing change from the electronics of inwardness. Back to structure, then, with a blatant relish for people in their own right and endlessly interacting. The novel can never do without the hedonism which rejoices in human encounter, marvelling at the diversity of temperaments but exclaiming at the similarities of people busily being themselves.

It is to be hoped that the endeavours of Snow, Cary and Durrell will not only set an example of how to keep the novel on course but also revive interest (or create it for the first time) in at least two of their predecessors: Ford Madox Ford and L. H. Myers. Before we consider the achievement of those two forgotten men, notice must be taken of Galsworthy (1867–1933) and the accumulated roughage of *The Forsyte Saga*.

Galsworthy's attempt to assess his times through analysis of class fails because, in the first place, his conception of 'Beauty' (Irene) is too abstract. In his preface to the *Saga* he announced that

> This long tale is no scientific study of the period; it is rather an intimate incarnation of the disturbances that Beauty effects in the lives of men. The figure of Irene, never present except through the sense of the other characters, is a concretion of disturbing beauty impinging on a possessive world.

No wonder, then, that Irene never comes to life; those who report on her cannot tell a beautiful woman from a football whistle or the beauty of art from a neatly printed billhead. Galsworthy in-fibulated himself from the start, and all we get is sustained in-sight into men whose only pride is in ownership. Galsworthy might have made something out of this theme; in one way he anticipated Sartre's point about the impossibility of love without reducing the loved person to an object. But Irene is nothing to start with, so she cannot be reduced. In both senses of the word she is a property. Soames Forsyte secures, through marriage, Irene's services both sexually and socially. Because Galsworthy sympathizes with him, Soames dominates the chronicle and eventually, in the novels coming after the saga and grouped together as *A Modern Comedy*, becomes Galsworthy's mouth-piece.

What a muddled saga it is. Setting out to satirize, Galsworthy ends up in whimsical tenderness: Old Jolyon is a feeble concep-tion because Galsworthy's own convictions were half-hearted. Setting out to explain the psychology of the upper-middle class, Galsworthy slid into the twenties which he did not understand: Jon, Mont and Fleur amount to nothing more than guesswork. And Bosinney versus Soames is no contest at all. The trouble with Galsworthy is that, even in the solid documentary of the first novel, *The Man of Property* (1906), he provides less than he intends to provide, and nothing inadvertently. We cannot enjoy the saga for things which crept in without his realizing. When C. P. Snow in the preface to *The Conscience of the Rich* explains that his own chronicle, while giving 'some insights into society', is meant to convey an 'inner design' with, as motif, the 'resonance between what Lewis Eliot sees and what he feels', he is drawing attention to something we ourselves may neither find nor need. For Snow provides an abundance and density which feed even those who miss his main point. He does not, as Galsworthy did, take sides; he blurs his thesis with the very fulness of life.

Galsworthy could not endure the essential loneliness of the satirist; he needed a sense of belonging more than the self-fulfil-ment of being seen to be rational. His characters cannot reason and he belongs to them; the apprentice who could not go it alone. And they, just like Soames exacting his marital rights, exact from Galsworthy the mindless loyalty he set out to ridicule. The satire is general rather than of class; when it comes off, it has an air of improvised joking—almost as if it were a special entertainment laid on as part of the dinners or the at-homes. Galsworthy could animate his puppets only through sympathizing with them; and the degree of their deadness, aesthetic not spiritual, is the measure of Galsworthy's own incapacity for perfidy. It is noteworthy that in his plays he makes only the feeblest attempts to explain the mentality of his rebels. His contenders, fugitives, deserters, backsliders and baby-killers are mere melodramatic forces dressed as people. In a word, he never analysed himself enough to be able to project his own motives; and no richness of texture, weight of documentation, mastery of atmosphere or relentless pity can conceal this deficiency.

Similar sagas came from 'Henry Handel Richardson' (Henrietta Robertson, *née* Richardson), whose *The Fortunes of Richard Mahony* (1917–29) has a loping vigour quite absent from Galsworthy, and G. B. Stern (*The Rakonitz Chronicles*, 1932). But the chronicle-novelist most likely to engage the modern reader is Ford Madox Ford (1873–1939) (he changed his name from Hueffer in 1919). Ford's universe is the absurd one of Camus. His writing is intensely personal, intrusively so; and for sound and fury, signifying only the self-command attainable through self-expression, his early novel, *The Good Soldier* (1915), cannot be matched in its own time. The narrator, Dowell, tells of the friendships between himself and his wife, and the Ashburnams. What he does not know, and so cannot tell, is that the Ashburnams and his wife ingeniously keep from him the liaison between his wife and Ashburnam, the *viveur* and Tory pillar. Technically the novel is a brilliant feat of counterpoint and integration; emotionally it never lets up. One of the oddest and cleverest things about it is the prose: Dowell expresses himself in an elated, friendly style which also can be read as the kind of irony he might indulge in if he knew. A slight element of overstatement keeps the reader warned; and Ford creates both Dowell as he is and Dowell as he might be. Bitterness is extreme; it ironically exaggerates the best; and so does Dowell, serenely *cocu* and gliding along in the heady sophisticated quartet that might have come out of Scott Fitzgerald. The four of them are so well in tune with one another, but only because Dowell is duped. The novel ends with a change of partners, but the distressing foursome goes on.

The Ashburnams, keeping up appearances, not letting Dowell down (at least according to their own surreptitious ethics), embody Ford's favourite theme of the stoical invalid. His Philoctetes never gives up. In Ford's tetralogy of Tietjens—*Some Do Not* (1924), *No More Parades* (1925), *A Man Could Stand Up* (1926) and *The Last Post* (1928)—his stoical doctrine reaches its fullest and most persuasive expression. Tietjen's wife, Sylvia, gradually ruins him with her infidelities; he assists in the process by taking her back after she has left him and by sticking to his code: no genuine gentleman divorces his wife. The wife, in this case, is a Catholic, so she cannot release him either. So there he is, the perfect Ford Prometheus. He might have said, with Gide, *il faut avoir un aigle*. His undeclared love for Valentine Wannup merely adds to Sylvia's means of destroying him. In public life, as in the war, he remains the epitome of gentlemanliness, which incenses Sylvia even more. But he gets nowhere, sapped from within.

In some ways Tietjens is a well-to-do Scobie, but Ford presents him not with the dispassionateness of Greene but with the partisan hyperbole of Galsworthy. Suddenly, as we read, a stereotype blots out Tietjens the individual; he becomes a diagram of the worst that can happen to a man of impossible integrity. Ford keeps wandering off into a region of near-hagiography; Tietjens becomes Ford, and Ford a sophisticated Bunyan. What saves the tetralogy is Ford's unflagging artifice, showing his man from many points of view. A great deal of the narrative is oblique and refracted through the consciousness of the other characters. This is a simpler version of the technique employed in Lawrence Durrell's own four-decker chronicle; Durrell, however, applies the multiple method to several characters and so creates an effect of greater complexity. Tietjens does not develop much: by definition, he cannot; and this means that his intelligent appraisals of what is happening to him cannot be translated into action. At his most active he is always repressing himself. Ford was therefore obliged to resort to some kind of stream technique and deft, swift applications of the blanket method. It is all highly readable—a tribute to Ford's skill in keeping things moving round a static hero. Finally there emerges the vital contrast: between unprincipled busyness and the energetic integrity that will not budge on moral issues: 'Some Do Not'. Ford manages to convey this without, as it were, enacting it in the construction as feverish activity and sluggish stillness. A more direct method than he chose would have crippled the books from the start. As it is, the Tietjens series is an impressive feat of the reflective intelligence at work without any loss to the main impression of lives streaming and tumbling forwards.

Ford's indictment of a morally bankrupt (although slightly mythical) ruling class resembles L. H. Myers's strictures in *The Root and the Flower* (1935) on the Trivial (as distinguished from the Fastidious). Myers's trilogy is both romantic and highly intellectual, proposing both a revolutionary view of human relationships and condemning the society of his time as lost to materialism. Myers (1881–1944) feels and reasons his way towards the light. There is something of Lawrence and Forster in him, as well as something of the tightly wound intellect of a Huxley. His main concern is that personal relationships should be spontaneous and unprescribed even though they have to exist in a society which can, as he says in *The Orissers* (1921),

see no excellence excepting in service to itself and which gradually but infallibly loses sight of all but material values. It consequently exacts terrible renunciations from its members— the deadliest and easiest being the suppression of a sense of renunciation.

Myers, of course, like Ford, is thinking of a particular section of society: the wealthy and the powerful. His Indian novels are all Rajahs and potentates; the 'Clio' is the most expensive steam-yacht known to man; Paulina in *Strange Glory* (1936) is a millionairess. He dealt also in moral extremes; the Fastidious must never parley with the Trivial—for the Fastidious are the bearers of a trust and eloquent of the dignity man can attain even while immersed in the destructive element.

The Fastidious are typified by the Orissers, isolated through choice and yet aware of the sterility of seclusion. Nicholas, inwardly refined but outwardly doubtful about everything, has no animal appetite for what the Maynes consider the good things of life. Lilian Orisser is a hermit of exquisite taste but unfulfilled in her marriage to Allen Allen, the wisest of the recluses. Cosmo's revolutionary impulses fade out, and Sir Charles kills himself. Obviously, there cannot be a great deal of action or of trivial talk. These serious people, although intimately in contact with one another, are not in touch with the vulgar: the least self-conscious, whose torments and elations fill the world with a very necessary noise. (In Forster's story, 'The Machine Stops', people go mad when the humming noise stops. Forster, of course, almost apotheosizes vulgarity and animal vigour, which Myers could never do.) The point is that if you secede, it is no use expecting to have the same moral challenges as you would find in the outside world. So any moral code evolved in seclusion is bound to be exiguous and inflexible. The Orissers suffer from a feeling of being untested, and it is indeed hard to conceive of them as people with appetites or faces. We are told they are there and we have to take that on trust. The writing is fulsome and yet arid— like the Orissers' intimate lives.

The Clio (1925) supplies a gorgeous symbol of affluence in the form of the eponymous yacht, and the prose is tighter. But we have to turn to *The Root and the Flower* to find any development in Myers's thought. This novel gives a vision of power, policy and turbulent India. Prince Jali quails a little at the 'heartless splendours' of the Durbar, and the materialism growing in India is rebuked in Daniyal's 'Pleasance of the Arts', a colony of fake aesthetes who have rejected the gross world for the grosser one of effete artificiality. The Pleasance demands conformity so that it may present a uniform front for disapproval. The colony stands on a marsh whose smell symbolizes some kind of moral decay— the kind of decay that Myers condemned in Proust in the introduction to *The Root and the Flower*: 'inverted cant . . . artistic snobbery . . . treating all sorts of sensibility as equal in importance, and all manifestations of character as standing on the same plane of significance'. There is a world of difference between what Myers calls 'emotional response to the universe in its august and divine aspect' and an undiscriminating response which, finding all kinds of conduct equally interesting, neglects to discriminate on moral grounds. Myers, like Greene's Scobie, does not want to offend God. He works on three levels: reverence for the created;

moral appraisal; and the scrutiny of the man beneath the *persona* —which is the novel's traditional role. The whole effort is towards a principled, discriminating awareness of creation.

To modern minds this all seems bloodless and defunct. The Fastidious, seen in the frustrated Orissers and the much less cut-off figures of Amar, Sita, Gokal, Hari and Jali, know they cannot be both human and isolated. Life calls them into play. All that preoccupies Myers is that the ruling class should be the best people: morally, in matters of taste and in self-knowledge. In some ways, the taste apart perhaps, he anticipates the inquiries of Snow. When Daniyal the aesthete and voluptuary treads on a cat's head, Amar, who is strongly tempted to withdraw from the world, strikes him and so re-enters into his obligations. Again, in *Strange Glory* Paulina decides to go to Russia. The choice is simple but Myers does not simplify it further. It is between a prison morality, which may become just as corrupt in its narrowness as that of the world, and a morality that has to be fought for outside. Although over-illustrating the first, Myers insists on the second; and although his characters and their names seem almost perversely remote, his argument has some bearing on totalitarianism and the democratic delegation of authority.

The Pool of Vishnu (1940), the sequel to *The Root and the Flower*, takes the responsibility theme a stage farther. Not only must we seek the responsibilities and the authority we are fitted for; we must never justify an action on non-personal grounds. Myers continually attacks the temptation to regard people as things. He argues fiercely against such notions as 'the masses' and against any shift which seems to work the impersonal against the personal. 'Every action', he says, 'is personal at its roots'; therefore the flower should never be artificial. Wentworth believes too that 'in addition to contact through individual relationships, there is a contact through the earth'. In *The Pool of Vishnu* this is brought out in words that might have come from Ignazio Silone's explanation in *The Seed beneath the Snow* that 'companion' derives from the taking of bread together:

> If one sees a man struggling at the bottom of a well, one is moved to do all one can to pull him out. If a man is starving, one's natural impulse is to share one's food with him. Surely it

is only on second thoughts that people don't do these things? Society seems to me to be like an organized system of rather mean second thoughts.

He perhaps forgets that an indoctrinated charitable reflex might strengthen the natural impulse and correct its lapses; but his point in all its emphasis of heart against intellect is clear and noble. The ideal is to have the ruler of both natural charity and practised taste—the humanist humanitarian. We must not, according to Myers's code, presume to protect people too much from what we think they cannot bear to know: that is worthy of a Lewis Eliot. Myers says that anyone who acts so 'is really being protective not of the other but himself'.

I do not want to labour parallels, but I have to here because they are what makes Myers interesting. Damayanti, having to choose between her self-centred father and her love for Mohan, is straight out of Sartre. (The young man mentioned in *Existentialism and Humanism* had to choose between an ailing mother and joining the Free French in England. Sartre, asked for his advice, gave it but does not say what it was. He thinks it should be obvious.) Myers pursues the dilemma with exemplary honesty. The Guru reminds Damayanti that 'in making one's personal life satisfactory, one automatically makes one's public life satisfactory too'. The individual must shape himself: in acting on his own behalf he is also acting for others. Myers is not preaching a facile doctrine of self-gratification; he is going by the heart, which makes many things clear. In this he is surely right. But it is here that one realizes he is outlining the human situation rather than giving rules. He is more concerned to separate the socially acceptable self from the real self: an easier undertaking than the solution of dilemmas in which the heart speaks equally on both sides. The plea is for the individual against the stereotype; once again it is the Guru who speaks:

'The personal alone is universal. The popular leader, the subtle statesman or lawyer—they speak only for the monster of the day and their words die. But the man who speaks out of his own personal depths, speaks for all men, is heard by all men, and his words do not die.'

There is a moral in that for all novelists: the faithfully explored particular will always generalize itself. That is why the *roman-fleuve*, even though it may bore us for long stretches, strikes home; and that is why even Myers, for all his far-fetched nomenclature and settings, eventually makes an important point unforgettably. He rejects the naturalist view, stresses free will ('You know that you are not the slave of mechanical fate, but the master of divine destiny'), shows his characters making up their minds and yet cannot lose himself in them. We are too much aware of the argument, the thesis: when Mohan shares his money with the peasants, the woodenness of the characters is also the wood of the moralist's structure showing through. Any homiletic pageant daunts the reader; but Myers's Indian novels, in their cumbersome way, tackle ideas which later novelists have presented more journalistically and less passionately.

Within his own clearly defined limits—ambitious man, man in powerful committee and man discovering the impossible—C. P. Snow (1905-) has created one of the masterworks of the modern English novel. For sheer experience he is hard to beat. A scientist who has published papers on molecular structure, a Cambridge don, a Civil Service Commissioner, a former chief of Scientific Personnel for the Ministry of Labour, he also knows about unofficial man. He offers no ideology but a potent, sane humanism. He may at times seem to be fondling the notion of power in much the same voluptuary way as Camus fondles the idea of justice. Certainly he writes of power with loving familiarity and indulges from time to time in The Voice of Experience. But why not? Few other novelists have dared to tackle his major theme, and Snow shows not only what goes on behind the scenes but also how power affects the wielder's private life. As against this, he cares too much for the individual as a social unit; his novels have so far shown little awareness of the religious side of man; and he thinks ecstasy unreliable and inferior to contentment. He seems to dismiss as slack romanticism a great deal which, while not making society more efficient, heartens people to go on living. And his notion of love seems peculiarly tepid; love is a good thing sometimes, because it oils the wheels of society. A hostile critic, determined to see the worst and make the most of it, would describe Snow's novels as school stories writ large: all is teamspirit, knuckling down, stiffening the lip and being decent. But that would be to exaggerate his ecological bent. It would be truer to say that Snow is too pragmatic and that sometimes the flavour of the moral primer becomes too strong. Writing as he does of the cares of office, he has good reason to omit the sheer joy of living but not to half-romanticize as he does the shufflings of power-seekers. He appeals mostly to the kind of reader who thinks himself a bit public-spirited, a bit short of passion and well endowed with gumption. Above all, he does not write the novel of ideas; he writes about the corrosive element in which good ideas are immersed.

He is the least flamboyant of novelists. His matter is solid: marriage, possessiveness, liberal politics, scientific research, the meaning of the cold war and of integrity. His view of man is not cheering: he sees conflicting motives, turpitude, misplaced idealism and equally misplaced cynicism, selfishness, envy, arrogant confidence and timid consciences. He does not extend his inquiry into the Malraux-Camus-Sartre region of genocide, massacre, torture and metaphysical striving. But he does offer (less romantically than Malraux his 'virile fraternity', Camus his *'mesure'* and Sartre his 'anguish') a saving grace of his own formulation: an 'idiot hope', as Roy Calvert, the self-torturing sensitive in *The Masters*, describes it. Lewis Eliot, abiding presence and occasional hero, manages to keep trying in spite of a miserable marriage, a thwarted career and a nascent pride in his very disillusionment. He manages this because, as far as he humanly can, he remains open to experience; he argues that, just as no one can forecast his own failure, so a man should not leap melodramatically into facile despair because of a few setbacks. He does not expect to retrieve but to rebuild. And, eventually, of course, this is what he does: he has the sense to recognize how.

The hero of Snow's early novel, *The Search* (1935), is a young scientist feeling his way both amorously and in committee: a theme is being tried out in muted Stendhal. Next comes *Strangers and Brothers* (1940), the first of the series bearing that general title. This is a more documentary piece, more insistent and more uniform in presenting the world of caucus touched on in the previous book. Instead of tracking a mind about, Snow elects to study several in close confinement. Lewis Eliot, the central figure in two novels of the series, narrates in the others the results of quests similar, or relevant, to his own. *The Light and the Dark* (1947) and *Time of Hope* (1949) describe a period of storm and stress in which hope (here 'idiot' in ignorance of, not despite, the facts) alternates with the despair of being a floater. Even so, Lewis Eliot survives in *Time of Hope* and reappears in *The Masters* (1951), perhaps the most tense although the most garrulous of the series. Eliot learns, through the stresses of a college election, how men expose themselves only gradually; and Snow knows, technically speaking, how such exposure (one man has military decorations; another drinks in secret; another lets his sense of sin drive him into a reckless avowal) keeps quickening the reader's interest. The character-study in this novel is wonderfully subtle, as it is in the succeeding one, *The New Men* (1954). Perhaps Snow needs the sense of complication, not between a couple, but that produced by a close-knit group: the Fellows of a college or 'the new men' working on the atom bomb. He has so much to say and demonstrate about the workings of groups that he becomes at times almost impatient with men in comparative isolation. The difference to be noted is that between Lewis Eliot, now emerging from, now fading into, the background of professional society, and Lewis Eliot *vis-à-vis* his wife, Sheila. It is clear that Snow prefers the first field of study, perhaps because Eliot needs as much colour as he can get from his surroundings and from as many crossing relationships as possible, but perhaps too because Snow for reasons of his own avoids the kind of obsessed peeling of the nerves managed so beautifully by Rosamond Lehmann in *The Echoing Grove* (1953) or, indeed, less poetically, by Pamela Hansford Johnson in *An Impossible Marriage* (1955). Snow is sometimes too solemn, not feline enough.

The next novels, *Homecomings* (1957) and *The Conscience of the Rich* (1958), are almost perfect achievements; even perversely so. *Homecomings* puts Lewis Eliot to the front again; in *Time of Hope* he grapples with a monopolizing mother, escapes into an unsatisfactory marriage and seeks consolation in his career. But, for his second turn as protagonist, Eliot is chastened, world-used, and willing to surrender his jealous regard for himself. His eventual happiness in marriage rebukes his mother, his brother Martin in *The New Men* and March's father in *The Conscience of the Rich.* To feel that you possess a human being, Snow seems to say, denatures that person; we can attach ourselves only by using generosity as the adhesive. This is one reason for Eliot's apparent shadowiness: he starts out like an Isherwood listener, except that all of him is not in play; he is not risking all of himself. He ends, much cannier, but willing to risk his all. Between reserve masked in self-offering and risk taken in rueful 'idiot hope', we lose the distinct man. But that means we can fit ourselves in without injuring the *persona*: Eliot is not typed, like Sawbridge or George Passant, or a clear abdicator like his brother Martin. Lewis's way amounts to 'Being well-meaning all the time, and thinking of nothing worse than our own safety'. This is not the way of the opportunist, the muddler or the doctrinaire. Only a dedicated humility entitles men to wield power while having to regard as 'strangers' men they know as 'brothers'. The worst crime in Snow's world leads to all others: being a stranger to oneself: not knowing one's nature. This is what Lewis Eliot learns in pain and loneliness, in joy and community—a condition as necessary in public affairs as in private: the heart's availability while vulnerable, even through the political shadow-boxing so clearly examined in *The Affair* (1960).

Like Snow, Joyce Cary (1888–1957) believed that the novel is a moral agent. 'All novels', he said in his Clark Lectures, *Art and Reality* (1958), 'are concerned from first to last with morality: all serious artists preach.' Cary thought that our actions have consequences beyond the immediate and that art can help us to gain a degree of long-sightedness. His novels show characters engaged in the fearful exercise of deciding on their own moralities; not, like Graham Greene's transgressors, in conflict with prescribed codes but defying amorality or the void. In this he is as empirical as Snow: a man has to open himself to all the facts; then create his principles. And if he seems unorthodox, he must bear with that, for he is really denying the safety-loving part of himself. Living dangerously according to a private code is Cary's ideal.

No wonder, then, that he creates so many characters of Dickensian richness. His people are always in the course of making themselves. In the trilogy of *Herself Surprised* (1941), *To Be a Pilgrim* (1942) and *The Horse's Mouth* (1944) the same events are seen through the eyes of Sarah Munday, the generous-hearted slattern cook; Wilsher, the acute eccentric old lawyer; and Gully Jimson, hot-bowelled painter of uncertain genius. The ventriloquism is brilliant, and he captures them both melting and fixed in their chosen ways. As life floods on, they rumble along with it, dissenting and acquiescing, but manically resolved to define themselves as they think fit. Cary creates what Greene does not: character with all its incidentals, and always with a leaning to the spectacular. He does not pursue one thesis like Snow, but showers us with hot fragments. For exuberance and freedom he has few rivals; but his very rage for gamut leads him into occasional unproductive muddle. In style:

> Far be it from me to claim that the prejudice of my genera-tion in favour of a certain reticence in respect of the details of private life is a law of the Medes—the more modern practice of, as it is said, coming clean which so often appears to us the opposite, may be indeed, as it is urged, a salutary blow against a dangerous prudery. (*Except the Lord*, 1953)

and in structure: too many threads being twisted together at once; too many observations of differing kinds; some meant to be taken in their own right only, others to be regarded as symbolic. His characteristic method of writing in trilogies relates him to the Durrell of the Alexandria tetralogy. Cary wants his own kind of synoptic view but, unlike Durrell, does not risk the completely symphonic novel. Something holds him back: in fact, fondness for character—for all its rumbustious centrifugal fertility—takes him only as far as his moralizing can survive. Cary's artistry is not quite equal to his combined Falstaffian and didactic impulses; the one is always impeding the other. His prodigious inventiveness is always a little curbed; his anxiety to show moral principles in the process of being established never quite disappears. Conse-quently there is always enough relish for living to distract us from the dogmatizing and to make it look forced, while there is, in the characterization, enough suggestion of type to spoil the pleasures of personality. Between the morality and the bravura Cary gets into difficulties which no skill can dispel.

A clue to this uncertainty is given in his Clark Lectures.

Repudiating Croce's beliefs that 'art is simply intuition' and 'intuition and expression are the same thing', Cary exposed his own dilemma. Caught between his gift for riotous pageant (in which he recalls Smollett) and his determination to *make something of* that pageant, he fumbles and cannot make that fumbling significant in itself. In other words, his struggle to reconcile his hedonism with his moral sense scars the novels aesthetically and adds nothing to their overt import. This is an extraordinary pity, and he knew it, even going so far as to define art as *any* attempt at communication. Failing to separate art from a telephone call or from sky-writing, he betrays his own imperfect fidelity to art. Because he continually obstructs his own creative fecundity, he has to widen his notion of what art is; and he has to rationalize the interference of Cary the moralist as necessary manipulation. Of course such manipulation goes on all the time (he himself was always shelving manuscripts and later chopping them about); but Cary chose not to distinguish too carefully between technical refurbishing and adaptation to moral purpose. At first glance he seems a highly articulate Lord of Misrule of the novel; on a closer look he can be seen, surreptitiously damping down the fireworks. His celebration of life is too often dogmatic; and the fact that his characters' morals are unorthodox does not alter the fact of his tampering. Gusto made tendentious becomes zeal; it cannot be judged morally; it can only be measured.

Hence the disappointment caused by his second trilogy. *Prisoner of Grace* (1952) gave the story of Chester Nimmo, an early twentieth-century politician, through the eyes of his wife Nina. It is a moving, spirited piece of writing. But the succeeding volumes, *Except the Lord* (1953) and *Not Honour More* (1955), became parasitically laborious. In getting close to his characters so as to study their moral alchemy, Cary wastes his supervisory status. Often it is hard to know whether the moralizing is Cary breaking fictional convention or the character exemplifying a certain attitude. Once again, Cary is uncertain because he is too close to his characters to resist the temptation to speak out through them, and yet, being close, thinks that temptation a part of the creative act itself. When he is being Procrustean he thinks he is still adding to abundance. It is a very muddled novelist indeed who canot help the reader to separate author's comment from deliberately offered examples. Such muddle seriously hinders the reader of Cary just as it hinders readers of Faulkner, Joyce, and, sometimes, of Proust.

Cary's unsatisfactoriness (failing to maintain his own illusion) can be explained by one of D. H. Lawrence's dicta in *Morality and the Novel*. Lawrence said that 'morality is that delicate, for ever trembling and changing balance between me and my circumambient universe . . . by life, we mean something that gleams, that has the fourth-dimensional quality'. This is what Cary was after: in many ways a latter-day Bunyan, he shows both the 'gleam' and the 'balance' but in so doing re-enters the creative process itself. The result is that he confuses creation of character with what, according to evidence we are given, the character might seem to create for himself. In other words, Cary pokes into the developing moral sense of his creations without realizing that he himself is not a character. The novelist is obliged to seem to give his characters a life which excludes him save as the one who understands them best. Whether or not he understands *himself* is irrelevant. So Cary cannot help but make the abounding vitality of his characters seem occasionally gratuitous. He loves to create but even more to explore what he has created. And the vitality tends to strike the reader as a lively show which engages the eye while the real work, that of moralizing, goes on. The panorama is always there, and often the gusto; but Cary manages to make the novel-trilogy not so much a composite view of men in society as a baroque stimulus to his own theorizings.

Anthony Powell (1905–) has considerably refined his technique since the Waugh-like laughs at totalitarianism in *Venusberg* (1932). His other early novels, *Afternoon Men* (1931), *From a View to a Death* (1933), *Agents and Patients* (1936) and *What's Become of Waring?* (1939), showed an uncommon ability to combine cranky matter-of-factness with hyperbolical inventiveness. His gift for comedy has learned by now to take its time. In *The Music of Time* (1951), a chronicle novel thus far running to six volumes, knockabout and the quick spatter of laughter have given way to poring. Powell stretches adolescence like elastic and pores over the expanded fibres in *A Question of Upbringing* (1951), *Buyer's Market* (1952) and *The Acceptance World* (1955). The music of his time is *largo*, the ethos is either upper-class or

Bohemian, and the theme is class-consciousness. A Widmerpool
bursts into the tight circle of the Stringhams, Gorings and
Walpole-Wilsons: this is the matter of comedy of manners. But
Widmerpool with sugar poured on his head, or breaking his en-
gagement to one of the high-born because he is impotent, is
almost the matter of farce. And the two do not quite mix. Both
come into being because Powell is detached: he can see the dog
beneath the skin, separate the genuine motive from what is
meant to conceal it and suddenly set the naked self performing
preposterous tricks.

But his grotesques are of limited appeal, like over-nourished
Wodehouse. Or at least they were until *At Lady Molly's* (1957)
introduced an inversion of Powell's usual type: Erridge, who has
grown a beard and lives as a tramp in the Midlands. He is a
shabby man with a slightly shabby conscience. His clothes are
good but he looks scruffy; he cares about Spain (this is the
thirties) and thinks of starting a new periodical, but he is also a
dangerous type—the diffident egoist. Set in his own mansion,
Thrubworth Park, he is a figure of endless fun and typical of
Powell's creations. He could have been sentimentalized or turned
into a walking idea. But Powell keeps him at arm's length, refusing to subject so rich a character to formulas. *Casanova's
Chinese Restaurant* (1960), set in the period of the Spanish Civil
War and the Abdication, presents the same characters with a
bland effrontery and skidding inconsequentiality which make the
volume interesting in itself but also warn us that the essence of
this *roman-fleuve* is improvisation. It was originally to be complete in two volumes, but now—as the scrutiny of two marriages
descends from high, narratorial analysis to low gossip in that
restaurant and the sociological purpose lapses into Powell's
Report on his Fictional Familiars—one sees no end. Speakers
end, the garrulous do not. Too much happens offstage. And it is
hard to see how any large-scale novelist can afford the reticences
of the short-story or obituary without anaesthetizing us to what
we badly need to have before us and without turning the comedy
into club-jokes. Powell is enveloped in his own world twice over:
what he himself *is* dictated his choice of subject, and now the
characters' own standards dictate the novel's nature. *The Kindly
Ones* (1962) maintains the ingenuity but also suggests possession

by the demon of mannerism; in this case working a good thing to death.

I have already suggested that the novelist who delights in the creation of characters for their own sake has difficulty in making moral points. Delight in human abundance and human variety somehow sap the moral sense;[1] and especially so in the mind of the novelist. There is another difficulty too: anyone with an eye for the complexity of personality will soon end up with the problem of definition. We can gain a more accurate idea of what X is like if we have the views of Y and Z; and we can be even more accurate if we know what, over a span of years, X thought of Y and Z, what Y thought of Z, of Z's opinion of X, and so on. Once begun, the quest becomes hopelessly complex. Just as there is no realism (realism is more of a desire than it is anything), neither is there absolute knowledge of character, personality or identity. Man and the novelist have to rely on a rough idea based on behaviour's repetitions. So a Joyce Cary, for example, already contending with a passion for expansive creation and another passion for scrutiny of the growing moral sense, decides to present a story from several points of view. Truth thus becomes a synthesis, and the reader has to work hard for what he finally assembles. Eventually we have to add to the abstract, social and private views of man another view: man as a relative animal. All views are incomplete, so the novelist might be justified in cultivating the incomplete. No truth is absolute because all statements are limited by the point of view from which they are made. It is not just a matter of a character's having a false notion of himself and having it exposed by the novelist. It is that the novelist, even though he plays a game of supposed omniscience, either imitates life by giving us an incomplete version or cheers us up with an illusion of someone's, for once, understanding completely. The stream novelist is entitled to his belief that one person's responses, fully explored, give as accurate an account of another person as does the combined testimony of fifty observers.

Even the chronicle novel is bound to give an incomplete account. Snow neglects progress through time for an inevitability which depends less on time than on common sense, recep-

1. Cf. Lawrence Durrell's narrator: '. . . all ideas seem equally good to me; the fact of their existence proves that someone is creating'.

tivity and experience. Lewis Eliot develops, it is true; but Snow makes his points thematically rather than chronologically. His *Strangers and Brothers* novels have not appeared in narrative order. Joyce Cary goes light on chronology; Anthony Powell's view is that of the social botanist—he goes for themes and uses them as occasions for near-caricature; and Lawrence Durrell works at a relativism of his own, with scant regard for chronological presentation. One is reminded of Dostoevsky's account, in *The Brothers Karamazov*, of how Fyodor Pavlovitch responded to the death of his first wife: there were two versions, but, adds Dostoevsky, 'It is quite possible that both versions were true, that he rejoiced at his release, and at the same time wept for her who released him.' And, of course, human complexity can go a great deal farther than that. The novelist has to decide for himself how much complexity he can convey. On the one hand, the *Bildungsroman* piles up the facts towards a total conception of a character; on the other, the picaresque novel presents life as just one thing after another, with the minimum of manipulation. At one extreme a Dorothy Richardson emancipates consciousness from time; an Anthony Powell does the same thing without letting the stream become undisciplined. At the other extreme, Doris Lessing creates the 'Martha Quest' series in which she herself is the omniscient narrator, judging and choosing the light her people will appear in. Martha Quest, closely watched as she grows up through the title novel (1952), into and out of *A Proper Marriage* (1954) and into maturity in *A Ripple from the Storm* (1958), is solid, vivid but never too close to us, which is more than can be said for Anna Wulf, the heroine and demandingly intellectual woman in *The Golden Notebook* (1962). Anna, the novelist-philosopher, writing about Ella, the Anna-like heroine of Anna's new novel, is too much; we are suffocated with information about Anna and her *personae*, and yet she is not distinct. In allowing herself almost 600 pages Mrs Lessing wastes her talent for self-discipline and falls victim to the grandiosity (rather than the usefulness) of narrator-omniscience.

The question, finally, becomes one of narrative point of view. C. P. Snow chooses Lewis Eliot, an academic lawyer, and Anthony Powell chooses Nicholas Jenkins, who publishes art books. Their judgments, indeed their reports, of experience are therefore distorted in ways we are meant to comprehend. Snow and Powell do not assume, as Virginia Woolf did, that 'To believe that your impressions hold good for others is to be released from the cramp and confinement of personality'; on the contrary, they stress the 'cramp' without trying to evade it. Their theme is the limitedness of human perception. They demonstrate it whereas Doris Lessing, for all her deft, uncompromising and brisk handling of her matter, takes the limitedness upon herself. In one case, the narrators prove the point; in the other, the novelist is subject to it. We return to ineluctable conditions I mentioned earlier; art is manipulation, permitting both the illusion of omniscience and the acknowledgment of limitedness. The important difference is between the novelist who does in fiction what is impossible in life, and admits to it, and the one who does in fiction only what is possible in life and, in asking nothing of us, makes us wonder why we are reading him at all. Fiction's main asset is that it can increase our awareness without deluding us. As long as we know the novelist's self-imposed limits, we know what kind of statements he is making; and as long as we are aware of limits we are in the presence of art. It is only when we ignore the assumptions on which art is based (primarily its freedom to ignore human ignorances) that we get into a muddle. Art can deepen our understanding of what exists by offering something which can exist only in the imagination. Art is an eloquent, self-contained means of referring to anything. It is not a mirror but an eye seeing what it wants to see, and is subject to one law only: the imagination has no control over things it does not imagine. So, whether we prefer fable to documentary, or *vice versa*, those preferences are essentially temperamental. Art is free to choose its method but not to extend its boundaries.

One typically documentary series of novels is that of Henry Williamson (1897–). Still in progress, *A Chronicle of Ancient Sunlight* re-creates in vast detail the life of Phillip Maddison from birth and childhood in Edwardian suburbia to his early manhood in the 1914–18 war. This unpretentious, untricksy chronicle has, so to speak, no more control over reality than has Williamson's saga about Tarka the Otter, Salar the Salmon, Brock the Badger and Chakchek the Peregrine. The battle scenes in *The Golden*

Virgin (1957) and *A Test to Destruction* (1960) are enthralling and vivid; but Phillip himself is a fairly ordinary chap, convinced of his duty to soldier on without much hope or much regret. He is explored with almost fanatical thoroughness; the other characters tend to fade into the background, leaving Phillip not very substantially holding the stage. No doubt this is part of Henry Williamson's intention: Phillip is average; such men exist, therefore we must accept his seeming lack of stature—even when it makes the novels both grey and torpid. But must we? Cannot ordinariness be treated in an extraordinary way? In such a way as to make us attend to it fixedly? If not, art has no advantages over life.

These problems have been ingeniously solved by Lawrence Durrell (1912–); which is not to say that Durrell has not created others. In the first novel of his Alexandria quartet, *Justine* (1957), Durrell presents a story set in Alexandria, and in the second, *Balthazar* (1958), presents the same events from a different point of view. The two succeeding novels, *Mountolive* (1958) and *Clea* (1960), complete the picture. In the prefatory note to *Balthazar* Durrell says his series is 'based on the relativity proposition. Three sides of space and one of time constitute the soup-mix recipe of a continuum.' The first three parts are 'deployed spatially. . . . They interlap, interweave, in a purely spatial relation. Time is stayed. The fourth part alone will represent time and be a true sequel.' Durrell has also explained the series in terms of 'subjective and objective modes' related to a common axis. Darley, the narrator, for instance, lets Balthazar gloss his account, and refers to the gloss as the 'Interlinear'. The result is, as Balthazar says, a novel with 'sliding panels'. In this way realities are 'intercalated', which is 'the only way to be faithful to time'.

When he is theorizing, Durrell sounds pretentious and pompous. What is more, the Alexandria quartet is more muddled than he seems to realize: it would be truer, and simpler, to say that it combines (often without warning) the stream of consciousness of several people, all of them doing their best to articulate recollections and their present impressions. Various texts are interspersed in the narrative, from the 'Interlinear' and Justine's diary to the autobiographical novel *Mœurs*, written by Justine's

first lover, and the writings of Pursewarden. All these float about
in 'The continuous present, which is the real history of that
collective anecdote, the human mind', and require brilliant use of
vocabulary. Sometimes Durrell's writing is too brilliant: his
monologues are a little too self-consciously gorgeous; characters
of average intelligence talk brilliantly (like Ivy Compton-
Burnett's); and a good many things are more Durrell than anyone else. 'I know,' says Pursewarden, 'my prose is touched with
plum pudding, but then all the prose belonging to the poetic
continuum is; it is intended to give a stereoscopic effect to
character.' So be it; it is hard to know what such observations as
the following do for stereoscopic effect: '. . . a splinter lodged in
the optic nerve. Pordre's eye kindled . . .' Or such speech as this:

> Her words rattled down like hail of sods on an empty coffin.
> 'How is it that you can feel no resentment against me? To
> forgive such treachery so easily—why, it is unmanly. . . . And
> yet, in truth, I enjoyed deceiving you. . . . But also there was
> regret in only offering you the pitiful simulacrum of a love
> (Ha! that word again!) which was sapped by deceit. I suppose
> this betrays the bottomless female vanity again. . . .'

This is like the bad fiction of the late nineteenth century; perhaps
Durrell intends to evoke the unidiomatic stereotypes of melo-
drama; but, if so, he over-evokes them. He has no need to do so.
Against his magnificent tapestry, in which there is little that is not
exotic, plain language looks like ivory. His expatriates are Jews,
Greeks, Syrians, English, French, Egyptians and Italians. Their
very names (like those of Myers's characters) make them remote:
Mountolive, the British plenipotentiary; Pombal the diplomat;
Narouz, living alone at the edge of the desert, with his hare-lip;
Capodistria, the satyr-*noir* who has ruined Justine; Scobie who,
with crucifix and remorse, could be Graham Greene's character
extrapolated to eighty-five; Pursewarden, the acerb, sex-fed successful writer; plus Athena, Trasha, Pierre Balbz, Cervonis,
Martinego, Zoltan, Amaril, Anselm, Semira. It is like reading
Byron crossed with Firbank. But how wonderfully precise,
enamelled and life-drinking most of Durrell's prose is. It is a rare
thing to find anyone even capable of over-writing, who can make

a world that is both lavish and deathly, both crammed and minutely realized.

Durrell needs the exotic before he can even begin to write; he intensifies all he touches and the quartet, like Pursewarden's Alexandria, has a strong flavour without 'having any real character'. Durrell's vision is restless, an aquarium of busy fish. He, of all novelists writing now, is the voluptuary of sexual anguish, as well as being a master of atmosphere and teeming variety. Reckless, exuberant, savage, awkward, self-indulgent and addicted to seeing everything in terms of everything else, Durrell achieves the desideratum of making his four novels dissolve into one another. Put through a receptive mind they coalesce into a spectrum of love's psychology. Durrell is just the type of novelist the English tradition needed; he teaches one to see, to use all the senses, and to relish the luxury that words can create from a tragic sense of life. No one suggests more vividly than he the imminence of chaos; the way life perpetuates itself at human expense, leaving men and women to get what joy they can while they are part of the process. Above all, his is a feat of imagination: first creating a world and then re-imagining it until it dazzles like a complex mosaic. Life, as he sees it, rewards us in its details and in its major outlines. What is in between he presents in a dozen forlorn love-stories in the most daring, most fastidious prose of our time. An almost intolerable sadness has rarely been made so delicious.

Oddly enough, an earlier novelist whose practice differed considerably from Durrell's wrote something in his *Journals* which in places reads like a Durrell credo:

The novelist of contemporary manners needs to be *saturated with a sense of the picturesque* in modern things. . . . Every scene, even the commonest, is wonderful, if only one can detach oneself, *casting off all memory* of use and custom, and behold it (as it were) for the first time; in its own right, authentic colours; *without making comparisons*. The novelist should cherish and burnish this faculty of seeing crudely, simply, artlessly, ignorantly; of seeing like a baby or a lunatic, *who lives each moment by itself* and tarnishes the present by no remembrance of the past (italics mine).

The author of that, Arnold Bennett, will have no comparisons or memories, but he does want the picturesque and the moment-by-moment vision. The difference is that Durrell wants everything; Bennett wants to pare. Both respond acutely to the surfaces of life: they celebrate life for what it is. But we have only to compare Durrell's quartet with, say, Bennett's trilogy of *Clayhanger* (1910), *Hilda Lessways* (1911) and *These Twain* (1916) to realize that, although both are introducing a new ethos into English fiction, Bennett is documenting and Durrell is working in metaphor. The Five Towns were grim to live in; Durrell's Alexandria is an image of heaven-hell. Bennett, especially in the moving *Anna of the Five Towns* (1902) and in his lovely Caravaggio-like contrasts between the two sisters in *The Old Wives' Tale* (1908), offers the stoicism of surrender to time. Durrell offers the tragedy of the fact that our bodies live in time while our minds do not. Bennett narrows his view as an act of stoicism itself; Durrell widens his in protest. Bennett restrains emotion through objectivity; Durrell turns it into atmosphere and poignant metaphor. Bennett curbs, Durrell is expansive. Where Bennett marvels at the ordinary, Durrell makes the exceptional seem commonplace. Edwin Clayhanger gradually opens up to life, Durrell's Darley increasingly looks inwards.

These distinctions between two creators of ethos reveal something about the English tradition, about the Dickens hyperbole that reappears in Durrell and the naturalism that continues in such of the younger comic writers as Kingsley Amis. We go back to the attack C. P. Snow launched on the aesthetic novel as distinct from the novel of social documentary. It is hard to write the novel of sensibility without seeming to wander from everyday reality; and, sooner or later, to wander from that reality, from quotidian trivia, is to produce hyperbole. The sensibility of Virginia Woolf is closer to the hyperbole of Dickens than to the documentary of Bennett. What we find in Mrs Woolf, Dickens and Durrell is the imagination used for its own sake. What we find in the tradition that comes from Bennett and Wells, *via* Gerhardi, is the imagination used for a usually comic purpose, not self-indulgently as in Dickens, but almost impersonally. It is the old distinction between romantic and classical: between the inward, the irregular, the grotesque, and the exoteric, the regular, the usual. What is new is the use of the comic as an anti-romantic gesture, lest any hyperbole be construed as self-indulgent laxity. Even philistinism has come to have a place in this comic tradition in which a dozen or so novelists, without attempting any kind of chronicle-novel, study modern society in a variety of ways ranging from the pithy to the picaresque, from the Wellsian to the deadpan. It is almost as if many of these writers shy away from grandeur, especially the grandeur of such projects as Snow, Powell and Durrell have undertaken. So now, then, to realism without a scheme and a factuality that is often laughed at as it arrives on the page.

(c) Samples and documentaries

I

It is a peculiarly English habit of English novelists to alleviate social message with humour. We find the habit in the great novelists of the eighteenth century, in Dickens and in H. G. Wells. To explain it we can invoke the English national character, its quipping stoicism and unmetaphysical sense of order. We might go further and invoke the English distaste for abstract ideas or the insularity which has created codes, regimens and attitudes to be found nowhere else. Whatever the reasons, the English novel tackles social reportage in a singularly unsolemn way. Fundamentally, I think, the humour is a sign of great or little confidence —an index to an extreme state. It is thrown in so that we shall not take solemnly what is meant seriously, or because the author does not want his excessive confidence to alienate us. It also appears because we enjoy laughing; and we laugh because some incident brings to mind a standard to which human behaviour should, but does not, correspond. It may be a standard of logic or decorum; whatever it is, it derives from an ingrained sense of the fitting. Humour, in fact, is aesthetic, a primitive form of art capable of being raised to great sophistication.

Wells (1866–1946), for example, although he took seriously his Little Man in the ascendant, could also see the comedy of his own optimism. Even he, and he could be a tremendous bore (*The World of William Clissold*, 1926), laced his anthems to rebels with reminders that he, too, knew human aspiration was part of the incessant human comedy. That comedy was not going to stop just because the lower-middles were ready to inherit the newly decent earth. He was both a Rousseau and a Dickens. His scientific romances are still readable: at least, *The Invisible Man* (1897), *The War of the Worlds* (1898), *When the Sleeper Wakes* (1899) and *The First Men in the Moon* (1901) have an appeal of caricature, however inaccurate they may be scientifically. The serious Wells, the educative and slightly parsonical specialist in hope, appeared in *The Food of the Gods* (1904) and pushed on into *Ann Veronica* (1909) and *The New Machiavelli* (1911), two novels that now seem

124

dated. The portrait of the emancipated woman and the conflict between love and political calling hang heavy now: there is no irony, no exuberant clap of hands. Wells could never express the tragic view without drifting off into essays. But what he could do extremely well was to imagine copiously, whether the result was funny chaps in cricket caps or ant-like Selenites on the Moon, whether Kipps or Quap, the radioactive earth. There is a link between Wells's scientific ingenuities and his human simples. Both transcend the state of society. Going to the moon was just as possible as going up in the commercial world.

Wells's most endearing achievements are comedies of human rockets: *Love and Mr Lewisham* (1900), *Kipps* (1905), *Tono-Bungay* (1909) and *The History of Mr Polly* (1910). Kipps, Polly and Uncle Ponderevo have something of Joyce: they beam phantasmagoric images against the dull walls of the world of cash. Mr Polly's fantasies and Uncle Ponderevo's delirium about serene palaces (after becoming a millionaire out of the patent medicine, Tono-Bungay) are means of beating the world on its own terms or one's own. They have in their bellies the spiritual equivalent of Falstaff's Manningtree Ox. And, in so far as they surfeit themselves with dreams or with success, they are funny as well as moving. Mr Polly, dabbling with suicide and arson, intensely trying to get beyond the world in which he has to live, is both a visionary and a buffoon. Social as well as metaphysical accusations are made through him. His type reappears in the work of the fifties novelists. It is the type of the preternaturally honest person who, like Camus's Meursault, refuses to pretend, whatever society might think of him. To protest and to transcend are the type's aims: to achieve an uncommitted individualism.

But in recent novels we find not only vestigial Wells but also George Gissing's concern with failure, isolation and being put upon. There is no fun in Gissing (1857–1903). *The Private Papers of Henry Ryecroft* (1903) is more genial than *New Grub Street* (1891); but the sense of resentment is the same. Gissing's scowling disdain for a smug and meretricious society is something that has come up again in the younger English novelists. Man as a passive dissenter, in retreat (like Henry Ryecroft) or eternally in harness, is Gissing's contribution to the anti-hero of our own time. Explaining the characters of *The Unclassed*, Gissing said: 'They refuse the statistic badge.' So do a good many modern blob-heroes, stirring their own peculiar broth of self-pity, isolation, lack of fulfilment, fear of risk, class-pride or class-shame, establishment-baiting, apathy and hubris. Godwin Peake in *Born in Exile* (1892) has a great deal in common with Mr Polly: both are out of touch, and both fight their environment. But usually it is the Wellsian hero who cocks a snoot at the social mesh and the Gissing type who surrenders. Both themes—cockiness and capitulation—appear in the novels of the fifties: *Room at the Top* means *Room at the Bottom* (as the titles chosen by John Braine and Noel Woodin make plain); and for every picaresque young man there is someone else who, like a character of Iris Murdoch's, goes to bed for days on end for lack of anything else to do.

The new realists of the English novel have little in common with another, parallel tradition which includes James Stephens's whimsical Dublin slum story, *The Charwoman's Daughter* (1912), Liam O'Flaherty's *The Informer* (1925), Frank O'Connor's wan tribute to broken hearts that smile, *Dutch Interior* (1940), and Sean O'Faolain's study in *A Nest of Simple Folk* (1923) of a cloddish rebel and the rain-dowsed scurry of Cork. The new realism is neither whimsical nor Dostoevskian; its exponents seem to fear nothing more than being caught in high-flown attitudes. Part of it continues the solid, matter-of-fact manner preferred by Walter Allen (*Innocence is Drowned*, 1938, *Blind Man's Ditch*, 1939, *Living Space*, 1940, *Rogue Elephant*, 1946, *Dead Man Over All*, 1950) and given a new depth and exquisitely focused intensity in *All in a Lifetime* (1959). It shows something of Nancy Mitford's zig-zag effervescence but little of the well-bred glitter conspicuous over the superficial psychology of *The Pursuit of Love* (1945) and *Love in a Cold Climate* (1949). It has something of her off-handedness regarding plot and her disregard of needed information. But between her shadowy sophisticates (Charles-Edouard de Valhubert in *The Blessing*, 1951, Lady Leone in *Don't Tell Alfred*, 1960) and, say, William Cooper's Joe Lunn, who appears in *Scenes from Provincial Life* (1950) and *Scenes from Married Life* (1960), there is a difference of social assumptions. Joe Lunn, a Labour voter not much taken with politics, shrewd but no intellectual, an agnostic humanitarian and author of three novels, advances from a freebooting interest in wonderful girls to being a

Principal in the Civil Service and a slightly bemused husband. He becomes a father too. In whatever he does he displays a Wellsian gusto. He keeps on acquiescing and stays euphoric. Partly Philistine, partly a lower-middle-class *arriviste*, Joe is nihilistically busy. In some ways he resembles the kind of Englishman ('decent', not urbane) whom Martin Green idealizes in *A Mirror for Anglo-Saxons* (1961): 'small, neat, quick-moving, with a fresh-coloured, neat-featured, unemphatic face, without physical stateliness, wheeling a bicycle, carelessly dressed, open-necked, plain-mannered, shrewd, skeptical, friendly-jeering in tone, hostile to all elaborateness or eccentricity, unwilling to talk his emotions, but quick in his sympathies . . .' That is, a priggishly nondescript, breakfast-cereal type of person whose ordinariness comes from his being either *déclassé* or obsessed about some difference between 'life' (apocalyptic, mystagogical) and the artificial 'gentlemanly' demeanour allegedly absent from Green's heroes, Lawrence, Orwell, F. R. Leavis, Kingsley Amis and the Mellors of *Lady Chatterley's Lover*. Of Nancy Mitford's proud francophilia not a jot in Green's apotheosis. Instead, and this no doubt reflects increased social mobility in Britain, the Joe Lunns and the Green-man scoff at the pruderies, the hierarchical cant and the cynical gentilities of the Establishment—all towards what Green dauntingly calls 'self-questioning sanativeness'.

It is self-questioning that redeems the new fictional hero and makes him tolerable. Jaunty Joe Lunn is not quite as priggish as Green's *homo decens*, and he does not *care* enough either. He hovers between self-seeking and careless kindness. According to his creator, Joe gets a great deal out of writing, but we never see him writing or thinking about his next novel. He does, however, in *Scenes from Provincial Life*, exclaim 'ah, novels, novels, Art, Art, pounds sterling!' In short, Joe enthuses like Kipps without really embracing a Cause. He rides the flux, the type of chap who, if he could stir himself, might argue for the 'common culture' envisioned by Raymond Williams (*Culture and Society*) and Richard Wollheim (*Socialism and Culture*). Such a person fits well into the capricious, knockabout comedy typified in *Scenes from Married Life*, Amis's *Lucky Jim* and Bradbury's *Eating People is Wrong*. This type of comedy came from Chekhov, *via* William Gerhardi, Evelyn Waugh and Cooper. It fits admirably an age of social turbulence in which some kind of plural culture is coming into being under the guidance of a welfare capitalism.

It is logical that, when society itself is in flux, and when at the same time aestheticism has been condemned, the novel should tackle both in its own way. The picaresque young man living an unsystematic life embodies one answer, and his self-centredness the other. Where the aesthetic flux was a device of texture overcoming structure, the philistine flux comes out as a device of structure supporting a texture empty of self-conscious 'style'. Yet, plain as the fifties novelists like to be thought, they refurbish an old romanticism. Their uncommittedness and fondness for samples of society rather than for an organized view (such as Snow, Powell and Durrell give) make the free association of the flux device reappear in the free career of the modern *picaro*. The flux has now become narrative; the urge to shape—whether according to myth or cycle-theory—is repudiated in the same way as aestheticism; and the romantic now collects encounters and snapshots with no purpose in mind beyond suggesting the flavour of modern society and keeping himself independent. Whereas Nancy Mitford's rebellious Radletts accept, without really knowing it, the status and roles imposed by the family, the Jim Dixons construct their code and creed as they go along. The Radletts inherit a type of rebellion; the Jim Dixons are anxious to inherit nothing, for they represent a whole generation of uprooted, unclassed, intelligent floaters wondering what they can make of themselves. The spectacle is both touching and hilarious. We are back. in fact, to the comedy of situations: people defining themselves according to vicissitude, not tradition.

The least-known novels of William Cooper (1910–) define the theme. *Young People* (1958) is set in the thirties but is not like its predecessor *Disquiet and Peace* (1956), a period piece. His young people are the post-war sort. They have been to university and now find themselves obliged to choose a career, their only link with their university days being recourse to pints or cafés. This is hardly the slick, genteel world of Nancy Mitford, Huxley and Waugh. Most of the characters are industrious, fairly earnest souls; but one, Leonard Harris, is a charlatan who married prematurely and tries to remedy the mess by aiming preposterously high. A combination of wide boy and climber, Harris typifies a character we first meet in Spanish picaresque. Unfortunately Cooper exposes him too quickly, whereas he should have left us to make up our own minds. To some extent Cooper has over-used the academic milieu: *The Struggles of Albert Woods* (1952) and *The Ever-Interesting Topic* (1953) illustrate, perhaps inadvertently, how the academic life on any level can become a way of clinging to youth—to the phase in which one's own course was pretty well mapped out. Most of the characters, Joe Lunn included, cast backward glances in the intervals of rough-and-tumble. Wanting to float, they find themselves pulled down into leaden routine, marriage, rainy days to be planned against, Responsibility, Decisions, Keeping Up. At his best Cooper is extremely funny; he finds the incongruous in the ordinary— whether in a prosecution for obscenity or in Lunnville Grammar School. When he is less than good, however, he is expecting the ordinary to sustain itself, to make itself funny or significant. Although sometimes lamely, his theme keeps in step with the times. But when Joe Lunn is established and respectable, he tends to bore; and Cooper then resorts to mere perkiness of style as a substitute for the excitement of social uncertainty.

So far none of the aggrieved heroes of Kingsley Amis (1922–) has become established or quite respectable. One can see life's mills grinding them into hurt acquiescence; and one has heard of Amis's heroes as instruments for exposing the shams and hypocrisies of post-war Britain, as archetypal buffoons, as carefully chosen specimens of a new era in education. None of these castings is entirely true, though all are right in some degree. *Lucky Jim* (1954) picked up threads left dangling by Wells: Dixon, like Kipps, Mr Polly and George Ponderevo, is of the lower middles and grudgingly proud of the fact. But he is different in that he combines pride with confident inquisitorial habits and intelligent, philistine scepticism. Nothing coy about Jim. He concerns himself with self-definition, rebuffing the blandishments of lip-service, wealth, sodality and taste. His censoriousness is a means of saving his integrity; when things get too tough he begins to go through his own private performance. As long as *he* knows he is not being taken in by idealistic or mercenary schemes, he sees no need to advertise the fact. In his soberest moments he acknowledges that his kind of revolt is metaphysical or private—furtive pranks on the telephone, lonely grimaces. He is not quite sure what he is, unless an embodied motive; but he does know what he refuses to be. *Lucky Jim*, in fact, is an assembly of social samples. A young man tries on various attitudes and takes some time to realize that all attitudes partly falsify the individual beneath; but, equally, that no one can recognize the individual until there are attitudes associated with him. The man of absolute integrity is like Robert Musil's conception of 'the man without qualities'. The result is paradox and farce; not so much a 'social document' as a comedy that inevitably typifies aspects of society.

Amis's subsequent novels have necessarily fallen a little flat. Seen to be what he has always declared himself to be—a comic novelist, and not a sociologist or a rain-gauge—he seemed in *That Uncertain Feeling* (1955) to be repeating himself to no significance. But not so. John Lewis, the librarian in the small Welsh town of Aberdarcy, escaping in a long skirt and a pigtailed wig, dismally regarding the backyard, the used dishes and removing caked sugar with his fingernail from the inside of a cup, is domesticated, libidinous man having to acknowledge his environment. But, he decides: 'It was luck, again, not self-restraint, that had stopped similar interests of mine from coming to anything during my five and a bit years of marriage.' The temptation which is Elizabeth Gruffydd-Williams is also linked to her husband, Chairman of the Library Committee. Lewis fecklessly waits for life to happen to him, always willing to take things or not. The novel ends with his escaping again, from the eager Lisa Watkins. He and his wife, standing at the pub door, look as if they too are coming with the colliers 'off shift'. Back to middling virtue he goes, making a go of things with what there is. Amis always ends on a chastened note.

I Like It Here (1958) varies the theme slightly. Garnet Bowen, an apparently successful writer without being prolific, is sent to Portugal by an American publisher: his mission, to determine the genuineness of a manuscript. But Bowen resents his Fairy Godmother, consoling himself that at least he has to go to Portugal and not Italy ('all those rotten old churches and museums and art galleries'). Amis is always careful to stress the necessity of Philistinism; it is part of ungullibility. Partly true as a response to aesthetes, it becomes monotonous when constantly exemplified in the same hero under different names. Amis's type of comedy is becoming his own cliché. We expect a drunk scene, an escape, some academic frivolity, a series of Chaucerian escapades and the usual anti-style, anti-literary dogma. Amis's novels, like those of Françoise Sagan, merge together. They have no more 'meaning' than Chaucer's tales have; and they are robustly funny. Perhaps this Chaucerian spirit has in him a *Troilus and Criseyde*.

Take A Girl Like You (1960), in which Patrick Standish, a young Latin teacher, occupies the usual length of a novel trying to seduce a young infant-teacher called Jenny Bunn, is not it; not quite. But the novel has an underlying moral seriousness all the more impressive because Amis seems to create it accidentally. He shows it in action, he does not militate. Patrick Standish lives and breathes, which Garnet Bowen does not. He also covets girls. Unfortunately his desires are more convincingly presented than Jenny is, for all the cataloguing of her physical attributes. In one sense Patrick is alone with his urges and his tortuous fidelity. He is a splendid creation: a pulsing individual, whereas she is the eternal feminine and an instance of a certain attitude. If this novel is Amis's version of the trouble between the sexes, he has made his point rather too powerfully—almost as if to say men are individuals and women all of a kind. The undomesticable male, coping with so firm a Jenny, becomes something of a stereotype himself. Once again, Chaucer comes to mind; so does Fielding, for Amis, morally serious rather than offering specific dogma, can make fun out of the most passionate individual's unwitting assumption of stock attitudes. Better joke than grieve about it, anyway, even if the joke is shaggy and the prose sometimes costive. There is roughage enough in Amis to compensate. What we need from him now is a real heroine and some exploration of older people. Otherwise, even his best performances will seem like self-parody—as *I Like It Here* did to an alarming extent.

John Wain's first novel, *Hurry on Down* (1953), was an exercise in picaresque; his young man bumped through various sectors of the post-war world; the situations were funny, the settings brilliantly vivid, but the characters were little more than faces in a crowd. In his next novel, *Living in the Present* (1955), he tidied up the picaresque into a quest; and a suicidal protagonist gave the narrative not so much more melodrama as an erratic meta-physical dimension. With *The Contenders* (1958) Wain showed a surer touch; the picaresque element is subdued to a more complex purpose. Joe Shaw, the narrator, plump and permissive, introduces himself and his cronies, Ned Roper and Robert Lamb, as at school in a Potteries town. Soon Roper has become a tycoon and Lamb, now a recognized painter, has married a famous fashion model. Before long, however, she quits Lamb for Roper; and Lamb takes up with, then leaves, an Italian girl who is eventually acquired by Joe Shaw, now a provincial journalist.

It all sounds thin and unprofitable. The characters—squat Lamb and blond, long Roper—are not convincing; and Joe Shaw talks much too slickly for what he is supposed to be. The style is full of Joe's exaggerations (some of which would do for Mickey Spillane), and one begins to wonder if Wain is creating such characters out of some sense of obligation to modern banality. He writes vigorously and gaily, but seems to have trouble in getting far below personal surfaces. His people are arid not just because many people in fact are arid but because he does not give a sufficiently imaginative account of their minds. Perhaps the accomplished critic (which Wain certainly is) tries not to *think* too much in his novels; if so, that is a pity.

Wain (1925–) so far seems content merely to have selected and tracked a few post-war types; his only advance has been from picaresque to pattern. His most promising performance is the title story in the collection called *Nuncle* (1960), in which Tom Rogers, an established novelist now dried up, lets his father-in-law write his books. The consequences are sinister: Rogers loses almost all, including his wife. This story, giving both high emotional temperature and intimate conflict, might have produced a masterpiece from a Lawrence. As it is, Wain finds the theme too literary and reassures himself with near-farce. Another story in the same book, 'The Quickest Way out of Manchester', deals with the emotional conflicts of a bank-clerk approaching middle age. It is deftly and ironically done, with not a word wasted. Wain perhaps needs to tackle themes of great emotional intensity—as in *Strike the Father Dead* (1962). He lets himself go for farce, rarely for adult passion. If he did let himself go, he might take as much notice of inward activity as of external bustle. Most of his characters seem to be busy because he prefers not to investigate their inner workings. So far he has attempted the busyness only. But perhaps he is working towards the deep end and a prose to match. One hopes so, for he has a fine, unpretentious intelligence.[1]

It is only natural that descriptions of junior living should require a picaresque main character. In Elaine Dundy's *The Dud Avocado* (1958) Sally Jay Gorce, daughter of an American cosmetics executive, bounces into Paris all Dewey-eyed and willing. Seduced by an Italian but slighted by an American, she lets her inquisitiveness feed on its own surfeit. A Daisy Miller in elated high gear, she neither has nor gains discrimination; experience to her is a matter of quantity, and she concludes her addition by marrying an English photographer and flying off to Japan in a suit of billiard-table baize. The writing is mordant and deliciously swift. As long as things keep happening to, and around, her Sally does not bother to make up her green mind about anything. And, of course, things keep happening just because of that.

John Braine (1922–) is a much less self-consciously brilliant writer than Miss Dundy. *Room at the Top* (1957) contributed a phrase to national idiom and darkened the usual picaresque progress with reports on a world not made for innocents to earn in. For all his frankness and agile narrative technique, Braine seemed to find the picaresque thwarting. Not content to pursue the accumulative rather than the evaluative method, he went oblique and philosophical in *The Vodi* (1959) and revisited his first theme mechanically in *Life at the Top* (1962). He is already beyond the academic-vernacular mixture of Amis and Wain, less interested in the world of objects than they are, and far from their version of the curmudgeonly jocose. So too is Brian Glanville, the author of several novels by twenty-seven, the best of which are *Along the Arno* (1956) and the more rambling *The Bankrupts* (1958). In the latter novel Glanville makes more of the Jewish bourgeois adults than of their children, Rosemary and Bernard. The young, it seems, are not interminably interesting even to the young; not even in the claustrophobic discussions at which Glanville is superb, as *Diamond* (1962) proved once again.

1. His affectionate memoir 'Meyerstein' (*Encounter*, August 1962) is one of his best compositions by far; the preparations in this piece seem those of major ability being gradually informed by a sense of the tragic.

All the novels of Iris Murdoch (1919–) have a touch of the poetic. More than any English novelist writing now, she can integrate in an unostentatious prose several different elements. For once, wit, dream, realism and mind-probing are made to consort decorously together. *The Flight from the Enchanter* (1956) and *The Sandcastle* (1957) were brilliant and imaginative rather than moving. Her main problem, it seems, is the over-activity of a well-trained mind. When she starts to analyse she can make a vast amount out of next to nothing; the performance is ingenious and astounding, but it tempts her into undue length. And, to make full claim on the reader's emotions, she has to bring all of herself into action: so that with complete statement comes the over-cerebral. In her first novel, *Under the Net* (1954), she keeps things on the move; and Jake Donoghue, the struggling peripatetic writer, convinces entirely. The comedy is beautifully timed, deftly varied, and the progress of Jake's self-discovery is illustrated rather than explained. In *The Bell* (1958), however, the tensions within the bizarre religious community prompt her into unhappy symbolism: the Abbey, the new bell, the legend. She adds a dimension by turning religious theorizing into fantasy, and the experiment does not quite succeed. Miss Murdoch's difficulties resemble those of Muriel Spark: religious experience, and differing religious convictions, have to be made to seem recognizable extensions of daily reality. So far, Miss Murdoch's wry comedy leads us away from her attempt at persistent fable. *A Severed Head* (1961) is intricate in both plot and texture; the amorous characters are made to play a kind of musical chairs, and Miss Murdoch relentlessly analyses each new permutation of people. Her articulate solicitude sometimes leads her into Jamesian casuistries which, taken at the hectic pace she sets, leave the reader baffled and unimplicated. So many liaisons at such speed take the novel nearer to farce than it is meant to be; but lately, in *An Unofficial Rose* (1962), she has written more loosely, more lushly, and is displaying her gifts with less strain.

Angus Wilson (1913–), a considerable novelist who scrupulously prolongs the tradition running from Trollope to Hugh Walpole, made his first attempt at fiction in *The Wrong Set* (1949), a collection of short stories. In the following year he published another collection, *Such Darling Dodos*: the title story shows Tony,

an aging homosexual dandy, visiting his cousins Robin and
Priscilla, both of them righteous humanitarians. Robin is dying of
cancer, but his dated idealism provokes Tony into the cruel 'dodo'
image. Tony, who has always felt morally inferior to the pair of
them, suddenly realizes that time has moved farther ahead of
them than of him. This concern with attitudes—how they possess
people and dehumanize them—appears in Wilson's novels in
massive, unsparingly realistic form.

In *Hemlock and After* (1953) he analyses the roles of Bernard
Sands: liberal humanist, cheerer-on of the underdog, enlightened
democrat, novelist and, especially for his arranging to have Vardon
Hall turned into a colony for young writers, patron. Sands is also
a homosexual and has a neurotic wife. It is a disorganized novel
about disintegration—post-war society's and Sands's. Realism
consorts here with extravaganza: Wilson has written a study of
Zola and has profitably studied his Dickens. At times the characterization is preposterous (the plebeian homosexuals especially),
but the main theme, the conflict between the need for external
authority and the reluctance to wield power, comes burning
through. Bernard Sands's death is an end of personal incertitude,
but he has served to instance painfully a situation which Wilson
handles with virile imagination and unshowy compassion. *Anglo-
Saxon Attitudes* (1956) is a well-organized, beautifully measured
novel about Gerald Middleton, a Professor emeritus who cannot
bring himself either to end his sham of a marriage or to expose the
archaeological hoax known as 'The Melpham Burial'. The heathen
idol that Gilbert Stokesay planted in the tomb of Bishop Eorpwald
is no more obscene than the sky-blue sentimentality of Inge,
Gerald's ample, beautiful Danish wife is to Gerald. Wilson explores the nature of middle-class worry and its impact on the
children of those involved. It is a horrifying experience to watch
trouble seeping from one generation into the next, from one concern into another. Gerald, locked in marital stocks of his own
devising, gives in, letting his will fail and his mind atrophy behind
its busy front. To find such a full-scale, trenchant and character-
packed anatomy of failure we have to go back to the nineteenth
century. Angus Wilson spots humbug everywhere and his novels
do the old-fashioned but eternally fascinating job of separating
the person from the *personae*. No English novelist save Graham

Greene has conveyed so poignantly, and none so exuberantly, the moments in life at which people stop trying to correct, or sever themselves from, the muddles they create. Wilson is harsh on fake living, on hypocrisy and vanity, but he is also an addict of frailty. He squeezes pretence until it screams at us. The short stories in *A Bit Off the Map* (1957) demolish coffee-bar intellectuals who adopt a self-styled Angry, the popular Press that supplies delinquents with the cant of self-justification, and other varieties of modern sham. It is Wilson's peculiar triumph to explode the superficies of life without seeming shallow himself. He knows the times backwards and, if he does find more freaks than most of us do, we must surely accept the exaggeration as his own defence against seeming a mere classifier. In *The Old Men at the Zoo* (1961) he studies the dilemma of the ageing still in power when confronted by complex and sudden events. Such a study takes him into the region of Snow, and he brings to it the passion for human enormity, and the irony, that Snow eschews. As yet, however, Wilson has more weight than power. For all his attention to Zola, he still retains something of the mildness of a Trollope, even when distributing damnation.

Another novelist who studies the modern scene with fanatical closeness, but without creating character on the same generous scale as Wilson, is Colin MacInnes. *City of Spades* (1957) describes the coloured population of London—not just African but West Indians or American negroes. Two worlds confront each other in the persons of Montgomery Pew (Assistant Welfare Officer at the Colonial Office) and the dynamic, contradictory Johnny Macdonald Fortune, fresh from Lagos. It is a vivacious, probing novel, both moving and informative. Colin MacInnes is at home with every aspect of his theme, although he prefers the Spades' euphoric carelessness to the cramped decorum of the Jumbles (John Bulls). Above all, he understands the young, their life-eating velleities and their ignorance of time (*Absolute Beginners*, 1959). His third novel, *Mr Love and Justice* (1960), the wryest of his tracts for the times, establishes him as the Hogarth of the cleared-streets era. Frankie Love, an out-of-work merchant seaman, 'adrift in Yokohama and repatriated at official expense', makes a fruitless visit to Stepney Labour Exchange and from that moment abandons the straight and narrow. P.C. Edward Justice, whose girl-friend has a shady father, is promoted to the C.I.D. about the same time as Frankie Love becomes a ponce. Gradually their courses through the field of vice converge; allegory begins to hover over them; and eventually they are in collision and collusion. Frankie develops a fey yearning for gaol but suddenly finds himself in hospital with ex-P.C. Justice whose erratic private life has ended his police career. Justice thinks of starting a dress-shop and Frankie, himself tempted to set up as a private eye, suggests using the shop as a brothel. Justice muses on the twists of fate.

These correspondences and transpositions are never blatant: the action is tortuous enough to mute the allegory without, however, burying the Defoe-like revelations that occur on every page. MacInnes communicates life's untidiness and a nagging sense of its sinister coincidences. A connoisseur of underdogs, Flash Harrys and wanglers, he is also a lover of paraphernalia and data: a sulking whore does her nails nineteen times each; in the 'heroic phase' of *pissoir* architecture 'the larva-hued earthenware, the huge brass pipes, the great slate walls dividing the compartments, are all built on an Egyptian scale'. He pores assiduously over the behaviour of narks, coppers and pimps; anomalies intrigue him: it is the vice squad's star sleuth who conscientiously procures Justice's downfall, the star ponce who rats on Love. But MacInnes also conveys the idea that the two novices are really toppled by anticipatory images of themselves as Detective Sergeant and Ponce Regent—roles that preclude Justice's petty ignominy no less than Love's defective sense of vocation.

Unfortunately MacInnes's documentary concern makes his characters explain their callings to each other, and to others, at wearisome length. By the time they have reached hospital and have time to talk, they have talked themselves out. There is not quite enough irrelevance coming out of them, and there are too many lame jokes from MacInnes as narrator: 'He looked at Edward like a brother (as Cain, for example, did on Abel)'; 'One could have heard an ice-cube drop'. One complains only because this vivid, perhaps too relentless novel could have been made defter, swifter and (the demerit of MacInnes's virtues) less proudly knowing.

Over a period of only three years Muriel Spark has produced

half a dozen novels and a book of short stories. After *The Comforters* (1957) and *Robinson* (1958) she published *Memento Mori* (1959), in which Death telephones the valetudinarian characters one by one, reminding them that they must eventually die. This cosmic snigger demoralizes them; they cannot fight, buy or disdain it. But the idea, funny in its flat way, led nowhere: it was negative and seemed to thwart imagination itself. But in her next novel, *The Ballad of Peckham Rye* (1960), Miss Spark dispensed with allegory and created a riot around a picaresque hero. Dougal Douglas is a charlatan. He cavorts, jives, rocks, bamboozles, postures, perverts and disdains until he has unnerved the whole community of Peckham Rye. Coming as an Arts man to do Personnel work for a textile firm, he ends up working simultaneously for a rival concern, undermining several affairs of the heart and precipitating a *crime passionel*. Deformed by a high shoulder, he adds Byronic paranoia to the inventive malice of a Till Eulenspiegel. All fall, for or because of him—including Merle Coverdale, head of typing pool, Miss Belle Frierne, his landlady (who once had an experience with a Highlander's kilt but survived), Trevor Lomas, the top local Teddy, and Mr Druce, the worldsad, wife-spurned managing director. Such a character might easily have blotted out the rest of the novel; but Miss Spark's almost fierce sense of human variety provides a crowd of solid, distinct and stingingly funny minor oafs as well as the delicious company of Dawn Waghorn, cone-winder, Annette Wren, traineeseamer, Elaine Kent, process-controller, and Odette Hill, uptwister. Dougal arrives, prevails, then departs for Africa to sell tape-recorders to witch-doctors. A Chaucerian normality is restored. Miss Spark has a deadly ear for the banalities of daily chatter and a tender sense of human hesitancy. Immaculately planned, the novel foams with life and the style is cunningly offhand, making the ridiculous irresistible.

But it is Miss Spark's other, metaphysical side which gives *The Ballad* its punch. Dougal Douglas, the wizard from across the river, is a supernatural force. His behaviour implies the presence of unmentioned devils, and so makes a macabre point more tellingly than the ingenuities of *Memento Mori*. *The Bachelors* (1960) is a funny account of bachelors involved with spiritualism. The plot is clever, the gallery of grotesques fuller and madder than ever, and the logic of the fable impeccable. Yet this mixture of 'The Wider Infinity' with lonely freaks does not quite come off. Miss Spark is a Catholic and this is Charles Williams territory, in which it is almost impossible to succeed. Walter Prett, the critic drunkenly denouncing the middle classes, Patrick Seaton the crook, Ronald the epileptic graphologist—these are diverting, and their trivialities imply the condition of their souls. But in this novel there are just too many specimens; the comprehensiveness seems too deliberate; and the metaphysical dimensions suggested in Ronald's fits seems *voulu*, especially when applied to a clutter of minor characters—rich widow, waitress, Alice's friend Elsie, Father Socket and a homosexual friend. . . . If *The Bachelors* is a fable, and Miss Spark keeps twisting our minds in that direction, then it ought to be more economical of minor illustrations; if it is a piece of social documentary, then the religious-spiritualist elements should not seem to express the author's 'philosophy'. Miss Spark is like a Bernanos trapped in an Anthony Powell. The one will have to come into the open or yield to the other altogether. At present Miss Spark's characters are too picturesque to make religious points without implying parody. She is attempting satire in which the opposite of the serious is the trivial. It is to be hoped that she will not decide that the funny has to go. What she has to do is to link the serious to the trivial funnily; not, as she does now, link the serious to the funny trivially.

It is hard for documentary novels not to appear trivial, and it is just as hard to attempt a documentary fable without seeming to waste all one's facts. It is not surprising, then, that many young novelists leave extraction of significances to the reader: they create the Joe Lunns, the Jim Dixons, the Jake Donaghues, and float them among closely observed details. We find circumstances presented in their own right, without reference to traditions or precedents; and such presentation necessarily makes us think of uninstructed man. It is almost as if we have been taken back to the beginning of life; except that the unexperienced hero has to reckon with modern phenomena. The fable is ironic; the picaro, trying to work things out, has all the handicaps of Adam and none of social man's guiding principles. Such a theme perfectly exemplifies the confusion of young people released from their class, from shibboleths and regimen. They hold hard to the material world: Kingsley Amis, for example, records detail with almost distracted precision. They do not compare events with standards but event with event. They induce, they rarely deduce. Like scientists investigating a previously unscrutinized process of nature, they keep on watching while they decide how much a representative sample can prove. They wonder when it is just to sum things up. Fearful of not having enough information, they keep on accumulating instances—just as Sally Jay Gorce does.

The picaresque repudiates the organizing mind and exemplifies inability to use the immediate literary past. It also gives the iconoclast, as well as the man who can connect nothing with nothing, an ideal medium. When a coherent world-view is lacking, the picaresque can still make points with the minimum of manipulation and communicate the flavour of experiences that seem incapable of being interpreted. And young writers, themselves caught between old houses and housing estates, old and redbrick universities, Empire and Welfare State, the Suez débâcle and Ban-the-Bomb marches, between working-class and the lower-middles, either try on all views or profess none. Until the 'plural' culture is a reality rather than a talking-point in the weeklies, the young novelist with an eye for comedy will be obliged to study the cultural muddle: not so much to explore the depths of individual psychology as to compare fronts and get behind arbitrary masks. The opportunity is ready-made for comedy of manners. A society of abrupt contrasts—especially between the not quite dislodged old and the not quite installed new—is bound to produce experts in surfaces, experts less fixed in principle and place than, say, the urbanely elegiac Powell, the sane, sadistic Waugh or the hyperbolic, probing Angus Wilson.

The romp prevails. Alan Sillitoe (1928–) in *Saturday Night and Sunday Morning* (1958) enthusiastically lets loose a working-class hero who, having sown a few wild oats and learned the disadvantages to oneself of being selfish, settles into mediocre flaccidity. Nothing is taken on trust, except the value of scepticism—a point unequivocally made in the same writer's collection of stories, *The Loneliness of the Long Distance Runner* (1959). A whole generation is summed up in the Borstal boy who refuses to try in the race he can easily win:

The pop-eyed potbellied governor said to a pop-eyed potbellied Member of Parliament who sat next to his pop-eyed
potbellied whore of a wife that I was his only hope for getting
the Borstal Blue Ribbon Prize Cup for Long Distance Cross
Country Running (All England), which I was, and it set me
laughing to myself inside, and I didn't say a word to any potbellied pop-eyed bastard that might give them real hope, though
I knew the governor anyway took my quietness to mean he'd
got that cup already stuck on the bookshelf in his office among
the few other mildewed trophies.

This is Gissing's grudge with a difference: it takes the initiative.
Its repetitive obloquy split into thesis and antithesis by the nougat
of smugness in the middle, the passage in fact proves its point in
the first five words. It is not only, however, a matter of resentment; the speaker is making the same point as Satie made when
he said that to have refused the *Légion d'Honneur* is not enough—
one should never have deserved it. And plebeian Diogenes can
mouth and rail in an idiom that the well-educated Amises and
Wains covet in much the same way as the poets of the thirties
coveted underprivileged status. A combination of 'I'm all right,
Jack' and 'So what?' typifies the attitude of many fictional heroes
of the fifties and sixties. It leads nowhere, but steam being blown
confers opportunities for rhetoric. And of rhetoric we are short,
especially of the prose versions of this kind of thing:

> Birds of a feather flock together
> And so do pigs and swine
> Rats and mice do have their choice
> And so I have mine.

This is not just angriness; it is creative contempt. On the literary
level, it takes the form of John Osborne's attack in *The Observer*
(30 October 1960) on

> the belief that working-class or non-Gentleman writers wrote
> principally out of resentment at not being able to get into
> Literary Society and/or become Gentlemen. Eventually the

message did seep through that the complaint had never been that it wasn't possible to get in, but that it had never been worth getting into in the first place.

And, more generally, this:

The condition of being English is one of the last hideouts of guerrilla Romanticism. Now that Christians and Gentlemen are assumed to be safely muffled up in the catacombs of Cabinet room and television studio, what is left of Holy Mother Church but the pillars of our derelict Englishness?

It is an inverted snobbery identifiable with honesty—the kind of honesty that peacetime conscription threatened to wreck. The young men do not want to be messed about.

Robert Holles, a Salinger-Sillitoe, tells in *Captain Cat* (1960) how Harry Bell, a young army apprentice, recalls the lousy training camp at Harlingford and his loused-up friendship there with 'Gangster' Boone, a clever misfit parked in the army for knocking up his girl. This novel brilliantly captures the aimless verbal violence of plebeian and military complaint: 'Loving thy neighbour as thyself is all very well as long as your neighbour doesn't happen to be a thieving, arse-crawling, snot-gobbling bastard like Coster.' On it goes, the livid effing-and-blinding prompted by the codified imbecilities of the military way. Harry and Boone form their own élite, the 'Indes' (independent, inner-directed), to condemn the perfidious, sadistic world of Turkey, the 'Sah!'-screaming sergeant; Joicey who rides on Horse Chadwick's sodomite shoulders; Freddie Palmer with a navel as big as an egg-cup; and of crumpet, jankers, dark rituals of polishing, whitewashing and doubling. Harry soon conforms, an incipient lord of flies, but never quite loses his foul-minded, instinctive charity. A moving, spitting and unexaggerated book, *Captain Cat* is also dementedly funny, enough to send one (as Harlingford says) pale as a pox-doctoring turnip or give a statue the bellyache. Not far removed are Keith Waterhouse's brilliantly perceptive account of a Saturday in the life of a young undertaker's clerk (*Billy Liar*, 1959) and Sid Chaplin's *Day of the Sardine* (1961) which traces young

Arthur Haggerston's career through deadend jobs into petty
gangsterdom and eventual maturity with the loss of his girl.
These novels make caustic rhetoric out of the side of life which
the well-reared think 'ugly'. Frank Norman, himself having
served six gaol terms, has pushed the mode as far as it will go;
or rather, he has discovered its coincidence with his natural mode
of self-expression. Such an autobiography as *Stand on Me* (1959),
with its Runyon-like sketches of 'tealeaves' (thieves), layabouts,
pimps, whores and 'kayfs', con-men and queers, challenges the
imaginative novelist to more strenuous efforts. Norman's accre-
tion of anecdotes about his youth in Soho gives the facts, draws
no moral and offers no defence. Neither does Brendan Behan in
Borstal Boy (1958): just the loathed, pointless routine presented
in scatological formulae and crisp sentences. Never have the
opportunities for vicarious slumming been so numerous; never
has society indulged in such intense self-exploration: just to be in
the know.

Rather different versions of the knockabout comedy have come
from John Rae, whose *The Custard Boys* (1960) builds up to an
adolescent *acte gratuit* by grammar-school boys, Godfrey Smith,
whose *The Business of Loving* (1961) becomes almost Wagnerian
about a group of Hampshire adolescents, and Jeremy Brooks,
whose *Jampot Smith* (1959) tackles Welsh adolescents with a more
dispassionate eye. At the end of *The Business of Loving* we are told
that 'We live in the age of the picaresque hero and the positivist
philosophy. . . . There's no magic in the world, except what we put
into it.' That *aperçu* might have come from Colin Wilson's novel
Ritual in the Dark (1960), in which a cerebral young Shavian cycles
between the British Museum and seedy lodgings. Sorme, the quasi-
hero, picks up with Austin Nunne, a wealthy homosexual aesthete,
a bed-ridden worldly priest, a frigid Jehovah's Witness aunt of
Nunne's and her niece (both of whom he seduces), and a misanthropic painter infatuated with a girl of twelve. Nunne is another
Jack the Ripper, and there is a crazy octogenarian, himself a
connoisseur of the disembowelling sport. Sorme, an egotistic
Genet-Faust figure, keeps spouting or musing about Nijinsky,
Sade, Shaw and other familiars; and the whole farrago of vision
and vastation, chips and psychopathology, Victorian sexuality and
self-regarding earnestness amounts to either an exorcizing self-

parody or a limp obeisance to the mode. It is impossible, as Gide found, to make juvenile escapades satanic without a premiss of wit or mockery.

A rather more glamorous version of the picaresque is Honor Tracy's *A Number of Things* (1960): this time, a young writer scrambling among the gaudy fauna of the Caribbean. Less spirited and much less witty, Peter Greave's *Young Man in the Sun* (1958) tracks a Lucky Jim through the swarming backwaters of Calcutta. Beautifully defining the provenance of the picaro, David Storey's *Flight into Camden* (1960) shows a miner father educating his son and daughter into a classless emptiness which drives the one into becoming a gelid careerist and the other into flight with a worthless married man. This is a fascinating study of people's need to cling to objects or to make other people as reliable as objects. They all, parents and children, know something is wrong, something lost, and the tragedy is that substitutes are no more than substitutes. Here, for once, the class-theme is explored in depth and without throwaway frivolity. It is an intensely disturbing novel. Compared with such a stock recital as Thomas Hinde's *For the Good of the Company* (1961)—young climber joins vast London firm, sleeps with boss's daughter, etcetera—it sets a challenging example. Storey's is the way the picaresque drama of social displacement has to go if it is not to lapse into vacuous prankishness; and already such writers as Iris Murdoch and Muriel Spark are going beyond the immediate and contemporary (without neglecting the social antic) while Amis and Wain are attempting moral seriousness without pomposity.

The young picaresque hero steadies himself by asking for an unattainable perfection. By now (Joe Lunn first appeared in 1950) he has often enough been shown not finding perfection—in love, politics, philosophy, *actes gratuits*, career, family, perversion, honesty and contempt. It is almost as if all these young novelists have been compiling a vast *Bildungsroman* of the Welfare Hero's adolescence and early manhood. One hopes that the practitioners of picaresque will advance to a less merely racketing conception of their art: in other words, not do a Waugh, marking youthful time, or a Huxley, abandoning the novel altogether. One logical development would be towards something as Dickensian, as lively as J. B. Priestley's *The Good Companions* (1929), but less sentimental than that meaty jamboree. Of course, Priestley's type of national relish is unlikely to win favour in the sixties: the modern novel is rooted in romantic dissent. But such writers as Angus Wilson and Iris Murdoch seem to be working towards a complex genre—almost as if the Walpole of *The Cathedral* (1922) were setting his studies of English life under the aspect of a Dickensian eternity.

I cannot help feeling that the young picaresque writer must now turn to Dickens: to imagination regarded in itself as a life-creating power. This would be to follow the example of Angus Wilson and Joyce Cary and to put contempt in its place. It was contemptuousness which thinned out into dustiness the abilities of Rose Macaulay; it is what disappoints us in Waugh and what disjoints the early Huxley. At the moment there is a cult of the unliterary, and the stylists, the exponents of bravura, are out in the cold. True, a Durrell has broken through; but the young, in their unrestrained astringency, deplore his purple, ignoring its purpose. Durrell admits that fiction is a concoction, and sets about a concoction that is life-enhancing. The Amises and Wains, on the other hand, opt for energy without elegance, almost as if they think an unplanned novel less artificial than one of consummate architectonic and blatantly rich texture. And their documentary aim becomes tedious, a crypto-sham worked against an admitted fake.

One way of substituting for style and imagination is to write the novel of specialized knowledge. This is not to belittle such a novel but to notice what it does not entail: best written with an imagination capable of making the documentary reverberate beyond its own limits, it can also be done cold as a species of the exotic. David Storey's *This Sporting Life* (1960), one of the best of its kind, treats of Arthur Machin, a Rugby League star, who, thoughtful but awkward, lumbers through the elations of eventual stardom, seeking an anthithesis to brutish prowess and his growing realization that all—skill, fame, lust, even tenderness—diminishes in its very flourishing. He searches and learns: no more. Some stilted conversations apart ('But just how long can you grovel?'), the long account of his exacerbating affair with his widowed landlady is moving and unforced. And the whole ethos of glum Northern town, the steaming byre of the shower-room, the mud savagery and the backroom mish-mash of fees, selectors and hangers-on, comes throbbingly alive. John Bowen's *Storyboard* (1960) is much more of a documentary: keeping its eye firmly on the copywriters' stratagem to sell soap, it reminds one that Bowen has strong predilections for (and considerable ability with) myth and fable. His account is convincing and of great information value, but too much like a report—as if Bowen were curbing himself at every word. The people are a bit faint, as they tend to be in most primarily documentary novels. The exceptions include Noel Woodin's *Joncer* (1961), a spirited and intelligent story about a National Hunt jockey (far from the meretriciousness of Frank Harris); another, more farcical, racing novel, *Daughters of Mulberry* (1961), by Roger Longrigg (whose own copywriting novel, *A High-Pitched Buzz*, 1959, is brittler than Bowen's); Roy Fuller's *The Ruined Boys* (1959) and *The Father's Comedy* (1961), dealing with public school and a court-martial respectively; and— following riotously in the wake of Wells's *The New Machiavelli*— Wilfrid Fienburgh's *No Love for Johnny* (1959) and Maurice Edelman's *The Minister* (1961), two novels about the undertow between private life and public affairs. Such novels as these, like Frank Norman's rambling Soho autobiographies and Snow's steady portrayal of the powerful, satisfy an appetite for vicarious national tourism. The facts of the society are being patiently set down, and its incoherence is being tabulated. This is no doubt a preliminary stage before the return, by some of the younger novelists at least, to stern probings of the human conscience. It is like making sure they can get to Tolstoy before they attempt Dostoevsky.

II

I conclude this section on the English novel with a brief look at the unorthodox. What follows will be pretty much a matter of personal preference. I only hope it may send the reader to a rewarding novel or two and remind him how hard the experimental novel has to fight to gain an audience in contemporary Britain.

Philip Toynbee (1916–) has always had the courage of his compulsions; and he has usually been compelled towards poetry—or at least the poetic. So after the experimental structure and texture of *Tea with Mrs Goodman* (1947) and *The Garden to the Sea* (1954) it is no surprise to find him publishing *Pantaloon or The Valediction* (1961), the first volume of a picaresque series. The difference is that *Pantaloon* is written in verse, with occasional stretches of prose. Part epic, part masque, it is concerned with Dick Aberville, the old and only survivor of a titled family, looking back to his childhood, his various *personae* and especially to the lyrical moments which have sustained him. Once again we have to remind ourselves that, because life is heterogeneous, art is obliged neither to be, nor not to be, of the same kind. Toynbee's mixture-novel has something in common with A. O. Chater's *Julian Fairfield* (1961) in which what is said melts into the reactions the words produce. In some ways Chater's novel reverses the method of Nathalie Sarraute, who combines pre-speech in all its inchoateness with uttered words. Naturally such explorations lead to muddle, imprecision, lack of pointing (is it clumsy writing or a cleverly prepared specimen of pre-thought or instantaneous response?) and turgidity. They also, in Chater's novel, lead to concentration on episodes to the neglect of overall structure—an error into which Proust falls and which Patrick Leigh Fermor avoids in *The Violins of St Jacques* (1954), based on the volcanic destruction in 1902 of St Pierre, the capital of Martinique. The point here is not that Leigh Fermor goes back, in his brilliant mandarin prose, to the creole customs of nearly seventy years ago (which we have to take on trust), but that he is constructing a metaphor in which the people do not really matter. They exist only to be consumed by the natural catastrophe. The splendour of the Comte de Serindan's ball overshadows the people at it, just as the volcano overshadows everything. The high cones of ivory *chou coco* parody the disaster they prefigure. This thematic process entails so individual an impress from the style as to preclude our asking whether or not the fable is a recognizable extension of reality.[1] The English tradition is short of novelists whose style makes the impossible palatable; there is room for a Djuna Barnes or a Truman Capote. This is not to suggest that the novel is the right genre in which to exploit words in their own right; it is not.

1. See also Rumer Godden's *Take Three Tenses* (1945) and Rosamond Lehmann's *The Ballad and the Source* (1945).

But there is no reason why the novel, which makes its effects by accumulation, should not display a variety of effects: from the robust itemizations of a Falstaff to the lurid, exaggerative rhetoric in which William Golding in *Free Fall* expresses his concern (like Durrell's Pursewarden) at a world in which there is not enough tenderness. Few modern stylists have equalled the sharp, economical, imaginative prose of Chapman Mortimer's *Madrigal* (1960). Few modern fabulists have tied allegory so cleverly to reportage as John Bowen does in *After the Rain* (1958): the hero meets a rain-maker and follows him out to Texas; before long the hero finds himself rowing along the King's Road and eventually takes up with a girl he finds aboard a lavish raft originally launched to advertise a patent food. Compared with Faulkner's much more apocalyptic *Old Man*, this is like real life—and more like the 'real life' we expect from fiction. Bowen seems to have it all in his hand: a passion for symbol, a tenacious regard for the everyday world, and a scalpel wit. *After the Rain* is both an adventure and a revelation, splendidly unpompous.

Malcolm Lowry's *Under the Volcano* (1947), the overwhelming story of an Englishman who seeks to escape technological civilization by going to Mexico (shades of Lawrence), still stands as one of the most successful symbolist novels of the century. Lowry's alcoholic hero can stomach neither his wife nor the age of steel, and the novel chronicles in bewildering but exquisite phantasmagoric images the nightmare of his last day. Lowry's first novel, *Ultramarine* (1933), is based on his adventures as a deck-hand on a voyage he made to the Far East at seventeen; the hero is already a heavy drinker. It remains to be seen whether the cache of Lowry's manuscripts discovered in a squatter's shack on an island off Vancouver will add to his reputation. *Lunar Caustic*, a novel set in the psychiatric ward of New York's Bellevue Hospital, and another novel, *October Ferry to Gabriola*, about a Camus-type character who suffers because he influenced someone to kill himself, should ensure the second vogue he merits. His collection of stories, *Hear Us O Lord from Heaven Thy Dwelling Place* (1961), is mostly autobiographical fragments. One story, the longest, describes in the stream-of-consciousness style (and with an auxiliary narrative running down the margin) a freighter voyage through the Panama Canal. The other stories deal with expatriate writers

and the Canadian squatter camp where Lowry (1909–1957) eventually settled. His febrile, desperate manner may not appeal to
everyone; but he had an astounding ability to combine virile
luxuriance with coherent structure.

A few young writers, although handicapped by the unadven-
turous tastes of English critics and readers—as well as by the
vogue for 'good, solid, sensible' novels—have nevertheless managed to make almost religious points in oblique ways. Seeming to
draw their superficies from the shelf that holds Compton Mackenzie, Louis Bromfield and Eric Linklater, they add something
philosophical. The best of these is Robert Shaw, an apprentice
Greene, who after a brilliantly imaginative and partly allegorical
first novel, *The Hiding Place* (1959), turned in an almost Dostoevskian second performance, *The Sun Doctor* (1961). Dr Benjamin
Halliday returns, to a knighthood, from twenty-five years in a
West African hospital. Almost a 'burnt-out case', he is haunted by
the vitiating memory of a personal blunder. Eventually he achieves
an adjustment; Shaw's exploration of the doctor's spiritual progress is both moving and massive—an earnest of impressive work
to come from a writer who can be intense, lavish and deep-
reaching without indulging in the self-mocking irony too common
in the English novelist. Shaw's understanding of desolation is as
profound as Beckett's; and he achieves it by hemming in his
characters with colour and social fabric, whereas Beckett pares
all that away.

III

The English novel, then, has recovered from the flux, and only
Lawrence Durrell makes much use of it. Structure, loose in
Powell, firm in Snow, haphazard in Cary, has been brought back
to help the reader through and the novelist to create suggestive patterns. It was inevitable that the English novelist, so uneasily concerned with the comedy of class, should push the novel of manners
towards a world of fantasy in which he could transform his self-
consciousness into caricatures and express unselfconsciousness by
delving into the minds of children. After all, the class-conscious
person of whatever stratum regards people not as individuals but

as types; and his response to individuals outside his own class is inadequate, impaired by shyness or disdain. So it is easy to turn people not of one's own class into objects of fun; preoccupation with class facilitates this, and England supports many professional entertainers who specialize in impersonating representative class figures. From the hyperbole of Dickens to the spoofs of Waugh, an inhibiting self-consciousness provokes compensatory caricature. The impersonality of class-detecting sanctions the inhumanity implicit in farce, and the personal *persona* is mingled with class drill. Both the established and the climbing have clear ideas about manners; and what is held in common by members of the same class is held to with ritualistic tenacity, as J. B. Priestley's warfactory novel, *Daylight on Saturday* (1943), tells us long before Sillitoe, and the riper Priestley's *Festival at Farbridge* (1951) reveals more voluminously than any comic panorama since *Pickwick*.

Small wonder that the human ecologists, ranging from Snow and Balchin to Powell and Nevil Shute, outnumber the metaphysical novelists. No raw metaphysics for the socially fixated English: nothing like the cosmic particularities of Camus, Malraux, Mann and Bernanos. Instead, the abstract-minded use society and manners to reassure themselves while tackling fantasy. They also reassure themselves with plain language, as if suspecting that bravura dissolves everything into personal haze all over again. Angus Wilson, for instance, sets *The Old Men at the Zoo* in the 1970s, at London Zoo. A sick giraffe kicks a keeper to death; the zoo administrators argue about shifting the animals to a game reserve; but war erupts and England is occupied. It is all very tenuous and oblique. The best parts are the administrators' quarrels, which have the reassuring sound of 'Colonel Bogey' heard in the middle of an Arctic waste. The book obviously overreaches: far into the portentous from too idiosyncratic and too slender a base.

Even English heroic is often mock. So when a novelist like Snow arrives and says he is unironically serious, he is hailed as a marvel. After all, so many English novelists have found excuses for private jokes: Anthony Powell, for example, says of his characters: 'the participants act their parts without consideration either for suitability of scene or for the words spoken by the rest of the cast. The result is a general tendency for things to be brought to the level of farce even when the theme is serious enough.' As long as the English novelist persists in his passion for deprecatory self-parody *via* the idioms of the various classes, the English novel will seem parochial and trivial, a tribal festivity. This is where the English novel differs from the American, in which violence and portentous outline are often assumed to be enough, and the French, which Germaine Brée has characterized through the example of Proust:

> We can distinguish [she writes] in Proust's work the two great temptations of the contemporary novel: to delete the story from the novel to the advantage of metaphysics, making it an essay in concrete metaphysics, and to project a closed and autonomous world so subjective that the reader no longer knows how to penetrate into it.[1]

With a few changes, we can discover the English novel as modern in that same sense, but also distinct according to its own lights. It deletes metaphysics to the advantage of the story (the fun of confecting) and so creates essays in concrete hyperbole which refer to a 'closed and autonomous world' just as impenetrable to many as that of Proust.

Already, Wilson, Snow, Hartley and Amis, to name a few, seem to be marking time, repeating themselves. On the one hand, it might be a good idea for the younger novelists to read their Rebecca West again, for her knack with people who are unusual, and for the gleaming fusion of decorum and density conspicuous in *The Thinking Reed* (1936) and *The Fountain Overflows* (1957). Or the Priestley of *Bright Day* (1946), for the generous and deft manipulation of family history against a shifting social scene. Or Pamela Hansford Johnson's best—*An Avenue of Stone* (1947), *The Philistines* (1949) and *The Last Resort* (1956)—for their sheer naturalness throughout the complexities of character-defining. Some of Rose Macaulay's caustic (*And No Man's Wit*, 1940; *Potterism*, 1920) would be salutary; it is not enough to have fun and just document *mores*. Alan Sillitoe is deepening in *Key to*

1. Germaine Brée, *Du Temps perdu au temps retrouvé* (1950), p. 268 (my translation).

the Door (1961) and, according to an article he wrote in *The Times*, even reading Sholom Aleichem. Again, William Golding is steering away from Orwell in the direction of Arthur Koestler's meticulous depiction of evil's social and political face, and a new religious intensity. James Hanley, plugging away without much acclaim, is an English Conrad-Camus who deserves more attention, especially for *Levine* (1956); he has come a long way from his working-class novels, *The Furys* (1935) and *The Secret Journey* (1936), which, however, the Gillian Freemans and the Sillitoes would do well to study. And Francis King, deftly and quietly unblurring the secrets of unspectacular spirits, is already a novelist of impressive achievement although perhaps too consistently mild in manner. *The Widow* (1957) is one of the least strained of his novels and possibly the most moving, while *The Custom House* (1961) reveals him as more descriptive, more expansive than usual—a rare feat considering that the theme is love and cowardice in modern Japan; he might have gone deeper than ever and thus destroyed the power of the Japanese milieu. The most publicized is not always the best, but it is usually the nation's most characteristic: that is to say, socially conscious to the point of fantasy. There are English novelists who have more in common with, say, Camus or Faulkner, with Kafka or Silone, than with novelists among their own countrymen. Anthony Burgess, Rex Warner, J. P. Donleavy, P. H. Newby, Rayner Heppenstall, Constantine Fitzgibbon, Gabriel Fielding, David Hughes, William Sansom, Paul Scott and Andrew Sinclair are among these, and their presence is reassuring at a time when the class-picaresque holds the ascendant over the poetic, the subjective and the metaphysical.

The fifties supplied anti-mandarin, anti-climactic, unpompous novels which mixed a type of Methodism with irritability. After Amis's 'filthy Mozart', it could hardly be expected that Art should save the novelist's and protagonist's soul; but cash and respectability did. Welfare England has her nostalgic Powells and her earnest Snows, her ingeniously rebellious Compton-Burnetts and Durrells; but she has, except for Greene and Golding, few novelists with anything like a powerfully profound vision of life. One's abiding impression is of pettiness, anaemia, triviality, pub-jokes and tuck-shop pranks, mild pints and insipid prose. But to ask for more than a few exceptions to this stolid stuff is to ask that the English should become a different nation and cultivate the energy, the passion, the mania of their outsiders—Shakespeare, Hardy, Lawrence—rather than remain their usual, carefully self-regimenting selves.

2

France

Today in many countries, particularly in
France, there is a conspiracy of silence.
Writers are constantly haunted by qualms of
conscience about the means or about the
ends, with the result that we are always keeping something back.

(JEAN-PAUL SARTRE)

I

ANYONE who contends, as he reasonably might, that the modern
French novel has fallen a victim to abstraction, should try to explain the neglect of Anatole France (1844–1924). This wry, philosophizing satirist tried, a little too earnestly and deliberately, to
play Voltaire to an age that favoured naturalism and the exotic.
But his determination to create his own manner can hardly be
said to be an adequate substitute for the strict fervour of a
Voltaire. At his worst France seems contrived and posturing; at
his best, the master of a light-handed facetiousness which seems
to believe in nothing. *Le Crime de Sylvestre Bonnard* (1881), the
first book to win him attention, introduced an erudite, cloying
kind of irony that reappeared in the sacred-profane interaction
of *Thaïs* (1890) and *La Rôtisserie de la Reine Pédauque* (1893), a
rambling novel about the forthright eighteenth-century *abbé*
Jérôme Coignard. At this time France was trying to reconcile high
intellectual ambitions with his impossibly cluttered mind; no
wonder he became a kind of intellectual epicurean. Alchemy,
anti-clericalism, raw passion and ironic pessimism distracted him
this way and that. The four novels of *L'Histoire contemporaine*

(1896–1901) gave him room for all his interests and obsessions and supplied a mouthpiece in the person of Professor Bergeret. This extended scrutiny of provincial society helped him to get the playfulness out of his system, and subsequent works such as his smearing *Vie de Jeanne d'Arc* (1908) and satirical *tours de force*, *L'Île des pingouins* (1908) and *La Révolte des anges* (1914), show him both blinder and more disciplined. His political convictions gained substance from his exquisite grasp of history; *Les Dieux ont soif* (1912) is a sharp, colourful account of the French Revolution. Yet, for all his opinions and his respect for the rational, he has nothing coherent to say. He remains a mental dilettante, happier with abstractions although avid for data. Professor Bergeret addresses his most scintillating observations to his dog and in *La Révolte des anges* the angels turn into men of the world. Of this myriad-minded groper it is enough to say that he created a prose of immaculate concision ('*Et sur son beau rire un faune presse une grappe de raisin vermeil*') which only Camus and Colette have equalled. His pert fables show him at his best and typify an aspect of the French mind: an aspect which, in the work of Camus, Malraux and Sartre, predominates over all else.

Little that is sumptuous survives into the twentieth-century novel. The diabolism and mysticism of Huysmans (1848–1907) is not resumed. The early works of Maurice Barrès (1862–1923) have something in common with Huysmans's *La Cathédrale* (1898) and *L'Oblat* (1903); but after completing his edifice of temperament, *Le Culte du Moi* (1888–91), Barrès changed direction and brought out a second trilogy, *Le Roman de l'énergie nationale* (1897–1902), a conspectus of contemporary politics. His interests became social, national and regional. In *Les Déracinés*, the first novel in this trilogy, he shows young people from Lorraine trying to gain a footing in Paris, but failing. His best novel, both profound and highly emotional, is *La Colline inspirée* (1913), in which his devout attachment to Lorraine, his native province, receives its most exalted expression. After egoism, regionalism; and after that, the national as an integer of a prized civilization. *Leurs figures* (1902) pokes fun at his fellow-deputies; *Au service de l'Allemagne* and *Colette Baudoche* (1909) argue for the defence of such 'Eastern bastions' of civilization as Metz; and, finally, his *Chroniques de la grande guerre* (1920–4) in fourteen volumes proves his eye set relentlessly outwards. Yet his bizarre personality survives in the prose style's emphatic luxuriance.

Pierre Loti (1850–1923) devoted most of his novels to wistful love-stories set in exotic lands: Tahiti in *Rarahu* (1880), Senegal in *Le Roman d'un Spahi* (1881) and Japan in *Madame Chrysanthème* (1887) and *La Troisième Jeunesse de Madame Prune* (1905). Such novels suited the escapist mood of men who deplored the growing machine-worship of the time. Of course, Loti's account of the East looks whimsical beside the passionate documentary of a Malraux; Loti could not help mythologizing and idealizing, and this habit rewarded him handsomely in *Pêcheur d'Islande* (1886), helping him to create a convincing vision of death and endurance in which his Breton fisherfolk are both themselves and metaphors. *Les Désenchantées* (1906) traces the growth of feminism in Turkey and gives us a Loti combining documentary resolve with a characteristic nostalgia. During the nineties the 'psychological' novel came into being: its main interests were social, forensic and moral. Nothing exotic or romantic in this, unless one regards the behaviour and misbehaviour of the well-to-do as asiatically remote. Of the psychological novelists, the most readable was Paul Bourget (1852–1935) who progressed from an early phase devoted to salon society (*Un Cœur de femme*, 1890, is typical) to one in which, remembering his Balzac and also his Voltaire, he created ironic diagrams of the cosmos. *Le Disciple* (1889) tells how a youth wrecks his life by applying to it the precepts of a famous deterministic psychologist. *Cosmopolis* (1893) and *Une Idylle tragique* (1896) present a super-Laputa of world citizens unable to root themselves elsewhere. After that all was religion and sociology, families and lengthy soul-analysis. *L'Étape* (1902) gives his theories about the family and *Un Divorce* (1904) purports to be a dossier but also reveals his growing sympathy with Catholicism. A cruder stylist, Paul Adam (1862–1920), went one better than Bourget in *Le Temps et la vie* (1899–1903), an attempt to convey the group-psychology of a whole epoch from the beginning of the Napoleonic era to the end of the Romantic. Adam reveals his lineage by incorporating Balzacian personages into his backgrounds. By 1905, when an '*enquête*' decided in favour of broad reality rather than fiddling analyses, the emphasis is on the explicit and unfancy. René Boylesve (1867–1926) wrote probing studies of *la vie de province* in a dense, cerebral style similar to Proust's; but on the advice of pundits he cleaned up his prose and became a storyteller again.

II

With the new century come massive pretensions and meaningful evasions. Romain Rolland (1866–1944), by temperament an idealist, by calling a biographer, chose to epitomize human greatness and capacity for hero-worship in *Jean-Christophe*, first published periodically between 1904 and 1912. This ten-volume panorama is many things: a view of (need one say?) civilization; the biography of a musician for whom Beethoven was the model; and a blast against power politics. Jean-Christophe unites in himself both German and French cultures, thus demonstrating the futility of feuding. The book is full of high-flown humanitarianism and high ideals, but its presentation of the political climate is no more convincing than one can expect from a novel of minutely analysed sensibility. There are three phases: Christopher Krafft's German youth, his maturity in Paris and reconciliation with life. The best parts are *L'Aube*, mostly about Christopher's childhood, *L'Adolescent*, love affairs with girls respectively bovine and dynamic, *La Révolte*, the break with German provincialism and the departure for Paris, and *La Foire sur la place* in which Rolland condemns the cults of the boulevard and the coteries of high life. Christopher seeks for something less effete and finds it in a servant-girl. Eventually he moves into a circle of genuine people, gets into amorous and political difficulties and finally has to leave Paris after being involved in a riot. In Basle he falls in love again and develops into a sage for the younger generation.

The women are deftly varied; the scene keeps changing—either geographically or more subtly according to Rolland's degree of enthusiasm for the locale, and throughout the Tolstoyan corridors of it all there blows a wind of sheer exuberance, a '*grand souffle panthéiste*'. Such a minor character as Christopher's mother is made to come alive and to exist as a presence throughout. Naturally, too, whole sections drag; Rolland's earnestness cloys; we tire of the sermons on the virtues of rough-and-ready fraternity and the litanies of 'work' and 'will' and 'creative energy'. The idealism is moving but over-documented—so much so that the reader finds himself switching off now and then, only to pick up ten pages later without loss. Like Gide, Rolland set great store by youth and did his utmost to influence it; he also got through to as many leaders as possible, his one-man crusade including Tagore and Gandhi. Few writers have made such a *Bildungsroman* of their own lives.

Jean-Christophe set the fashion for the *roman-fleuve* and prompted many sequels, including those of Proust, Dreiser and Bennett. But Rolland had more to say, and between 1922 and 1934 he churned it out in the seven volumes of his second cyclical novel, *L'Âme enchantée*. The 'soul' is that of Annette Rivière, the story that of Annette and her sisters, an illegitimate son, and her eventual conversion to a doctrine of humanitarian action. The cycle ends with an almost febrile paean to communism. The whole thing is too much of a Rolland confession, but Annette's untidy course as she rears her wild son and nurtures a small circle of progressive intellectuals has a certain ragged fascination. She is not a Dorothy Richardson girl, being much less sophisticated and less casuistical; but she survives in the mind as an attractive principle robustly expounded. As a person, however, she is no-where near as immediate as Christopher Krafft. Rolland is always torn between art and social action; the one always seemed to laugh at the other. Essentially teutonic, he shovels away at his hills of data, now astounding us with sheer synoptic power, now putting us right off with righteous hysteria. He was a Rousseau out of his time, and he has often been dismissed as such: a volu-minous naïf lost in the complexities of a world too fast for him. Even so, his doctrines of fraternity and stoicism look forward to similar doctrines set in more classical form by Camus and Malraux.

The years between the wars witnessed the *roman-fleuve* in full spate. Jules Romains (1885–), Georges Duhamel (1884–), Roger Martin du Gard (1881–1961) and Jean-Richard Bloch (1884–1947) all undertook exhaustive, long-term documentations, most of them so flaccid as to vindicate their English counterparts' restriction of their inquiries to one segment of society. Snow, Powell and Durrell never seem to be straining as these writers do;

once again, it should be noted, that often-abused eclecticism of the English novelist pays dividends of integration, coherence and momentum.

Romains and du Gard had both subscribed to the Unanimist doctrines evolved from Zola and Verhaeren; but it was first of all in their poems that they tried to celebrate the collective entity of city, town, region and suburb. Compared with Paul Adam, they neglected the psychology of their highly anthemed guinea-pigs; you cannot talk, as Romains does for the twenty-seven volumes of *Les Hommes de bonne volonté* (1932–47), of group spirit without first of all exploring individuals. Romains goes from October 1908 to October 1933 and consistently pits his social thesis against the principles of art: whether or not the collective counts more than the individual, theoretically speaking, art's nature makes such doctrine impossible to express. Many Russian 'tractor' novels have proved that. We do not read novels to study the collectivity, sad as that may be to the public-minded; we read for recognition and vicarious intimacy. If we want data on the mass-man we can read Durkheim, Le Bon and Riesman. Romains's early novels make Unanimist points without destroying the novel's conventions of artifice: *Les Copains* (1913), for instance, shows a bunch of practical jokers reinforcing their solidarity through Gidean *actes gratuits*. *Lucienne* (1922) analyses the problem of a wife trying to emancipate her husband from his engrossing bourgeois family. This novel, in fact, is the first in a trilogy entitled *Psyche* which goes on to study the same couple's sexual life in *Dieu des corps* (1928) and *Quand le navire* (1929). Romains is at his best here: deft, witty and penetrating. He is all of that in a really serious novel, *Le Dictateur* (1926), in which a revolutionary politician deserts his associates in order to stand alone in autarky. These novels dabble in none of the mystical materialisms to be found in Romains's major *roman-fleuve*; instead, the individual is explored in his impact on others. Whether the occasion is death (*Mort de quelqu'un*, 1911) or love (*Psyche*) Romains's investigation remains jargon-free and agile: no pseudo-scientific magniloquence intrudes, and the novels further understanding of the human enigma.

In *Les Hommes de bonne volonté*, however, over a hundred characters are introduced in the early volumes; the first volume covers only one day's miscellany of lives; and it takes a dozen volumes to get from 1908 to 1915. The whole thing is neither deliberate enough nor careless enough. In the Preface Romains explains that there is no central character because society itself is his theme. So we get crafty switches of our attention and careless counterpointing—the humble against the arrogant, the debauchee against the dedicated scientist. In fact Romains has said that such a method of writing—uncertain progress and confidently made interruptions—gives the feel of life itself. Once again, we note the fallacy of mimicry—cropping up here on a stupendous scale. What, then, we may well ask, are we supposed to get from the inserted technical *dossiers*? Why deal in sample cases as well as in individuals? Who defines a type? Are we to regard what Romains says in the same way as we regard attempts, made in actual life, to type ourselves? Are these tensions illuminating or simply the detritus of an overworked theory?

The text does not answer us. It certainly stirs the mind to protest. Not that a plan or pattern is essential; but if there is no scheme, does the novel end at all or end without warning, or with a decline, as life does? Supposedly art, this novel is not life, and yet it acts upon us as if it were life and not just representation. Wearied of questioning the text, we attend more closely to the pageant of industrial suburb, Normaliens, city workers, idlers, prowlers and escapists: on many levels '*l'inquiétude aux cent visages*', all seeking relief in the illicit or the impossible. The war-shadow covers an increasing area; while politicians wrangle, the car-factories increase production and the Cubists display their discoveries. Romains took pains to inform himself of the business, political and artisan worlds, and then set two students, Jallez and Jerphanion, promenading through the synthesis of it all. Perhaps we are to follow them carefully without narrowing our minds into theirs. For there is, besides axe-grinding, dusty fodder, superficial psychology and wilful mystagogy, a brilliant kaleidoscope of a swarming epoch. The reader has to submit, amalgamating himself just as the Unanimist wants.

Georges Duhamel (1884–) adopted a rather different method for his first *roman-fleuve*. *La Vie et aventures de Salavin* (1920–32) has a hero, or at least a hero *manqué*. Salavin, an average type, tries his best to adjust to life; but he is too introverted, too sensitive about himself, too diffident. No one seems to want his friendship; his attempt to take an active part in social life merely gets him into trouble; trying to be generous to others, he only victimizes himself. Eventually he leaves France, still hoping to be of service. Something between a dehydrated Don Quixote and Samuel Beckett's 'Worm', Salavin seems too helpless to be true, too diligent to fail entirely. By the standards of the materialistic society that Duhamel despised he does fail; but he dies telling his wife that he has discovered how to live. Duhamel has suggested that Salavin is not a type but what any of us might become if our own meaner or most reckless actions happened at the worst possible time. The narrative shifts from first to third person and back again—a refreshing rather than bewildering expedient. Duhamel's second cycle, *La Chronique des Pasquier* (1933–45), deals with a family and its satellites, its internal feuds and social encounters. Running from the nineties to the 1920s, it anatomizes the bourgeoisie and bourgeois ideals through careful, compassionate study of the meek, self-sacrificing mother, the opsimath of a father who became a doctor late in life, and the five children of whom Laurent, a scientist, is the nearest to Duhamel's ideal of self-respecting self-denial. Again, the narrative point of view is shifted about, increasingly as the various members of the family become implicated in concerns beyond the family. Sometimes glutinously sentimental, Duhamel presents an image of '*l'intélligence du cœur*'—something he learned about painfully during service with a hospital unit in the First World War. As a plea for compassionate empathy, *Salavin* looks forward to novels which have difficulty in separating empathy from pity, and humility from mere sluggishness. The *Pasquier* cycle is altogether more hardheaded, but logically so because it is primarily concerned with the responsibilities and ambitions of the exploding family. Duhamel's diatribe against mechanical civilization, *Scènes de la vie future* (1930) supports natural, companionable man against the comfort-loving cipher; a theme more likely to engender sentimentality than promote reform.

Of other *romans-fleuve*, Roger Martin du Gard's *Les Thibault* (1922–40) tackles much the same period as the *Pasquier* chronicle. Duhamel's dynamics are here too; but, rather than the fragmentation of a family, we witness that of a whole class: the bourgeoisie

once again. Of the two Thibault brothers on whom du Gard con-
centrates, one is a doctor, the other a progressive intellectual. The
war wrecks them both although it is presented as an almost abstract force. Other bourgeois survive, perhaps because they have
something to cling to, whereas the Thibault brothers are too enlightened to accept facile answers or superficial class-cant. There
have been few clearer, better-documented discussions of a light
that failed: the light, in this case, of scientific optimism. The
severe breakdown which du Gard experienced after the war adds
a sonorous pessimism not to be found in Duhamel but eloquent
of the fearful hope that prompted these vast chronicles. With so
many millions anxious to find some sort of happiness, with so
many virtuous aspirations to be discerned, why massacre? Why
war? Why the decline of a whole class? The answers occupy
thousands of documentary pages, and usually it is sentimentality
and humility *versus* cynicism and the Faustian urge. On this
colossal scale the truth about individuals is frightening indeed.

Similar panoramas were devised by Jean-Richard Bloch (1884–
1947) and the Belgian-born René Behaine (1888–). Bloch's *Et Cie*
('And Co.'), describing a Jewish-Alsatian family, is less ponderous
and more hopeful than Behaine's prodigious *Histoire d'une
société*. The longer the look, it seems, the more reason for pessimism. Bloch's work, comparatively speaking, is concise and
almost crisp. There is something to be said for the brevity of *War
and Peace*. Jacques de Lacretelle (1888–), best known as the author
of *Silbermann* (1922) which explores a Jewish boy's tormented
schooldays, has also written a highly subjective novel, *La Vie
inquiète de Jean Hermelin* (1920) and the four-volume *roman-
fleuve, Les Hauts-Ponts* (1932–5). The last-named is a discerning
though ponderous account of a woman's devotion to her family
estate. Jacques Chardonne (1884–) is best known for *Les Destinées sentimentales* (1934–5), a deft study of marital problems
against a backcloth of provincial business life. Henri de Montherlant (1896–) limits his *Les Jeunes Filles* (1935–40) to four volumes
throughout which the obnoxious hero, Costals, conducts a savage
inquest on modern woman. Another author working on these
lines was the Belgian, Charles Plisnier (1896–1952), with two cycles
to his credit: *Meurtres* (1939–41) and *Mères* (1946–9). Plisnier,
like Louis Aragon (1897–), studied social man as ideological man;

Plisnier, the ex-communist, retained and cleansed his social realism whereas Aragon, in *Le Monde Réel* (1934–), which he resumed after the war with *Les Communistes*, kept a dash of the poetic in his unchanged politics. Also after the war, Paul Vialar (1898–) began to publish a chronicle called, quite without irony, *La Mort est un commencement*.

The *roman-fleuve* goes on, becoming perhaps more idiosyncratic. Proust, of course, is the master of the unwitting elegiac that such works tend to be. He captures and extrapolates the unfinished relationships of lives that can go forward only by jettisoning; he refuses what has been fragmented, sets the past stalking the present until 'wasted' means 'unscrutinized' and 'loved' means 'fully interpreted'. *À la Recherche du temps perdu* (1913–27) makes decline its premise: after all, when love thrives best on absence, what matter that all we love disappears? It from us; we from it. All recedes from us; the stream cannot be held; so, when Proust sets about reclaiming a whole class and its standards, his method is the reverse of time's relentless jumble. He works his mind and memory hard, logically and ironically; he does not hesitate to circle round and round (like a dog preparing to sit) before capturing a zone of lost experience. There is nothing sloppy or muddled about his evocations; his remembering is a mode of systematic reasoning. And Time, of course, loses to Marcel, because he has already beaten it when he realizes, towards the end of the novel, that writing from the involuntary memory is what Malraux would call an 'anti-destiny'. Proust aims at no realism: observers make their own account of life, and writers necessarily make even more personal accounts of the fiction they invent. 'Perhaps', Proust himself said, 'the immobility of material objects is imposed upon them by the immobility of our mind as it looks upon them, by our certainty as to their identity.' Or again: 'quite as valuable discoveries as we could make in Pascal's *Thoughts* may be inspired by a soap advertisement'. Or, more extreme than ever: 'There is no reason why a real place, existing outside the mind, should conform to memory's images any more than to those of the fancy.' The point is that he applies to lived life the very standards the realist or naturalist writer neglects: in other words, those standards and principles I have suggested in Part One, Section 4. He had an almost visceral intelligence; no wonder he scattered himself in articulate repetition: he was noting messages as they came through, and kept repeating the doubtful memories in the presence of near-synonyms. So it is that, where the Romainses and the Duhamels, in recording transience, succumb to it, Proust proves that what is precious to us is subject to no processes but our own. Alongside the massed mounds of the chronicle-novels, that was a point worth making and, in fact, worth racing against his own death to make completely.

From the world of Proust, polarized between the fascination of decay and the triumph in arresting one's own motion through time, it is a considerable step to Jean-Paul Sartre (1905–) and the novel-cycle called *Les Chemins de la liberté* (1945–50). Like Proust, Sartre constructs a social panorama, applying to it the extra dimension of philosophy in much the same way as Proust applies time and memory and Tolstoy history. But Sartre's panorama is more limited than that of Proust: not because it reviews a narrower range of society (it does not) but because Sartre fails to make virtue out of his philosophical necessity whereas Proust's theories are made to give all their strength to the narrative. Proust integrates theory with behaviour; the two interact and produce bewitching syntheses. Sartre, caught between rather crass demonstration and the need to keep things moving forward, becomes woolly and tentative.

In an earlier novel, *La Nausée* (1938), Sartre set out to show a character in a state of hopeless indecision. There were few philosophical trappings to this persuasive short work. The same is true of the stories in *Le Mur* (1939): the brutal, matter-of-fact close-ups lock home the trapped people; hemmed in by their own circumstances, then by Sartre's relentless concentration on nouns and constant recourse to verbs denoting ineffectual responses, these people have a meaning beyond the immediate. Prisoners all, they are the antithesis to the hero of *La Nausée* whose existence nothing justifies, who is at once free and paralysed. These early fictions are among Sartre's best, and deserve attention. His longer efforts, however, suffer from too much ambition and too little pruning. Perhaps early doses of Dos Passos and Faulkner (about whom Sartre wrote critical essays in the *Nouvelle Revue française*) repeated on him when he began to emulate. In 1943 he published the 700-page philosophical tract *L'Être et le néant* which, towards the end, develops into a rather sketchy theory of psychoanalysis. So, aiming at density and continuum, as well as philosophically preoccupied, Sartre offered his fictional version of existentialism. Like Proust he held that reality is mental and that love, as a union of two humans, is an impossible and misleading ideal. But because reality cannot demonstrably exist for anything but minds does not mean that it exists only in minds. On the contrary, human reality is there all the time. What people try to do is to give themselves the same definiteness as an object without losing the human faculty of self-awareness. Those who over-define themselves (or others) lose humanity; those who indulge in excessive self-awareness lack clear edges. The trouble always begins when we try to define ourselves in relation to what we think the fixed identities of other people; for as soon as we 'fix' a person, we have created an inhuman person. The main problem, therefore, is to achieve lucid relationships with other people without regarding them as things or becoming things ourselves. It is impossible. Hence the constant blur in which most people live; hence the frustration and nausea of life. It is the old paradox about the flux and fixity. (Other writers, Camus and Malraux especially, but also Saint-Exupéry and Sartre's friend and disciple Simone de Beauvoir, have shown characters rebelling against this human impasse: bursting out into useful or provocative action either to defy the universe or simply to relieve the accumulated tension. I shall come to these shortly.) We shall always be incomplete and undefined. Man at his most human is tempted to annul his very humanity. The only way out, although Sartre has not suggested it, is to try to cultivate a respect for *things*, so that we respect whatever we have to make of ourselves or of others. It would then not be depreciatory to speak of other people as 'the Other'. Sartre's main problem is that he cannot forget the difference between what he knows of human consciousness and what he knows of things. Other views, such as those of Huxley or Santayana, recommend an all-embracing attentiveness in which people and things are not identified but given equal, *thoughtful* respect. After all, as Sartre has pointed out, although we can keep on choosing, our identities will not be completely defined until we have died. From such an agonizing view, ethics must grow although they will be tentative ethics at best; for there is always an unknown element depending

on how a multitude of individual consciousnesses will respond to
the doubleness of humanity. Ethics do not refer to things; but not
all people are more human than they are things. There is no slick
answer to all this. But man can keep on examining his predicament until he has over it the kind of power that only understanding can confer.

So to the triptych of *Les Chemins de la liberté*: *L'Âge de raison*
(1945), *Le Sursis* (1945) and *La Mort dans l'âme* (1950). It is intended as a tribute to 'the grandeur of humanity', 'without illusions' (i.e. religion), and to the possibility of a new humanism
'hard but without useless violence; passionate yet restrained;
striving to paint the metaphysical condition of man while fully
participating in the movements of society'. It sounds well and
sends us back to his precept, expressed in 'Qu'est-ce que la
littérature?' (*Situations*, II), of combining social complexity with
metaphysical ideas. Unfortunately, for the most part, we come
away from Sartre's panorama with social ideas and metaphysical
complexity.

Historical events whirl the people forward while they are trying
to define themselves. Nations at war, nations averting their
political eyes while neighbours are invaded, nations wondering
what to do and being overrun while they wonder—this is bad
enough to provoke an enduring disgust. But the cosmos, with its
unheeding renewal of sap, works on the characters too. So the
nausea is both social and cosmic; the portrait is of disintegration
and distraction. This is the account of life that the Catholic rejects
as irrelevant to the Beatific Vision and that the Marxist explains as
merely incompetent arrangement of society. Sartre writes in a
transitional period between a settled and a revolutionary view of
man: for various reasons, and under various labels, rugged individualism opposes the collectivity; and Sartre is showing how
unsatisfactory the result will have to be. Only this could explain
his fellow-travelling period and the varying degrees of intensity
evident in his life-long attachment to Marxist doctrine. This century has seen the individual beguiled into accepting creeds of
world domination, driven into fierce nationalism against those
creeds, fashionably paying the psychotherapist to adjust him to
society, confusedly turning to the safe, sometimes hermetic, world
of art (Malraux) and toying virtuously with noble but apparently

impotent ideas (Camus). Sartre himself has exaggerated, at one point claiming T. E. Lawrence for existentialism, at another laughing at systems from the security of his very German, very Italian, system. (He has German blood himself, and it is worth noting that many of his personages bear German names: Hoederer, Goetz, and more recently Franz von Gerlach in *Les Séquestrés d'Altona*. Perhaps this is a means of exorcizing the bogeyman of your philosophical system.) In the long run, and this makes any philosopher bad-tempered, reason outstrips our abilities to put things right. Therefore a great deal of reasoning is merely intellectual exercise; good for the muscles but ineffectual. Ignazio Silone has made this point better than most: he admits it, whereas Sartre grudgingly cannot help letting it emerge.

Not surprisingly the hero of *L'Âge de raison* is a young philosophy teacher, Mathieu Delarue, '*l'homme*', as his circle of Bohemian intellectuals call him, '*qui veut être libre*'. Exhaustively analysing himself, Mathieu tries to take full control of, and full responsibility for, himself. He is not trying to rationalize the Gidean *acte gratuit*, having indulged in such acts in his youth to no enduring advantage. He is trying to give a rational account of all his actions. Unfortunately, however, Marcelle, his mistress, becomes pregnant and all his good reasoning cannot alter the fact. After some squalid efforts to muster an abortionist's fee, he begins to consider marrying Marcelle. He recoils from the idea of destroying a human embryo; and if he married Marcelle he could tell himself his self-assertion was not ended: after all, he does not have to marry her. Mathieu's brother, a sensible bourgeois solicitor, advises marriage; and that is enough to make Mathieu prefer the opposite. He is now infatuated with a young student, Ivich, not least because she is unconnected with his main dilemma. (He fails to realize that in distracting him from one problem she is confronting him with another.) Suddenly, however, Daniel, a young homosexual, suggests to Mathieu that he himself is responsible for Marcelle's condition. At once Mathieu welcomes the news; he resents it too: his rights have been infringed. His self-esteem continually battles with his instinct for self-preservation. He wants to get out of complications until he can deliberately bring on himself complications of his own choosing. The unheroic hero, indeed, he exemplifies the futility of theorizing while you are leading any kind of life. A thoroughgoing theorist would have had no Marcelle in the first place; but he might have caught a cold, been mutilated in a traffic accident or become a prey to melancholia. Sartre makes these points almost garishly in sinuous but sometimes deliberately stumbling prose. Finally he makes Mathieu, now bogged down in self-despising indecision, steal the money for an abortion. Too late; Marcelle inveigles him into saying he no longer loves her and then decides to marry Daniel. The cosmic joke is now played in full: a practical, fertile joke, at that. Mathieu asked too much, trying to cut his physical cloak out of metaphysical cloth.

Characteristically Sartre chooses his examples from an unstable, groping set. Most people could get into the same scrape, but would not approach it or get out of it with such a wealth of theorizing. Sartre is making a special point pertinent to himself and to all theoreticians. Another point, which does not seem to occur to him, is that most people remedy problems with principles or a spin of a coin. His disgust is with formularized living, the bourgeois way that a C. P. Snow finds imperative if we are not to have chaos. In the second volume of the group, *Le Sursis*, Sartre turns from his bohemian rebels to the atmosphere before Munich. He exchanges the test-tube method for that of the cinema; rather than tabulating and listing the main events of the period (as Romains and Duhamel do), he jerks us away to the atmosphere of Marseilles, Munich, Biarritz and Paris. The stench of appeasement wafts away from the Daladiers and the Chamberlains to yield creatures of its own making: Gros-Louis the illiterate mental pigmy in the vast physical frame; Philippe the pacifist; and Pierre who dotes on all his sensations, pleasant or otherwise. Personal tension gives way to national. By now in the background, Daniel has adjusted to marriage; Mathieu has regained the confidence to muddle onwards with Ivich. When mobilization hits, there are disintegrations of a nobler kind than the merely sexual: Daniel, for example, becomes a Roman Catholic. But, they find, war is not coming, after all. Reintegrations do not follow: in fact, this phase of the novel is handled in an incredibly deft, Tolstoyan way. The intersection of the international with the personal has rarely been more movingly, more discerningly, portrayed. The rebels have been rebelled upon; and their own personal acts of defiance have been engulfed by a crisis which affects a whole nation, both ennobling and destroying. Suddenly, it appears that not only cannot the Mathieus make sense of their own lives; they cannot even in the vaguest way anticipate the collective fate. Hence all the guilt in Sartre's writings: man can conceive of the deliberately lived life but he cannot, individually or collectively, bring it into being. Sartre ties the two themes together in another paradox: 'definitions are never settled; one cannot define a man before he has died, or humanity before it has vanished'. That is a religious point—the compassionate but brutal answer to all ego-centric neurotics who want to postpone their lives until they can be in full control. Neither microcosm nor macrocosm will be entirely sensible until we stop them and put them right: that is why the universe is absurd. Freedom, as Mathieu comes to realize, is sheer terror—whether on the personal plane or on the national, as when in *La Mort dans l'âme* the national disintegrates because the known does not indicate in any way the nature of the unknown.

Sartre's vision must ultimately be interpreted as one of the com-pensatory games we play with ourselves once we have admitted our ineffectuality. His dithering adolescents personify the French mind-game. Theorizing is an effective way of cheering ourselves up, but not of constructing principles. Not afraid to get his hands dirty or to present his own type unflatteringly, Sartre has created a contrapuntal type of novel in which the evasions and vain ambi-tions of a whole era add up to rhetoric while a culture burns. Where do we come out? In narcissism or political action? The choice, Sartre implies, is false. He himself has spoken up on many occasions, believing that something might be achieved; but he has also created the hero of the play *Les Séquestrés d'Altona*: Franz von Gerlach, immured in a bedroom in the family mansion. Franz is out of touch; he prefers life that way, and spends his time ad-dressing speeches to the crabs he supposes to have taken over the earth in the year 3000. 'Listen', he tells them, 'to the plea of man-kind: "We were betrayed by our deeds. By our words, by our lousy lives." ' Franz not only is having an incestuous relationship with his sister but refuses to have any contact with his father who is dying of cancer. It is the father who eventually drives himself and Franz off to suicide: Franz, it is revealed at the end of the play, had tortured Russian prisoners in Smolensk. So the father assumes his own part of the responsibility. The play ends with a recorded speech by Franz which is really a protest from the acute self-awareness of modern man: 'The century might have been a good one had not man been watched from time immemorial by the cruel enemy who had sworn to destroy him, that hairless, evil, flesh-eating beast—man himself.' Thus the complaint of the honest theoretician. It speaks of all that Sartre has impotently fought with theory, of his almost masochistic self-exposure, of his more than political view of humanity, and also of the forces which other writers from Gide to Robbe-Grillet have opposed with all the resources of individuality.

III

The thought of Albert Camus (1913–1960) was always intricately ambitious but, perhaps because of his lyrical streak and his impatience with extreme attitudes, seems less coherent in detail than in outline. His work shows all of Gide's care for the individual without Gide's inability to see farther: the clarity of Gide's outlines is that of an unmitigated self-concern; Camus's is that of a man more concerned with the predicament of any individual human rather than with himself in particular. A search for moderation, for the Greek middle way, has always characterized Camus's much-publicized 'positions'. His early essays in *L'Envers et l'endroit* (1937) and *Noces* (1939) shuttled between instinctive atheism and physical delight. He learned early that happiness is not easily won by the questing mind: between exultation and despair there is only the realization of the absurd —the lack of correspondence between coherent ideals and incoherent actuality. This disparity, as he pointed out in *Le Mythe de Sisyphe* (1942), can prompt suicide, physical or mental, neither of which is in accord with his view that 'the absurd depends as much on man as on the world for its existence'. The fact that we perceive the absurd increases the amount of absurdity. For the absurd is irremediable: to this truth men must stoically attend, all the same. We tread a 'vertiginous ridge' between self-destruction and escapism; and, it is true, the act of 'keeping faith with the earth' is a sentimental choice. It must not be allowed to

deceive us into being adamantly idealistic. But, as Camus explains
in his own peculiar choosy and occasionally cloudy way, we can
revolt: we can 'refuse' the universe.

Man has refused the universe in two principal ways: meta-
physically and politically, as Camus points out in *L'Homme
révolté* (1951). From such perceptions he extracts a resolute
humanism that seeks a way between romantic self-deceit and
revolutionary inhumanity. Neither self-deceit nor murder (to
which all political rebellion leads) makes life any more meaningful
or more tolerable. Within each individual there is something that
the absurd affronts; that is sufficient reason to go on living,
although Camus infers no divine intention from it. To confront
the universe, in whatever way, is an emotional gamble, not a
logical step. Confrontation has to be based on some such concept
as the 'sunlit thought' with which Camus vaguely concludes
L'Homme révolté. The cultivation of the middle way, *mesure*,
entails lowering our sights even at the expense of *mesure* itself.
Camus really means we should knuckle down to things and not,
like the saint or sinner, expect too much: the old Senecan *sustine*,
all over again.

When we turn to Camus's fiction (the word 'novel' does not
quite fit his narratives, any more than it does Gide's) we find a
mind too cerebrally alert, and not quite in command of the world
of daily triviality. *L'Étranger* (1942) demonstrates that there are
no explanations of life other than those man creates for himself.
Such explanations are a form of self-deceit—what Sartre calls
mauvaise foi; and Meursault, the unheroic hero, the animated
robot who accidentally commits a pointless murder, is punished
by society not so much for that act as for refusing to utter things
he does not believe in. Meursault refuses to fool himself; he is the
archetypally honest man, made what he is by the universe as it
is. In fact he is the kind of automaton that a society of different
automatons lusts to expunge. In his personal life—in his attitude
to his mother's death, to his girl-friend and his acquaintances—
he neither pretends to feelings he does not have nor dissimulates
those he cannot help having. Ultimately he realizes that his death-
sentence binds him to all other men; and that realization is the
basis upon which Camus constructs his doctrine of charity and
compassion. The individual at once counts and does not: because

he is thus merged into the universe's consumption of humans, he has a basis on which to operate as an individual entity. Meursault can therefore reject the priest's belief in divine purpose; in the same way the death of the priest in *La Peste* (1947), the novelfable Camus worked on during the war, symbolizes the irrelevance of religion when all men have united in a common purpose that reflects their eventual common fate.

La Peste is narrated by the central character, Dr Rieux. He tells how Oran, a city in North Africa, is shaken into life by an outbreak of plague, and how it responds when the scourge is over. Some men fight the plague; others reconcile themselves to it. The plague is Nature in all her power; the city, Oran, is the embodiment of human routine in all its mindlessness. The streets fill with rats; the citizenry are shaken out of the torpor they cannot, of their own volition, dispel. The sea cannot be reached; the gates of the city are closed. The people are enclosed with the bubonic plague that kills them by the thousand. Nature is implacable; but several men, whom we are to see in close-up, band together to resist. The priest, Father Paneloux, interprets the plague as retribution for sins, but later comes to think it a God-inflicted test in the true epic style. He dies believing this. But another man, Tarrou, a brawny extrovert, who once witnessed a decapitation, sees the plague as just another manifestation of Nature's destructive urge. He firmly believes that good in this world arrives as the result of exerting our will-power. He dies hating Nature's brutish ways, and exalting man's power to change the natural order. The main figure, Dr Rieux, is a dedicated automaton; at least he is until he sees a small child die, and hears the priest interpret its death as punishment. The doctor cannot see how punishment should be indiscriminate. Why should the child be killed when many of the guilty survive? The only one to survive the plague, he compiles his chronicle of outrage and injustice at the hands of impersonal Nature. His work has to go on protecting man against the blind powers of the cosmos. Only in rebelling against the human condition can man prove, as Camus says, his essential nobility.

After relinquishing all hope of epiphany, Rieux accepts the mystique of brotherhood. He and Tarrou turn one night from the plague to swim in the sea. Thus they renew their capacity for joy as well as their will to fight on others' behalf. But this is no leap of faith: Camus offers, instead, the conviction compactly expressed in *Le Mythe de Sisyphe* that 'tenderness, creativity, action, human nobility will take their place again in this insensate world'. This conviction defies all plagues, physical or mental: 'the wine of the absurd and the bread of indifference' will nourish man's 'greatness'—and not necessarily within a theological framework. According to Camus, 'there are only two universes for a human spirit; that of the sacred (or in Christian language, of grace) and that of revolt'. Hence the near-liturgy, assembled in *L'Homme révolté*, of revolt mythological, literary and actual from Prometheus to Ivan Karamazov and Sade. Camus makes faith a deliberate act, excluding from it such irrational leaps as those of the Christian existentialists. But he commends Buber's doctrine of awareness and distance, as well as defining 'the sacred' as 'that presence felt in the silence during a moment of genuine awareness'. Camus the elated pagan continually disturbed the edifice of rational thought erected by Camus the humanist. Perhaps the doves that, in *La Chute* (1956), spiral in the Dutch sky denote something less matter-of-fact than human solidarity; something to which his death adds an ironic new twist. *La Chute* confronts us with a successful Parisian lawyer who has abandoned his practice for the waterfront of Amsterdam. He feels a failure as a man: he once failed to prevent a girl from drowning herself. So, in Camus's terms, he has repudiated his bond with other men. He does not, especially in his own eyes, qualify to be a member of the human community. So he secedes in an attempt to expiate and to requalify. Once again, Camus stresses the privileges and commitments of individual self-awareness. It was this fundamental view of man which continually led him to compose tracts disguised as novels and, in *Exil et le royaume* (1957), allegories that shimmer in the guise of technically immaculate short-stories. In fact, the farther he went, the more he attempted the universal and anagogic rather than the particular. From the beginning he preferred to deal in pregnant generalities, occasionally 'filling in' with everyday data when his theme became too abstract (which is just what he does in his published notebooks and journals).

Germaine Brée has described an unpublished novel called *La Vie heureuse*—a kind of Dostoevskian *Summa*—which she considers to be the matrix of all Camus's published writings. The hero, Mersault (foreshadowing Meursault), murders Zagreus, a Dionysus figure, as a protest or 'revolt' against death. Mersault, for one moment of time, arrogates to himself death's own power; he is a cosmic trespasser. He then goes off to Prague with money the murder has brought him. But in a Prague street he finds a body, returns to Algiers and re-thinks his whole position. He falls ill, but welcomes his decay and imminent death as the cosmos's supreme compliments. We are not very far from the English Romantics' talk of being made 'one with Nature'. The novel is a variation on the theme of the pilgrim's progress: it exemplifies Plotinus's view that all beings have fallen from a state of participation in the source of being and are constantly attempting, through various stages, to return. Mersault's stages are physical, intellectual and spiritual—a common enough triad. He lives out in his own career the three main stages of Camus's analysis of the human situation: the universe is 'absurd' ('utterly deaf' to human aspirations) and provokes 'revolt' either nihilistic (anarchy) or ideological (prophetism and revolution), neither of which compares favourably with a hopeful moderateness based on 'sunlit thought'. Camus, in fact, was a true stoic; and the theme of his writings is almost Christian: in tribulation, in this 'century of fear', we should seek neither solitude nor utter solidarity; we should be neither maenads nor ascetics, neither men of stone nor mock-gods, but simply 'present' to one another and responsible for ourselves.

This positive side of Camus is impressive and heartening. But, from *L'Envers et l'endroit* to *Exil et le royaume*, he maintained certain negative habits of mind which have been too little noted and too little discussed. The key to this unsatisfactoriness can be found in Sartre's rebuke to the effect that Camus loved humanity but mistrusted individuals. He had a feeble sense of social texture, of the stuff that makes Balzacian novels; of love between individuals in all their eccentricity and groping; of the fact that we fear not death, but the possibilities beyond it: rapture without hope, like heroic hedonism, is not enough. We must love life, he says; in his discussions of art, however, we find much talk of fraternity but little delight in man himself. He had an exaggerated respect for art; he once said: 'I must write as I swim'; and perhaps because modern societies are 'desacralized' he expected too much of art, and so joins Forster and Malraux. It is a considerable step from regarding art as the perfectionist's only outlet to adapting it into a religion. Writing, like swimming, may be dynamic; but it is not the full answer to the human craving for control over the world beyond death.

Camus's last book, announced as *Le Premier homme*, might demonstrate whether or not he was incapable of the novel of manners. Moderation's nympholept, he often found his middle way conducting him into an ordinariness his imagination spurned. He always seemed rather unheedful of life's mixtures. He put freedom of the body before the quality of the spirit, and once quoted Dostoevsky's remark that 'One must love life before loving its meaning . . . yes and when the love of life disappears, no meaning can console us.' Camus's love of life was selective; he preferred its primitive forms, pastorals and archetypes. Can he, on such a basis, create characters both anagogic and convincing? No, he cannot. When Rieux and Tarrou go off to swim in the sea they briefly reunite themselves with the beneficent side of Nature; they challenge the horror, complete the picture, refuse an absolute vision. So too Camus, stealing off from the 'century of fear' to lavish rhapsodies and abstract ideas. Swimming brought him 'the turbulent possession of the sea by my legs'; theorizing often brought him a similarly illusory hold over the world. His synoptic view—of the eternal and contemporary extremes: death, the pathos of ageing, summer's invincible recurrence, oppression, cold war, and French troops lording it in his native Algeria—has variety but not quite enough. One wonders whether his philosophy was communicable in terms of so much else that is muddled and intricate and not momentous, out of which our daily lives are made. *Le Premier homme* sounds as allegorical as ever. Chateaubriand's 'last and most gifted' heir was unlikely to become a Balzac without making serious inroads on his previous habits.

The novels, art-criticism, aesthetics and career of André Malraux (1901–), as well as having given considerable stimulus to Camus, have made Camus's points in a much subtler, more sophisticated way. It is impossible to separate Malraux's novels from his career, for all his writings are offered as records of and commentaries on his own spiritual progress. Malraux's is the worldly sanity of a man who has put himself at mankind's disposal and eventually, without bitterness, found it wanting. He is one of the greatest twentieth-century French writers: for versatility, depth and for faith in mankind as well as in his own idiosyncrasy. He speaks as an individual: where Camus's rhetoric is politically orientated, Malraux's is private—aimed at the aesthetic sense. His first three novels, *Les Conquérants* (1928), *La Voie royale* (1930) and the ample, compassionate *La Condition humaine* (1933) all deal with China and constantly suggest allegories of 'the human condition'. *Le Temps du mépris* (1935) presents with harrowing brevity the fate of a Czech communist in Nazi Germany; *L'Espoir* (1937), Malraux's most Hemingway-like novel, is about the Spanish Civil War, abounds in scenes of compassionate irony and signalizes Malraux's despair about man's inability to co-operate reliably with his fellows. *Les Noyers de l'Altenburg* (1948) marks his shift to straightforward allegory and to the pursuit of man's dignity not in politics or adventure but in the history of visual art. (So far, Malraux has not written about the history of literature, although he has extended his adoration of the visual into an almost Christopher Isherwood homage to the art of cinema. There seems no reason why the ennobling archetypes which turn up in art should not, to a man as well read as Malraux, turn up in literature too.)

The main feature of all these novels is the scrutiny of individual initiative and man's power to organize a better world. Against violence, confusion, revolution and torture Malraux creates images of hope: it is man's fate to have to construct a basis for hope. It would be idle to identify Malraux with any political or religious orthodoxy; he has always managed to keep a little out of step in order to comment generously and honestly. His most constant literary habit (from his early novels to his study of religious art, *La Métamorphose des dieux*, published in 1957) has been to illustrate or indicate secular epiphanies which, he says, give man grounds for hope and a basis for self-respect. Man, in fact, is the creature who can create his own epiphanies through acting in accordance with principles undecreed but inherited from century to century along with the colossal load of recurring human weakness.

'What *is* man?' That is the question substituted at the last moment for 'The Eternal Elements of Art', the topic for discussion at the colloquy in *Les Noyers de l'Altenburg*. Walter Berger, the host and moderator, has just learned of his brother's suicide; and his consequent shift to apparent basics is an augury of epiphanies to come. In the same novel German soldiers move forward after a gas-attack, only to return, shocked beyond all discipline, each bearing the body of a gassed Russian. Such incidents give the lie to beserk relativism. There *is* continuity of human nature across the ages; man does possess something eternal—something evinced when Katow, in *La Condition humaine*, gives to a fellow-prisoner the cyanide that would have saved him from his own barbarously cruel execution. Selflessness, like death, is ineluctable: we can no more talk ourselves into the former than we can talk ourselves out of dying. What Malraux calls 'the assault of pity' redeems our daily life; the timeless walnut trees, like the voices of silence we find in painting and sculpture, identify and stylize the undying in us. This much, even among the Malraux paradoxes of intellectual-adventurer and compassionate aesthete, stays clear.

An occasional rhetorical cloud obscures his meaning now and then, but the patient reader soon accustoms himself to the usual Malraux antitheses: dark and light, demonic and divine, desolation and communion, repugnance and love. These are trite enough as versions of Malraux's encounters with Saturn, the man-devouring ogre who cripples human enterprise with fear. But they become more arresting and less trite when related to a development that might be summed up thus: Historical initiative in the form of revolution or leadership certainly repudiates the concept of man as a helpless pawn; but such initiative is itself subject to the mechanicality of the universe—accusing but never rectifying. Art, on the other hand, is both supremely individual and supremely communal; it is not subject to the flaws that beset those who attempt to transcend the human condition through self-punishment (Perken in *La Voie royale*) or political commitment (Garine in *Les Conquérants*).

Such is the story of Malraux's own life; he has made himself the raw material of a profound and courageous experiment. The younger generation of Frenchmen (and perhaps some of his old political associates) may find him now rather *passé*, invincibly earnest and visibly misguided; but such vicissitudes are allowed for in his own view of his career as a whole. He intends it to be read as a meaningful instance. The ship-captain in *La Voie royale* calls Perken a 'mythomaniac'; the same term fits Malraux. Perken, who tries to mask the world from himself, to use it as a mirror, speaks slightingly of Mayrena, king of the Sedangs: 'I see him as a player-king, bent on acting his own biography. You Frenchmen usually have a weakness for that sort of man, who prefers giving a fine performance to actual success.' If we borrow that against Malraux himself, we shall not be far wrong.

Malraux has thought most deeply about, has sought action most avidly in, the realm of the mental possibilities between nihilism and the urge to conquer, between fatalism and the longing to be a god. The conqueror, all cosmic initiative and spiritual ardour, ends up devising such a lethal abstraction as Naziism. Hope precedes action; to be any use, action has to be organized, and all organization is a mode of the abstract. Perken fears a death not chosen; Clappique in *La Condition humaine*, idling while hostile forces gather, abdicates from choice. For action is human—initially; and, initially, so is choice. We are most haunted by what we choose not to do. So it is equally futile to try shaping the world to our ideal as to accept the cycle of eternal recurrence.

Such is the theme of *Les Conquérants* and *La Voie royale* and, a few privileged moments and beings apart, of the next three novels. Only with the transitional *Les Noyers* does Malraux begin to reinterpret his sense of 'numinous awe', of 'frail and humble communion' and post-Renaissance man's sense of power. Neither blind action nor cringing apathy is truly human. Awe outstrips all appearances; communion is not physical; power is to be defined as our response to the demons. And the artist's true job is a demiurgic onslaught on those demons, for he alone can offer, in default of faith, a universal testimony to the nature of our world.

IV

To consider André Gide (1869–1951) as a novelist at all is partly to misapprehend him; at the same time, to regard, say, *Les Faux-monnayeurs* (1925)—the only one of his books he called a

roman—and *La Porte étroite* (1909) as tracts or dissimulated autobiography is dishonest. They *look* like fiction and have to be
judged as such. Gide suffered from too many contradictions to
settle happily into any traditional genre save the journal. It is
noteworthy that he added to *Les Faux-monnayeurs* a sequel called
Le Journal des Faux-monnayeurs (1927) which purported to be a
log-book of commentary compiled during the writing of the
earlier volume. It does not excuse the woodenness of the adults
or detract from the elated pageantry that Gide makes out of
Parisian schoolboys and adolescents; neither does it illuminate
what has gone before. Gide suffered from restlessness and self-
consciousness. He was always itching to put things in a different
way, to revoke his current method of presentation, to intervene
and demonstrate the silliness of the categories the reader is trying
to apply. Sensual and ascetic, married but homosexual, essentially
a moralist but also highly imaginative, a master of classical prose
but self-obsessed, he was always shuffling about. To him, the
arbitrariness of categories—in art as in life—kills both *disponibilité* and sincerity.

L'*Immoraliste* (1902) is crypto-autobiography: the young hero
dabbles in theft and little crimes against himself, and eventually
causes the death of his wife. Gide, as ever, is extrapolating his
own situation. His *Retour de l'enfant prodige* (1907) is a parable
which he turns into a different parable. But *La Porte étroite* is
a parable all of his own in which Alissa sacrifices earthly love to
her sense of religious vocation. Much less moving and almost
cripplingly self-conscious is *La Symphonie pastorale* (1919),
offered as a diary concocted after the event. It records the mixed
motives of a Swiss pastor who devotes himself to an ignorant,
blind girl and in the process alienates his wife, falls in love and
finally capitulates in the face of a suicide attempt by the girl, her
conversion to Rome and her quoting of the abhorred St Paul. The
pastor rationalizes his love for the girl: 'I search the Gospels, I
search in vain for commands, threats, prohibitions. . . . All of
these come from St Paul'; 'Every living creature ought to tend to
joy.' The dialogue with himself is fascinating, especially the vel-
leity for the innocence before laws existed. It is some kind of
innocence (but a harmful one) which Lafcadio Wluiki in *Les
Caves du Vatican* (1914) seeks in the *acte gratuit*—pushing a

stranger out of a railway carriage. But this brittle *sotie*, with its fake Pope, its elaborate swindling in Paris and Rome, its puns and fluttering surface agitation, is more of an excursion into philosophical high spirits than a novel. The trilogy consisting of *L'École des femmes* (1929), *Robert* (1930) and *Geneviève* (1937) is Gide's most sustained effort to excel in one genre: he sensitively, although too sparingly, describes a failed marriage and its impact on the daughter. Because Gide here gives more psychology than is usual, he makes the reader want more. These novels are written with compassion and tender logic; but even they seem to skim the surface and their economy seems to come as much from per-functoriness as from the desire to be 'classical' in restraint.

If only he had painted in his novels as vividly as in such of his travel books as *Voyage au Congo* (1927) and *Retour du Tchad* (1928). Always, in the Gide of the *roman-journal* there is some-thing of the cynical schoolboy, both narcissistic and cerebrally indifferent. There is no doubt of his sincerity or of his hatred of 'counterfeiting' hypocrites. He was just too much aware of human possibilities, too fond of everything, to manage the deliberate limitations art requires. And when he limited himself, his self-consciousness erupted in the shape of the Edouard supposed to be writing *Les Faux-monnayeurs*. Too often he drew his immacu-late circles round areas of too little common experience. The cream is never in the meringues; the diet is stimulating, but not nourishing.

Compared with Sidonie-Gabrielle Colette (1873–1954) Gide is deficient in ordinary common sense. Their attitudes to writing are similar—Colette's 'Beware of "embellishments", beware of indiscreet poetry' fits the Gidean aesthetic perfectly—but Colette manages to search her soul without becoming self-obsessed. She delights in the physical world; like some voluptuous feline, she purrs in unselfconscious prose. '*Regarde*', she kept saying: there is no hierarchy of themes, for everything counts equally if you are attending fully. The 'Claudine' novels are vitiated by the mere-triciousness of her collaborator-husband Henry Gauthier-Villars. Writing in her own right in *La Vagabonde* (1910) she confessed herself a gentle sensualist but gradually grew more objective. *La Retraite sentimentale* (1907), *La Maison de Claudine* (1923) and *Le Fanal bleu* (1949) show her occasional urge to declare herself.

Her best novels, perhaps, are *Chéri* (1920) and *La Fin de Chéri* (1926) in which a middle-aged woman, Léa de Lonval, undertakes the sentimental education of the spoiled young Chéri. Léa knows what she is doing; she is bound to suffer. Chéri, on the other hand, does not; but, in the second novel, by now a tinny young war hero, he finds he cannot settle down. Verging on tragedy, these two novels achieve a depth and dimension not to be found in Colette's studies of adolescent love (*Le Blé en herbe*, 1923).

What we do not find in Colette anywhere is abstract ideas: she lives through her pulses, an 'earth-ecstatic', and shows especial empathy towards animals. How subtly she creates an entire, small world, to which her novels cross-refer. The physical world is always present; it has to be for her to present her main theme: loss. Those who survive loss discover that 'it is not normal that a human being, any more than an animal, should relish a state that would be a state of perfect happiness'. She opposes absolutes as resolutely as Camus: interviewed in 1937 she put the matter very clearly in a few words: 'Adapt oneself to what life brings, know how to pick up the pieces of a destroyed happiness and stick them together as well as possible so as to make another. And then suppress, energetically, all that is unbearable, or do something about it.' She sees that humans are still trying to do what animals learned long ago: to adapt to environment. She does not, however, fully explore the corollary of her view; people as perpetually adaptable as she recommends end up not wanting anything particularly. Their stoicism becomes a refusal of need and entails the dilution of one's humanity. Such is the unhoping *disponibilité* of Léa de Lonval, the wise *grande cocotte*, and perhaps in store for *Julie de Carneilhan* (1941). For a full dissection of that state of mind we have to go to Mauriac. It is the antithesis to the wistful reveries and elated schoolboy animality of Alain-Fournier's *Le Grand Meaulnes* (1913).

The twenties, which saw Colette and Gide writing the first few of their best novels, saw the rise of two gifted Catholic novelists, François Mauriac and Georges Bernanos, against a background of comparatively trivial stuff. The war produced some rather laboured novels, the most thoughtful of which are Adrien Bertrand's *Appel au Sol* (1916), battle-scenes mingled with heavy philosophizing, and his more pungent *L'Orage sur le jardin de Candide* (1918); H. Malherbe's *La Flamme au poing* (1917) and Duhamel's *La Vie des martyrs* (1917). These are works of rationalization, whereas other novels portray the bewilderment of the common soldier; René Benjamin's *Gaspard* (1915), for instance, centres on a boyish opportunist who passes from adolescent gallantry to mature resignation. War's shocking mixture of the ridiculous and the tragic, presented by Benjamin through the mixed slang of the trenches (soldier's *argot* plus the *blague* of Montparnasse), gives way in Henri Barbusse's *Le Feu* (1916) to a more absolute vision of horror which foreshadows Malraux. Barbusse overdoes things in order to make a moderate point. Roland Dorgelès's *Les Croix de bois* (1919), although just as infernal, is more resigned in tone: Sulphart, one of the soldiers, is both belligerent and wry; such a conception could not have come from Barbusse.

Just as exaggerative in its indiscriminate way was Louis-Ferdinand Céline's *Voyage au bout de la nuit* (1932), a caustic and frenetic assimilation of post-war nihilism into between-wars instability. This grotesque novel, the true sediment of 1914–18, has nothing in common with the twenties' most characteristic products. It is also the natural overflow of Céline's own picaresque, topsy-turvy life on several continents. It is much more than pornography, and here and there even less: the hero fumbles from one disaster to the next in a kind of emotional vagabondage and, like the Ferdinand of *Mort à crédit* (1936), finds everything dying and disintegrating as he looks at it. It is man that one must fear, not the processes of Nature; and 'man' includes religion, love, science and politics. There are two kinds: the evil and the mad; nothing else. It is no wonder that Céline has been reviled as a scatologist and a beast: born Louis Ferdinand Destouches in 1894, he died (as he had predicted) 'in disgrace, shame and poverty' in 1961. Anti-semitic, life-hating, self-despising, son of a seamstress and a failed teacher of a father, suffering always from a severe head wound earned after volunteering for a dangerous war mission, he is his own anathema. Anything we say about him applies to his volcanic novels. It is beside the point to regret his Nazi sympathies, his appointment as medical adviser to the ailing Pétain, his exile in Denmark, his arrest and imprisonment, his pellagra and eventual pardon. He returned to Paris in 1951, where he died. Visitors reported his insomnia, mania and diabolism; they could not tell whether the man was living the novel or the novel the man. Yet, in the Clichy slums, he had often worked himself to exhaustion, trying to save a child's life: in him, good was just as impulsive and instinctive as evil, and that was his view. Leon Trotsky reviewed *Voyage* in 1935 and declared that Céline 'walked into great literature as other men walked into their homes', and Gide wisely observed that 'It is not reality which Céline paints but the hallucinations which reality provokes. I find here the accents of a remarkable sensibility.'

Surely Gide was right. There was something prophetic about Céline's nihilism, something visionary in *Voyage* which is missing in such of his other writings as *Mea Culpa* (1937), or the ferociously anti-semitic *Bagatelles pour un massacre* (1938) or the onslaught on the French in *École des cadavres* (1938), although fitfully present in *Mort à crédit*. A sensitive maniac, this man, and very German in damning and trying to abolish what he cannot put right. He has something in common with Hemingway and Joyce; his charity, like his French, is perverted and nasty, but his two novels make a good many recent French novels look thin and timid.[1] His very misanthropy is creative and his prose is much more ingenious than that of Henry Miller, than whom he is supposed to be filthier. In fact he satisfied the three main requirements of the great novelist: he is avid, articulate and has vision. It is to be hoped that he will now begin to get the serious attention he deserves, even if only because he found Russia a miserable country. The true partners of his gift are Beckett (especially for the mud-epic *Comment c'est*, 1961), Genet and Bernanos.

The shallow sophistications of Paul Morand (*Ouvert la nuit*, 1922, *Fermé la nuit*, 1923, *L'Europe galante*, 1925, *Magie noire*, 1928) show some of the cavalier toughness used almost as a gimmick by Francis Carco (1886–) in *Rue Pigalle* (1927) and *Ténèbres* (1935). Jean Giraudoux's gossamer sophistries are the shallowest of all, the most exiguous response to a pervading nihilism: *Suzanne et le Pacifique* (1921) and *Siegfried et le limousin* (1922) ignite themselves here and there only to fizzle trivially on.

1. E.g. I take at random Françoise Sagan's *Les Merveilleux Nuages* and Paul Vercors's *Sylva*.

The caducity of Jean Cocteau's *Le Grand Écart* (1923) and *Thomas l'imposteur* (1925) constantly suggests that he has nothing to say; however, in *Les Enfants terribles* (1929) the rigmaroles and fantasies of adolescence are fondly sketched without being explored in the manner of, say, Henry Green or L. P. Hartley. Of *Les Enfants* Cocteau says in *Opium*; 'it was written during an obsession with "Make Believe" (*Show Boat*); those who like the book should buy the record and play it while re-reading'. We are reminded that Cocteau (1891–1963) is the capital *amuseur*, a child of the Jazz Age. Fantasy and somnambulism come naturally to him as the spiritual equivalents of Morand's heady steeplechases from capital to capital (always in weird company) or of Giraudoux's *couture*-minded female Crusoe. Such were the escapes from post-war frustration. They also provided their authors with the germ of more substantial works: Cocteau's drama, *Les Parents terribles* (1938), Morand's New York novel *Champions du monde* (1930) and his aviation study *Air indien* (1932), and Giradoux's analytical *Les Aventures de Jerôme Berdini* (1930). Another mode of fantasy appeared in André Maurois's psychological romance about Shelley, *Ariel* (1923) and (no doubt because the British and Irish are fantastic to start with) in the same writer's *Les Silences du Colonel Bramble* (1918) and *Les Discours du docteur O'Grady* (1922). Maurois has also written novels of a rather thin kind: *Bernard Quesnay* (1926), *Climats* (1932) and *Terre promise* (1945) are the best. Maurois is essentially a derivative writer; when he has to start from his own imagination he seems curiously lacking.

Imagination, often without any apparent bearing on daily life, turns up in its most garish form in the post-war revival of the adventure novel. Pierre Benoit's *Koenigsmark* (1918) and Pierre MacOrlan's *Le Chant de l'équipage* (1918) set the style with bewitching incredible heroines and techniques more or less cinematic. Aeroplanes and bullfighting figure in the adventure mythology raised to its highest power by Henri de Montherlant in *Les Bestiaires* (1926). The vogue stretches from Louis Bertrand's and the Tharaud brothers' novels about Africa and racial conflict (*La Fête Arabe*), central Europe and Jerusalem, to the P. C. Wren-like novels of Joseph Kessel. It is curious to see how champagne fantasy yields to colour and a dash of Kipling; post-war develops

into pre-war and enervated frivolity quickens up into yearning
for action. Another war soon satisfies the yearning.

François Mauriac (1885–) has succeeded in writing religious
novels without ever labouring the immanence or the seeming
absence of the supernatural. His work has a timeless quality
which he has secured by cutting out infinity. (This is not true of
Bernanos.) Combining a morbid psychological subtlety with a
gift for unhurried, expansive development of complex themes,
Mauriac also excels at landscape. The Bordeaux *landes* emblema-
tize for him as do the moors for Hardy. *L'Enfant chargé de chaînes*
(1913) and *Préséances* (1921) are confessional, a little uncontrolled, but all the same deeply disturbing accounts of a sore
adolescence. In his first thoroughly integrated novel, *Le Baiser au
lépreux* (1922), the wife's muted, stifled, sea-changing disgust with
her husband is rendered without the slightest monotony; which,
in itself, is a sufficient proof of Mauriac's keen sensitivity to distinct but similar-looking states of mind. *Le Fleuve du feu* (1923)
presents a Gidean theme: the conflict between sensual and pure.
A young couple are eventually swept away from purity, but
Mauriac is more interested (like Gide in *La Porte étroite*) in
making something *out of* the 'fire' than in communicating its
quality. Usually, in fact, Mauriac's account of sexual desire is
anaemic; he too often fails to supply the convincing detail, too
often tries to make points by blatant omission. With inordinate
mother-love, however, he is more at home, as *Génitrix* (1923)
proves. Félicité Gazenave is the first of Mauriac's monsters to be
poised between damnation and grace. Ruining her son's marriage,
she also seems to illustrate the destructive nature of all love—a
point that Colette made, but hardly in the terms of Mauriac. In
Mauriac, love sometimes seems no more than a front: 'love', says
Thérèse Desqueyroux in *La Fin de la nuit* (1935), 'is not necessarily wicked . . . but wickedness is an awful thing when it does
not wear the mask of love'. In the same novel the following
sinister exchange defines Mauriac's love even further:

'Anyone hearing you talk would think that you had loved
Argelouse.'
'Loved?—not exactly. But I endured such suffering there
that it comes to much the same thing.'

Already in *Le Désert de l'amour* (1925) Mauriac had shown a
father and son enslaved by love for the same woman: oddly
enough, the pair of them, identified in desire, separate themselves by being almost interchangeable: the father is virile and
fresh, his son rigid and negative. Mauriac shuffles the paradoxes
just enough to distort the stock triangle without making it seem
contrived.

Thérèse Desqueyroux (1927) introduced a vicious but pitiable
woman who, because she summed up so much of Mauriac's out-
look, haunted him for years. In the Foreword he addresses her
thus: 'Many, Thérèse, will say that you do not exist. But I who
for so many years have watched you closely, have sometimes
stopped you in your walks, and now lay bare your secret, I know
that you do. I remember, as a young man, seeing you in a stuffy
Courtroom, at the mercy of lawyers whose hearts were less hard
than those of the over-dressed women on the public benches.
Your small face was white, your lips scarcely visible. Later still, I
came on you again in a country drawing-room, a young and
ravaged woman plagued by the attentive care of aged relatives
and a foolish husband. . . .' Thérèse, driven to attempt the poisoning of her husband, Bernard, eventually turns up to give a guiding
hand to Marie, her daughter. In *La Fin de la nuit*, not intended
as a sequel, Mauriac explains his cryptic heroine:

> She took form in my mind as an example of that power,
> granted to all human beings—no matter how much they may
> seem to be the slaves of a hostile fate—of saying 'No' to the
> law which beats them down. . . . But she belongs to that class
> of human beings (and it is a huge family!) for whom night can
> end only when life itself ends.

Some concluding pages (giving Thérèse 'pardon and the peace of
God') he destroyed because he could not conceive of 'the priest
who would have possessed the qualifications necessary if he was
to hear her confession with understanding. Since then I have
found him . . . and I know now . . . just how Thérèse entered into
the eternal radiance of death.' Take Thérèse's libertine and
anguished career as we may, it is hard to ignore the almost
Byronic pose in these quotations. Fortunately, none of it gets into

the novels proper; and Mauriac's delineation and scrutiny of Thérèse is one of the most beautiful, least stagy pieces of writing in the modern French novel. *Le Nœud de vipères* (1932) is an even more intensely conceived account of hatred festering within one family, and *Le Mystère Frontenac* (1933) reads like a retort to *Génitrix*: this time the mother fosters family solidarity. *Les Anges noires* (1936) is about the crimes and consciences of a Don Juan of the provinces—a novel almost unrelievedly black. But then, Mauriac is interested in evil and makes it a matter of 'lighting', so that dark corners can be investigated and surface sensationalism made transparent.

Mauriac's favourite method, the retrospective confession, calls for both understatement and discipline. There are some things which need not be said heavily and others which must be trimmed lest they seem gaudy. The hot-house in the country-house imposes its own special requirements: the atmosphere transforms and inflates whatever is said or done. So the bourgeoisie with its petty pursuits and mercantile obsessions, its passion for decorum and its fur-coated celebration at midnight on Christmas of a child born in a manger, comes to seem monstrous. In order to effect this transformation, the novelist has to know everything about his characters; which is precisely what, in *Le Roman* and *Le Romancier et ses personnages*, Mauriac insists upon. The trouble is that when the novelist is too much in command, his characters never seem to hesitate: a certain glibness, a too impressive efficiency (which Sartre has criticized in Mauriac), wrecks the illusion of people's making up their own minds. But Sartre's objections are invalid: first because Mauriac is *expressing* life, not mimicking it, and second because Mauriac is in the tradition of the moralists (Pascal, Racine and Péguy), not that of the realists (Balzac, Flaubert, Zola), and seizes upon essences to turn into spiritual exercises rather than reproducing the surface of daily life. He triumphs, one might say, with a dazzling disregard of superficial actuality. In fact, Mauriac (like the Eliot of the plays) appeals to the non-Catholic precisely because (unlike the converts or reaffirmers, Bloy, Maritain, Péguy, Psichari, Du Bos, Rivière, Claudel, etc.) he wears his faith easily. He is confident: sufficiently so to dispense with exact portrayal of life as we know it and to let his conviction emerge without being insisted upon. His polish and *savoir-faire* come from an accurate idea of what art is and what the religious mind need not attempt. His technique is almost a representation of his theme and of the way in which he regards it. A text from St Paul's *Epistle to the Romans* suggests something of his preoccupations: 'For the good that I would I do not: but the evil which I would not, that I do.' He goes after essentials, leaving both reportage and protestation to less assured performers.

Mauriac is especially good at revealing the metaphysical terror which attends both sin and sex. As sex is the source of our being, it is also profoundly religious, and to regard it as not so is a blunder. That seems reasonable enough. But he seems unable to stress the religious force of sexuality without exaggerating the way in which the body impedes the spirit. This, in so intelligent a novelist, is an almost wilful sally into prurience. What he calls 'the filth of flesh' requires clear definition if it is to mean anything at all; unfortunately that definition is missing. Of the comedy of sex he knows nothing; he specializes in repressed lusts and ignores the equilibrium consequent on desire gratified. Because he wants emotion festering, he picks out the thwarted, which is well enough until he begins to construct a cosmology on that basis. At that point, not even daring to compare the electricity of pleasure with the electricity of religious joy, he becomes dishonest. To quote the original title of *Génitrix*, '*Il n'est qu'un seul amour*'. Exactly. Even lust in itself, untransfigured, has to be venerated even if not liked. The same source is evoked for lust, love and grace, and to pretend otherwise is to commit *mauvaise foi*. Even Maria Cross in *Le Désert de l'amour*, sensual-maternal-egoistic, really as lonely as any adolescent on the threshold of puberty, has to be revered for the power she embodies, whatever we may think of her disposition. Mauriac could do with a dose of Colette's emphasis on 'attending' to the world.

Also against him there are his irrelevances, his often facile symbols (wasted gardens, etc.) and his reluctance to celebrate the beauty of the physical world. There is too a certain monotony in his settings not quite counteracted by the exquisite phasing even of his best novels. It is always the same ethos with Mauriac. But when all is said, his ability with intense, dark emotions makes a good many English novelists look like tepid amateurs of melodrama. People *are* intense if you dig deep enough into them; and

Mauriac proves that point over and over again. His more recent novels, *La Pharisienne* (1941), *Le Sagouin* (1951), *Galigaï* (1952), consolidate his confined image of the world, combining the methods of Madame de La Fayette with the steadiness of Pascal. It is not surprising that this master of unwasteful dialogue should also have turned his hand to the theatre.

No French novelist except, oddly enough, Françoise Sagan achieves quite the dry precision of Mauriac. Georges Bernanos (1888–1948), in some ways Mauriac's extravagant antithesis, takes as his theme not only the dark springs of passion but also its embodiment of violence. (Bernanos enjoys quite a vogue in the United States.) His style is correspondingly more lurid. In *La grande peur des bien-pensants* (1931) he condemned the bourgeois obsession with getting and spending and, in *Les grands cimetières sous la lune* (1938), Franco and his backers. Bernanos the polemicist is inseparable from Bernanos the almost Gothic novelist. Much concerned with demonic possession, he wrote a tract, *La France contre les robots* (1947), and a novel, *Sous le soleil de Satan* (1926), which can profitably be read together. Munich, Vichy and the machine-civilization epitomize the extremes of intemperate rationalism which are personified, in this particular novel, in a caricature of Anatole France. The priest grapples with the supernatural (there are some vivid scenes of epiphany or apocalypse), while the humble, doomed hero of *Le Journal d'un curé de campagne* (1936) tackles things in a much less febrile way. The novels in between are intense, viscous and erratic: *L'Imposture* (1927) has a blurred vehemence and *La Joie* (1929) mixes pristine spirituality (typified in the girl, Chantal) with throbbing evocations of ineluctable cosmic forces. In *La Nouvelle Histoire de Mouchette* (1937) an adolescent girl disintegrates spiritually under the impact of enigmatic disasters, and Bernanos's last novel, *Monsieur Ouine* (1946), takes his obsession with damnation, brimstone and the devil beyond the possibilities of cogent art. There is something of Joyce in Bernanos: not afraid to pile up effects or to seem incoherent, he relies on vehemence to carry the reader with him. He deals in inspissation and impasto, mixing souls like pure colours, turning grace into terrible lava. In the line of descent from such as Léon Bloy, he is perhaps the most excitable of the French novelists. Of the flesh he is not afraid and about the possibility of being damned he is ferociously eloquent.

His royalism and his interest in violence relate him to Henri de Montherlant (1896–), except that the latter lacks Bernanos's cosmic preoccupations. Montherlant, believing that desire revitalizes and love corrupts, turned from Catholicism to Spanish mysticism, from France to Algeria, from writing to being a matador. He finds man the individual noble but man the herd-animal crass. As his *Carnets* reveal, he is both self-conscious and misanthropic. He wants readers and yet he wants to be independent. Always ready to indulge in mystification, he never published *La Rose de sable* (1954) in its complete form, which is a pity. The characters are interesting: Auligny the orthodox-minded young officer doing a tour in a solitary Sahara outpost, Guiscart the well-to-do painter who now devotes himself entirely to fornication, Ramie the little Arab girl with whom Auligny has a curious love-affair, and the desert itself. Parts of the novel are melodramatic and phoney, and some of the metaphors are preposterous, but the love-affair is delicately, hauntingly evoked, especially the surface charm of Ramie contrasted with her 'cold and inert' heart. They are all irremediably lonely, all but Ramie following the dictates of the heart. This, says Montherlant, is always a mistake: 'we should all be most suspicious of any venture of spirit or conscience which we knew had begun by being merely one of the heart'. The emphasis is surely on 'knew' and confers ample scope for the kind of self-deception that the restless, cynical, exalted post-war Montherlant badly needed in order to keep going. Compact of Barrès and Chateaubriand, the early Montherlant plunges fatalistically into rituals of war, bullfighting, Mithraic sun-worship and callisthenics. The novels of this period, *La Relève du matin* (1920), *Le Songe* (1925), *Les Bestiaires* (1926) and *Les Olympiques* (1927), are more like personal outpourings than considered works of art.

His nihilism (which led him to welcome the Occupation *'pour le plaisir de trahir'*) appears in *Solstice de juin 1941* (1942) and the first sign of a mature, objective novelist in *Les Célibataires* (1934). This is a masterpiece: two eccentric old men, an elderly uncle and his nephew, both bachelors and survivors of a line of the Breton nobility, share a small house. The uncle, Élie de Coëtquidan, is a baron and has to be catalogued: virgin, pariah, miser, coprophilic, noisome, his clothes held together with safety-pins. The nephew is a layabout, occasionally working as a labourer or coal-shoveller. He washes once a fortnight and is vexed with creditors whom his father incurred by the score. They both draw Octave the banker into their slough of tedium; this rich relative is reluctant, but eventually capitulates when Élie provokes his anti-semitic instincts by threatening to go and live with a Jewish mistress. The whole novel is appalling and enthralling. The old men, rolling bread pellets or lying hopelessly in bed, are very much like the valetudinarians of Samuel Beckett: these are the spectres of our own anticipations of age. There is more 'realism' in one paragraph of this novel than in all of Montherlant's techni-colour virility anthems put together. *Les Jeunes Filles* (1935–40) shows the method in full symphony: a precise eye, a voracious ear for the idiom of class, a paralysing irony and a stringent sense of the comic.

The cult of action which in the early Montherlant is a literary pose contrasts with the occupational commentaries of Antoine de Saint-Exupéry (1900–1944). This pioneer civil pilot disappeared during a wartime mission, thus clinching the dangerous mystique of which he wrote. His first book, the uneven and sentimental *Courrier-Sud* (1929), is his only novel although his subsequent writings, cast as autobiographical records, might well strike the reader as fiction. *Vol de nuit* (1931)—with preface by Gide, the visionary *Terre des hommes* (1939) and the story of a futile sortie in *Pilote de Guerre* (1942) are exciting for the dizzying experiences they present so austerely. But the writing is sometimes wooden or otiose, and *Citadelle* (1948), published posthumously, is just as opaque in places as Malraux's *Les Voix du silence*, to which it corresponds as the man-of-action's philosophical testament. The idea of self-definition through heroism may seem a little hack-neyed and rhetorical by now, but it necessarily retains a special power in France where intellectuals have often proved their points with their lives. Anarchy of much lower pressure but equally insistent about the nobility of man in his freedom to define himself appears in the writings of Simone de Beauvoir (1908–). A temperament's pessimism contends with philosophical optimism in her novels, *L'Invitée* (1943), *Le Sang des autres* (1945)

and *Tous les hommes sont mortels* (1946). Her touch is lighter than
Sartre's, and her handling of complex psychology more ingenious. *Les Mandarins* (1954) is noteworthy as a piece of contemporary cultural history in which she manages to make
interesting in their own right some thinly disguised portraits of
the intellectuals she has known.

V

Before considering the French contribution to the 'anti-novel'
or 'meta-novel', a few not easily classified novelists should be
mentioned. The Swiss, Charles-Ferdinand Ramuz (1878–1947),
author of almost thirty novels, specialized in portraits of the
countryfolk of Vaud, his native canton. Small craftsmen, wine-
growers and fishermen are lovingly explored in obtuse prose
flecked with regional idiom. Ramuz's main achievement was to
create, in the simplest terms, a whole pageant of life and death—
in which death is as natural as birth. His tragic sense shows to
best effect in *Le Règne de l'esprit malin* (1917), *Présence de la
mort* (1922) and *La Grande Peur dans la montagne* (1926). His
is not the idealized Switzerland of Hemingway, but as clearly and
unsparingly realized as Sherwood Anderson's Winesburg or
Mauriac's Landes. Jean Giono (1895–) is another regionalist with
power to transcend the local. Of mixed Italian and French blood,
he tends to overdo his contrast between the life of the soil and the
barrenness of machine civilization. A Greek pantheism haunts
his hymns to the peasantry. His early life at home in Provence
with his shoemaker father is delicately, sensuously evoked in *Jean
le bleu* (1932), his war experiences in the commanding *Le Grand
Troupeau* (1931) and his mystical, gaudy primitivism in a good
many rather repetitive novels ranging from *Les Vraies Richesses*
(1936), *Le Serpent d'étoiles* (1933) and *Le Poids du ciel* (1938) to
the well-known short story *La Femme du boulanger* (1939). His
most considerable achievement (although also the richest in preciosity and the most insistent about the religion of earth) is his
two trilogies: *Colline* (1920), *Un de Baumugnes* (1929), *Regain*
(1930) and *Le Chant du monde* (1934), *Que ma joie demeure* (1935)
and *Batailles dans la montagne* (1937). In some ways his prose

style resembles that of Bernanos: livid and full of elaborate metaphors. But he has the sense of humour Bernanos lacks. His more recent work has shown considerable variety, ranging from the sunny fun of *Le Hussard sur le toit* (1951) to the topicality of *Notes sur l'affaire Dominici* (1955).

André Chamson (1900–) is a more sombre, less dynamic regionalist. Having written a thesis for the École de Chartes on the geography of his native region, the Cévennes, he has combined fiction with intense political interests (left-wing), miscellaneous studies and government office. His world is less simplified than than of Giono and Ramuz: it calls for a tamer style and a curbing of self-indulgent lyricism. After *Roux le bandit* (1925) came his best-known novel, *Les Hommes de la route* (1927) and *Le Crime des justes* (1929), colourful but rather grim studies of the Cévenole peasants. *Heritages* (1932) goes beyond the pastoral and *La Galère* (1939) makes a frontal attack on contemporary French politics. In spite of his public-spirited ideals and his sympathy for men who work the earth, Chamson does not satisfy: his lyricism seems escape—all the more because half his interests are in the world of affairs. The *roman-fleuve* might have helped him to integrate his messages and avoid the roles in which he tends to appear, although by accident, the discontented countryman and the rural politician. *Le Dernier Village* (1946) and *La Neige et la fleur* (1951) have to be read for passages of spare beauty rather than for their general impact (on which Chamson is inclined to rely too much).

Henri Bosco (1888–) also turns the folkways and earth-atavism of Provence into captivating, unlaboured novels which neither idealize nor caricature the peasant mind. *L'Ane culotte* (1937), *Hyacinthe* (1940) and *Le Renard dans l'île* (1956), as well as *Barboche* (1957), relate him to Giono and Chamson, and, for a knack with fantasy, to a neglected and erratic novelist, Julien Gracq (1910–). The author of a study of André Breton, Gracq maintained a long silence after his *Le Rivage des Syrtes* won the Goncourt in 1951. Then, in 1958, he published *Un Balcon en forêt*, which certainly reads as if it has been long brooded over. A heavily anagogic account of a claustrophobic situation, it takes us back to autumn 1939. Young Lieutenant Grange, a Poe-lover caught between heroic pretensions and a more fundamental sense of *sauve qui peut*, commands an isolated, ill-equipped blockhouse on the Belgian frontier. His mission, never clearly stated by the dithering French General Staff, appears to be a spying-cum-rear-guard action against German tanks—if they come. To Grange and his three men the 'if' is unimportant, for they believe themselves exempted from the war. The sonorous forest drugs them. Each settles comfortably into a manless family in the nearby village, and Grange has a brief, intense affair with Mona, a phthisic young dryad straight out of Maeterlinck or Charles Morgan. Before the Germans can advance the village is evacuated, the affair is over and Grange a new man, fatalistically serene. Hardly has the attack begun when the blockhouse gets a direct hit; Grange and one of his men escape through the emergency tunnel, and the book ends with him climbing wounded into bed in Mona's deserted house.

Anyone with a taste for archetypes will have a feast here. With fey atavistic fervour Gracq elaborates his blockhouse in terms of a 'Red Riding Hood Hut', Verne's floating island and the Islands of the Blessed. The four men are now stranded fish, now unicorns; the forest is Arden. Grange, the most thoughtful of lieutenants, having too little to do, attends voraciously to everything. Consequently his perceptions are intense to the point of nausea; he fills the void with his racing, lavish mind. But when Gracq not only underlines his own Wagnerian-Jungian allegories but even thickens up every impression with snarled images and softly wadded repetitions, the reading becomes tedious. He also catalogues a good deal, perhaps intending an antithesis of hard objects (in rooms, bags, pockets) to the whimsy and soft degeneration of the isolated men. All he achieves, however, is a crammed fable, brisk and pappy by turns, but almost redeemed by an exciting, austere account of the German advance that surrounds Grange long before touching him.

Gracq, for all his involuted fantasies—some of them almost surrealist—at least does not, like the novelists of the anti-psychological school, ditch depth-psychology only to create a new version of the typical method of William James. What Gracq lacks is the ferocious, tormented religious impulse of such a novelist as Marcel Jouhandeau (1888–), whose Monsieur Godeau and town of Chaminadour remind one of Faulkner and Mauriac.

Gracq and Jouhandeau have symbolism and burlesque in common; Gracq is by far the milder of the two, but his delicacy
weakens his impact in much the same way as Jouhandeau's
bitterness weakens his. For ruthless introspection, savage comedy
of 'humours' and an almost brutal economy of prose style,
Jouhandeau's *Monsieur Godeau intime* (1926), *Monsieur Godeau
marié* (1933) and *Chroniques maritales* (1938) are outstanding. *Les
Térébinte* (1926), *Tite-le-long* (1932), *Bincho-Ana* (1933) and
Chaminadour I–III (1934–41) consist mainly of mordant vignettes
of his native town. He sometimes fails to move through pursuing
acerbity as much, it seems, for stylistic flourish as in uncalculated
vehemence. He pits cruelties of his own against those of life and
his most recent works, *Mémorial* (1948–58), *Ménagerie domestique*
(1948), *L'Éternel procès* (1959) and *Les Argonautes* (1959), show
him little changed.

Under his own name of Marcel Provence, Jouhandeau published the vitriolic *Les Allemands en Provence* (1919) and *Bauxite
et aluminium: L'Allemagne et l'après-guerre* (1920), both of which
match in grim modern aridity the novels of Maxence Van der
Meersch (1907–51). The three volumes of Meersch's *La Fille
pauvre* (1931–55) vividly and depressingly communicate the
sullen, sulphurous industrial north-east, and its power over men's
minds. *Masque de chair* (1958) shows the same punch as *Corps et
âmes* (193), his well-known diatribe against the medical profes-
sion. Concerning marriage, Jacques Chardonne (1884–) is every
bit as analytical but nowhere near so acerb as Jouhandeau. His
first novel, *L'Epithalame* (1921), presents views on the marital
state similar to those of D. H. Lawrence. The theme is resumed in
Éva (1930), *Claire* (1931) and, of course, in his cycle-novel *Les
Destinées sentimentales*. For Chardonne, the truth about life is to
be found in intimate relationships rather than in social pageant.
Unfortunately this conviction leads him into sanctimoniousness
and over-insistence. *L'Amour c'est beaucoup plus que l'amour*
(1957) is a title which can be taken, like most of Chardonne's
actual novels, as both mawkish and unrewardingly honest. Julien
Green (1900–), born in Paris of American parents, has at various
times been said to resemble Kafka, Faulkner, Melville, Hawthorne, Balzac, Emily Brontë and Bernanos. But he is very much
his own man. He combines, in a way sometimes astounding and

sometimes tedious, fantasy, whimsy, violence and an obsession with heredity. His early novels are too melodramatic—even when one allows the degree of melodrama his themes necessarily entail. *Le Voyageur sur la terre* (1924) and *Mont-Cinère* (1926) are neurotic, desperate works all the more difficult to swallow because the prose does not absorb and nurture the violence. The same is true of Green's best novels, *Adrienne Mesurat* (1927), *Léviathan* (1929), *Le Visionnaire* (1934) and *Minuit* (1936). His main deficiency emerges in comparison with Dostoevsky: Green, working out a tragic, hideous view of life, phases the structure cleverly but never quite knows when an emotion or an episode has exhausted itself locally; Dostoevsky never goes on for too long. Green, dealing almost exclusively in what Emerson called 'the soul's mumps and measles', cannot leave torment alone; the result is a plethora of symbolism: the setting exists within the torment, not the torment in the setting. Thus, *Le Malfaiteur* (1955) takes the passions of a bourgeois family, abstracts the passion, and then replaces the passionate characters in a lava of their own making. The result is inspissation; suggestion is too mild for him, and only insistence will do. Green's study of Hawthorne, published in 1928, expresses Green's own American inclinations in terms of the American.

Jean Schlumberger (1877–), Protestant and practical, writes of a family estate in Normandy (*Saint-Saturnin*, 1931) and of schemes of industrial management (*Histoire de quatre potiers*, 1935) in a completely opposite manner to that of the mystagogic Green. Schlumberger, until *Stéphane le glorieux* (1940)—an unflinching story of a soldier's remorse—is, if anything, too matter-of-fact, having separated off his questioning mind into *traités* on body and soul, and other metaphysical, psychosomatic themes. One novelist who turned matter-of-factness into a devastating classical manner was Raymond Radiguet (1903–1923), whose two short novels *Le Diable au corps* (1923) and *Le Bal du comte d'Orgel* (1924) respectively show the Longus-type fable and the novel of manners raised to a cutting, deft power. Radiguet is both acute and sensitive, excelling in both nuance and bold, compressed effects. Françoise Sagan (1935–), expert clinician of the spoiled, the rootless and the overreaching, writes short novels which merge together in the reader's mind. Unpretentious in style, *Bonjour, Tristesse* (1954), *Un certain sourire* (1956), and the less carefully conceived *Dans un mois, dans un an* (1957) and *Aimez-vous Brahms . . .* (1957), display the advantages of a straightforward narrative technique. She gains most of her effects from meaningful suppressions and laconic juxtapositions. The rhetoricians—Bernanos, Green—want to be admired in the act of communicating: they themselves want to be noticed—almost as if they forget the complicity between reader and author. Sagan, every bit as austere as Radiguet, has the knack of paring down an illustrative story almost to the point of curtness. Gide attempted this too, but rarely managed it without becoming perfunctory. Sagan suggests the fulness of life while teaching the reader to discriminate as he proceeds.

A similar trenchant intensity can be found in the work of Hervé Bazin, whose dozen or so novels are written in a staccato, succinct, rhythmical French: '*Baisez-vous, taisez-vous, les oreilles amies vous écoutent. Et coule, salive à romance, lessive à soupçons.*' Bazin, as *Vipère au poing* (1948) and *Au Nom du fils* (1960) demonstrate, can be both savage and mild, a drypoint Schlumberger. He observes his people intimately but often uses them as occasions for compactly manœuvred stylistic display. M. Astin in *Au Nom du Fils* is made to brood a great deal as he watches his three children growing up and away from him; while Astin broods, Bazin does prose geometry like a stealthy ballet. Less pungent than anything by Bazin, Philippe Sollers's first novel, *Une Solitude curieuse* (1960), deals with a Moravia-Colette type of theme: a young adolescent learns about love from the maid, Spanish and twice his age. Brilliant at conveying the atmosphere of an old shuttered house, of nocturnal city life and autumn vineyards and orchards, Sollers names rather than represents. His characters tend to have nothing between hallucination and mundane movements—the area that Sagan fills in so subtly. It is an unfortunate truth that lush style does not, of itself, thicken the psychology of a novel any more than austerity of style necessarily implies richness pared down. The art of the novel always suffers from any hardening of the categories.

Samuel Beckett (1906–) has sacrificed the conventional novel to dense explorations of states of mind and narrowed his props until what remains is appallingly vivid. In an early essay on Proust, published over thirty years ago, Beckett spoke of 'the vulgarity of a plausible concatenation'; in that sense, his novels are the least vulgar ever written. Watt, in the novel of that name (1953), goes to work in the house of a Mr Knott, has an unhappy experience at a railway station and ends up in an institution. Much of Watt's time is devoted to learning how to smile: he 'had watched people smile and thought he understood how it was done'. He also creates mental timetables for coincidences of the merest things— the feeding of a dog and the comings and goings of the mysterious Knott. Beckett's characters are aged beats: in *Murphy* (1938) the main character retires into his own mental privacy, which is divided into three layers: light, semi-dark and dark. In the light Murphy can defend himself; this is the region of the novel's caustic satire. The second layer is 'the Belacqua bliss'—sloth, day-dream; and the third is utter accidie where Murphy becomes a 'mote in the dark of absolute freedom'.

His characters advance from concentration to self-loss. The main character in *Molloy* (1951), the first novel in a trilogy (which perhaps exemplifies the three layers), spends considerable time working out how to distribute sixteen sucking stones among four pockets in such a way that no stone is sucked twice. Such doddering devotion to the world of objects reassures the Beckett heroes. As the trilogy goes on, their plights get worse. Malone in *Malone meurt* (1951) is confined to a room where, while dying, he receives meals and care. He counts his material possessions. And the 'hero' of *L'innommable* (1953) is really a kind of Arabian Nights victim. His name is Mahood but he dubs himself 'Worm'; well he might, incarcerated as he is in a large jar which stands on a pedestal in the street, just outside a chophouse. Mahood has neither arms nor legs; a collar attached to the jar's rim holds his head rigid. From time to time the chophouse-owner's wife feeds him, changes the sawdust and bedecks the jar with Chinese lanterns. Mahood the aged foetus weeps—his entire family died from sausage poisoning. His plaint is that of all Beckett's de-prived, wrecked, hopeless, ludicrous reductions of humanity:

I'm mute, what do they want, what have I done to them, what have I done to God, what have they done to God, what has God done to us, nothing, and we've done nothing to him, you can't do anything to him, he can't do anything to us, we're innocent, he's innocent, it's nobody's fault.

Once Beckett's characters pause to reflect, a spell seizes them. Vladimir and Estragon in *Waiting for Godot* have shed themselves of all superfluous things—of *all* things, that is. The characters in another Beckett play, *Fin de partie*, are put in ashcans. Yet, poor bare animals that Becket makes them, they retain some power of hope. They sit still. They spell to us the human essence. They inhabit the flux. Beckett is obsessed by the difference between man's romantic dreams and the very little that life needs in order to sustain itself. His portraits of animal existence are caricatures of paradise; the vast superstructure of society topples away; the dreams of simplistic Rousseaus, like the vast corpus of human pretensions (ambition, love, wit, 'fraternity', causes, metaphysics), look idiotic. This, says Beckett, is what man is; this is the source of all so-called civilization. The reader suddenly realizes that to laugh is to be brutal, to sympathize is to ignore man's tenacity.

Beckett rapidly passes from the fiercely macabre (as when the lunatic asylum holds its inquest on Murphy's body) to malicious irreverence. The characters of his novels, unlike the more pugnacious ones in his early stories, represent passivity: life has done things to them. Little pathetic ingenuities on the brink of darkness are all that remain beyond a diffident longing for companionship and the constant fear of not having food or shelter. In many ways, Beckett makes all over again the points of *King Lear*. Moran in *Molloy* starts out as an almost manic perfectionist—a man with a pattern complex—but gradually declines into a vegetable: he even welcomes a paralysis of the leg and wants further afflictions —dumbness, deafness, blindness, amnesia—with 'just enough brain intact to allow you to exult. And to dread death like a regeneration'. Beckett constantly implies the joy of oblivion without disregarding man's obstinate, nagging urge to preserve his life. Without pain, there is no life, without life there is, presumably, no pain. Beckett's choice is clear: it is life, no matter how much indignity it entails.

Such desperate conclusions come naturally from Beckett the Irishman who has adopted French as his medium. He is much closer to such French experimentalists as Robbe-Grillet, Butor

and Nathalie Sarraute than to anyone English. He picks the least
promising, most exiguous material and tries to redeem it through
sheer skill; and, because his prose is so accurate and lithe, he
succeeds. He writes with immense energy about next to nothing.
'It's not certain' is the phrase that recurs in his writings; but if
insistence and industriousness can supply some kind of certainty,
then Beckett does too. His obsession with the flux of identity
relates him to Nigel Dennis, who wrote a witty satire, *Cards of
Identity* (1955), on the same theme. In some ways, Beckett's concentration on uncertainty (mostly of the metaphysical kind)
parallels Amis's and Wain's accounts of social insecurity. His
aged heroes want something fixed where all is moving; so too do
the Jim Dixons and, in a different—almost religious—way, the
main personages of Robbe-Grillet and the anti-psychological
school. As Meister Eckhart said, to be poor in spirit is to 'possess
nothing, to know nothing, and to will nothing'. Beckett, with
considerable aesthetic courage, has tackled the theme of spiritual
poverty and, in doing so, has demonstrated the very poverty of
imagination which, in England, makes originality a thing to sniff
at. Beckett is not for plain tastes any more than what is fancy is
for him.

VI

There remain to be considered those novelists who have created
what Claude Mauriac calls '*L'Alittérature contemporaine*' (1958).
Of these the most prolific theorist is Alain Robbe-Grillet (1922–),
whose novels *Les Gommes* (1953), *Le Voyeur* (1955), *La Jalousie*
(1957) and *Dans le labyrinthe* (1959) have increasingly transformed
matter-of-factness into a perverse technique of mere annotation.
'It is a matter here, however,' Robbe-Grillet said in the introduction to *Dans le labyrinthe*, 'of a strictly material reality, which
is to say a reality without allegorical force.' In that instance the
labyrinth was one of streets through which a soldier wanders,
searching—without knowing why—for an address he has forgotten. So, having already dispensed with plot and psychology,
Robbe-Grillet also fended off the meaning-hunters. What was left
seemed exiguous and futile. Robbe-Grillet's finicking inventories
of the physical world bored rather than reassured, creating a

world in which the proffered solace of a hold on material things meant nothing because there was no one alive enough in the novel to need that kind of help. The home truth Robbe-Grillet seemed to be forgetting, or dodging, was the simple one that art is mimetic. Whether or not we decide to assume attitudes and obsessions presented in a novel depends on what the people in the novel get out of them. We were, in fact, in both *Le Voyeur*, the least rarefied of his novels, and *Dans le labyrinthe*, being offered a narrator's obsession: the narrator, a deliberate creation, took little part in the action (or rather in the procession of sentences), saw things defectively and should have been replaced by an observer with more information. It may be an arresting trick to present people as if they were unknown animals in an observation-chamber; it is also a wilful distortion of what most of us, in our rough-and-ready everyday way, think we *know*.

The same defect is to be found in *La Jalousie*. The narrator botanizes obsessively about the trivia of the daily round—and perhaps he does teach one to attend more carefully to the geometry of horizon, twig and window, to the structure of insects, the texture of wood and the sound of hair being combed. The English and American editions even include a plan of the house in which most of the selected incidents take place. The setting is tropical; the incessantly acute descriptions choke us, and the whole novel seems written expressly for critics to theorize about. A woman referred to as A . . . is having some kind of an affair with a neighbour, Franck. Nothing much happens, except that cocktails are taken on the terrace, meals quietly eaten; a trip into town is planned, and a novel is read. From time to time Franck crushes a centipede. Outside the house, the banana plantation swells; inside, the physical presence of A . . . confronts that of Franck. Their foreheads touch once; perhaps they kiss—the narrator does not say. Their car crashes on the way into town and catches fire; yet they are soon back on the terrace, sipping and serenely pondering, and exchanging banalities. Robbe-Grillet's main effort is towards repeating, regardless of chronology, accounts of the same incidents or occasions.

La Jalousie collates the similar and peels apart what is usually lumped together. It is all epitome and tension; unfortunately the epitomes, like wheels on ice, spin in grooves twenty pages long, and nothing moves forward. True, this technique does give one that extraordinary 'I-have-been-here-before' feeling—but too often. Prose, even when employed in a double fugue, is not music, and the unrepeated bits get lost simply because one is so surprised, put out, by the repetitions themselves. The narrator is importunate: at one point he tells the reader: 'This is the moment when the scene of the squashing of the centipede on the bare wall occurs.' One resents being nudged like that. Round we go—cocktails, centipede, the novel they are both reading, the letter she is writing, her walking, his tapering fingers, cocktails, centipede.... The whole is at least hypnotic and conveys harrowingly the vast part of our lives that is automatic. Robbe-Grillet is much subtler than a fact-fetichist; he really does communicate his keen response to minutiae.

In the long run, however, just one view of man is not enough. A novelist needs more than one trick. Robbe-Grillet should fit his one highly developed technique into a fairly orthodox novel: in fact *Le Voyeur* promised something rich and strange within familiar limits. *La Jalousie*, however, takes him into tricky country that lies somewhere between seed-catalogues and chamber music. Like Franck (who is listing the parts of his car engine), Robbe-Grillet 'performs this exhaustive inventory with a concern for exactitude which obliges him to mention a number of elements that are ordinarily understood without being referred to'. Robbe-Grillet's Bach-prose enthrals the reader with sense-data; but scrutiny of banana skins will never expose the fact that people, unlike bananas, are not identical inside.

Yet there is hope: even the narrator in *La Jalousie* speculates now and then; a few moods slip through. Robbe-Grillet's antithesis, Nathalie Sarraute, deals in inchoate, nascent thoughts and therefore unfinished sentences. Between her biological, plotless and pre-psychological cycles and his philatelic obsessions, there is little to choose. Each extreme represents a discovery, and one must hope for saner applications. Meanwhile, better than either is Michel Butor's subtle account, in *La Modification*, of a man's treadmilling thoughts as he lolls in the train taking him from his wife in Paris to his mistress in Rome. Robbe-Grillet's Seeing Eye, owing so much to Proust, would do well to borrow *all* that Proust offers. Psychology, as Proust and Butor have proved, is not

necessarily the sire of the trite. And obliquity is not the only way
of being original, any more than being direct precludes subtlety.

Robbe-Grillet, himself a director of the publishing house *Les
Éditions de Minuit* which has nurtured and published several of
the *'Alittérature'* group, has made various declarations of personal or group policy. 'The public's mistake', he wrote in the *New
Statesman* (19 February 1961), 'lies in thinking that the form of the
"real novel" was fixed once and for all in the Balzacian era
by strict, definite laws.' One agrees and would be glad to let things
rest at that if only, in pursuing his argument, he did not seem to
confuse genre with art, and the freedom of choice we have in
fixing a genre's limits with the immutable limits of art. Within art
a genre has no limits; but art in its very nature cannot be changed.
'The New Novel', Robbe-Grillet goes on, 'is concerned only with
man and his place in the world.' He means that just as, in swiftly
changing times, man gropes his way, so in the novel must the
characters grope, and so, in reading, must the reader. But, no
matter how much society alters, art remains the same: it is
always a version, a concocted version, of the world—just as, in
Robbe-Grillet's own novels, objects do not exist unperceived. To
try and push art beyond its established identity is just as futile as
asking what a bottle looks like when no one is perceiving it. It is
odd to find Robbe-Grillet claiming, almost in echo of Camus on
realism, that 'God alone can profess to be objective' while refusing
to acknowledge that, so to speak, God alone can create art that
transcends art's limits. He wants art to be not only mimetic but
to *be* the thing it portrays:

> Why strain to find out the name of a man in a novel when he
> doesn't tell us it? Every day we meet people whose names we
> don't know; and we can spend a whole evening talking to a
> stranger, without having taken the slightest notice of the
> introductions made by our hostess.

The answer to that is simple: talking with a stranger is not the
same as reading about a stranger in a novel. If we enjoy talking to
strangers, we go out and look for them; we do not turn to a novel.
When we read a novel we expect it, as a specimen of art, to do something which art (as distinct from talking to a stranger) alone can do.

Robbe-Grillet attacks fixed concepts, which is fine. But to attack Nature also, which we cannot change, is a different thing. It is, he says, 'the forms he [man] creates that give meaning to the world'. Just so: he is admitting that the world *is* intractable; but at the same time ignoring the fact that, when man began to create art, such creation was limited by the fact that man did not create the world. If man could, of his own accord, create a novel which no one knew was a novel, then he could be said to have extended the frontiers of art. But surely it is precisely on account of its limits that art interests us; without them it would merely become part of the world which art sets out to master. Art is subject to the laws of matter and it is extraordinary that Robbe-Grillet, an expert on agricultural machinery, should ignore this. It is as if he is asking that a tractor should, without being a tractor, do all that a tractor should. Art cannot be indistinguishable from what it represents until the nature of the universe is changed. And the novel which pretends it is not bound by the limits of art either is dealing with a world entirely of art or is cancelling itself out.

To this extent Robbe-Grillet's aesthetics misrepresents his own, and his associates', practice. When, in his own novels, he plays tricks with time, we know that he is deliberately manipulating things in order to evoke experiences we ourselves have had or is manipulating things in order to suggest experience as yet unknown. And if, in reading, say, *Les Gommes* (in which the time theme is paramount), we become able to formulate for the first time the nature of some hypothetical experience, then we still do not have that experience at first-hand. Either way—evocation or hypothesis—we are conscious of device. It is always experience-as-read-in-a-book. Similarly, when Butor in his fascinating but solemn *La Modification* (1957) works a dozen different journeys simultaneously into one man's stream of consciousness, we are conscious of both device and evocation: he is manipulating things to make a point, and encouraging us to re-live similar experiences of our own—all of this within the novel. But when Butor in *L'Emploi du temps* (1956) superimposes two temporal sequences and justifies the superimposition as 'quite natural since in real life one's mental analysis of past events takes place while other events are accumulating', he is both right and wrong. Right to evoke everyone's experience; wrong to justify *art* and *device* as 'natural'. Art is not natural.

A principle emerges: in other words, a formulated acknowledgment of a state of things we cannot seem to change. The only art that tempts us to recall our own experiences is that which echoes what we have experienced. Once we have begun to recall, we are willing to entertain manipulations which make special points. We need both correspondence and manipulation: the first without the second entertains us; the second without the first is like abstract art—unlikely to engage our whole being. So, within the context of her script, it is entirely fair (because unrealistic) of Marguerite Duras to set *Hiroshima, Mon Amour* in an unlikely place. Her introductory synopsis explains her choice:

> Between two beings geographically, philosophically, historically, racially, etc., as remote from each other as it is possible to be, Hiroshima is the common ground (perhaps the only one in the world) where the universals of eroticism, of love and of misery are pitilessly illuminated.

She wants to isolate and intensify the individual against an intensified universality. Most people have the same bodily needs, the same routines: their individuality consists in minor quirks which, according to Mme Duras, always manifest themselves externally. Hence her diligent cataloguing, in *Les Petits Chevaux de Tarquinia* (1953), of the behaviour of a group of bored friends on the Italian coast. Hence too her recourse to Robbe-Grillet's device of repeating the same sentence at regular intervals: that repetition is the routine of life, and it is made to throw idiosyncrasies into relief. She demonstrates rather than explains, and the reader has to work hard to interpret what is offered. Just as Hiroshima is theoretically apt and experimentally remote, so is each person's private self from his observable routines. *Le Square* (1955) and *Moderato Cantabile* (1958), which makes even adultery a compulsive, joyless routine, also show her willingness to distort common reality in order to express herself more pungently. But one wonders just how far our unique selves are available to the empirical observer who wants to photograph rather than explain. The '*chosiste*' prefers to deal in concrete details—in nouns—and so recalls the practice of the Goncourts. It is the reader who is supposed to establish the abstract significance of the details catalogued. Alternatively, of course, he can choose to follow the author to the letter and remain content with enumeration.

Once the usefulness of distorting a recognizable experience is seen, the achievement of the *anti-roman* writers or *chosistes* can be justified as art, and not for the reasons advanced by Robbe-Grillet. Since language itself is artificial, then the novelist is entitled to create (so long as he sticks to it) a terminology of his own. Henri Thomas, in *John Perkins* (1960), supplies two different endings; the hero's outbursts, occurring at the same time each night, make Thomas's point forcefully because they do not quite match our own experience—we do not quite credit them. The structure, so cunningly devised, is a trope in itself. So too Claude Simon, in *La Route des Flandres* (1960), chooses to suggest '*l'incohérent nonchalant impersonnel et déstructeur travail du temps*' through obsessively vivid hallucinations and a consistent disregard of conventional punctuation. Georges, recalling the débâcle in Flanders, 1940, makes no effort to organize his memories or to relate them to his present affair with the widow of a man under whom he served. Another novelist, Maurice Blanchot, who has published studies of Sade, Lautréamont and René Char, writes, in an essay on the last-named, of an attitude which manifests itself in the language of his own *Thomas l'obscur* (1950):

> No one stands present behind the written word: it gives voice to absent being, like the divine voice of the oracle . . . And like writing, the oracle refuses to justify, explain or defend itself . . . .

He is admitting the artificiality of art. A little farther on, he points out how art differs from life:

> what can this thing be, with its eternal immutability which is nothing but a semblance, a thing which speaks truth and yet with nothing but a void behind it, no possibility of discussion, so that in it the truth has nothing with which to confirm itself, appears without support, is only a scandalous semblance of truth, an image, and by its imagery and seeming draws away truth into depths where there is neither truth nor meaning, not even error?

'Nothing but a semblance'; yes, but because significant semblance is all that is aimed at. That is the justification of such novels as Roger Frison-Roche's mystical, mountaineering novels of which *La Piste Oubliée* (1950) is typical; René Daumal's *Mont Analogue* (1952), 'a novel of symbolically authentic non-Euclidean adventures in mountain-climbing'; and Nathalie Sarraute's *Le Planétarium* (1959) in which she attempts to 'study psychological movements while they are forming, at the very moment of birth, so to speak, or reactions which cannot be perceived directly' by posting 'another consciousness on the outer boundaries of the character's consciousness, one that is more clear-seeing than his own'. In *Le Planétarium* a young social climber and his wife wangle an elderly aunt's apartment from which to take off into 'social space'. Sarraute's earlier novels revealed the new technique in all its weaknesses. *Portrait d'un inconnu* (1948), complete with preface by Sartre, sacrifices names and physical exteriors for a scattershot version of the *roman d'analyse* in which all we have is 'I' and 'They', the 'I' being a psychological detective probing the appearances of an old man and his middle-aged daughter.[1] Sarraute (1900–), showing how we distort all we perceive, is doing nothing especially new: indeed, she may send us eagerly and perhaps

---

1. Cf. similarly difficult novels in which 'identity' becomes a ludicrous presumption. Vernier, in Michel Butor's *Degrés* (1960), starts as himself, then pretends he is Pierre the schoolboy and finally, in a third section, vanishes into such statements as this: '. . . you began writing the text that I am continuing, or more precisely that *you* are continuing by using *me*, for actually it's not I who is writing but you, you are speaking *through* me, trying to see things from my point of view, to imagine what I could know that you don't know, furnishing me the information which you possess and which would be out of my reach'. Similarly, Beckett's trilogy *L'Innommable* finishes by abolishing all the names (Molloy, Moran, Malone, Mahood, Worm, even Murphy and Watt) that have been offered, and the prostrate 'hero' of *Comment c'est* (1960) discovers that he himself has invented the personages— Pim, Bom, Krim and Kram—who have populated his mud hell. And even so sophisticated and articulate a novelist as Claude Mauriac—in a series of novels which begins narrowly with the egoism of Bertrand Carnéjoux (*Toutes les femmes sont fatales*, 1957), widens into the smart dinner party he gives (*Un Dîner en ville*, 1959) and then expands to include the whole of the Carrefour de Buci (*La Marquise sortit à cinq heures*, 1961)—offers a montage of interior monologues which blur the identity of characters whose preoccupations keep recurring. 'Being oneself', it seems, is too risky for novelists who find even '*l'exactitude littérale*' a quest of exasperating difficulty.

relievedly back to Choderlos de Laclos's *Les Liaisons dangereuses*. In *Martereau* (1953), the central figure is a consumptive young man living with his uncle's family and trying to work out the true nature of Martereau, his uncle's associate. This is a simpler novel, and the overlapping layers of narrative effectively demonstrate an all too common problem. But the attempt to achieve a *tachisme* of words—to patch together an immaculate, whole vision while persuading us that we have been given all the facts and have been spared none of the difficulties—produces a prose-style remarkably uneven and erratic. *L'Ère du soupçon* (1956) supplies a useful phrase with which to typify Sarraute and her time. It is not to be wondered at if younger French novelists, wearied of the interior flux and exasperated with the piecing-together of psychic clues, have gone to the other extreme and devised crossword-puzzle novels in which all the clues are material and the mind's swirling pool is boarded over, like a well, and then conspicuously avoided.

Another novelist, Michel Bernard, does his best to stimulate and intensify 'psychological movements while they are forming' by writing long, sensuous interior monologues (*La Plage*, 1960; *La Mise à nu*, 1961) while Alfred Kern, in *Le Bonheur fragile* (1960), contrasts mental mercury with the world of objects which, in fact, is never seen plain, and about which we know nothing when it is unperceived.

A good many of these experimental novels look back to, or at least evoke, André Breton's *Nadja* (1928). Surrealism has become sub-realism, and actuality something of one's own creation. The extremist formulation of this pursuit is perhaps André Gorz's *Le Traître* (1958) in which a young refugee from the Nazis (Gorz himself) writes a novel in order to define himself and, in fact, saves himself and his sanity by resorting to philosophical jargon. Sartre's lively preface speaks of this novel as a soliloquy swollen with retrospective particulars; and it is just that—a slow-motion record of a young man who, rootless and neurotic, envies the person who merely by filling out questionnaires can create for himself 'an objective identity . . . that is perfectly adapted to an anonymous order'. The record of these painful maieutics upon the self is curiously moving and brilliantly phrased. Maurice Blanchot has spoken of the therapeutic worth of writing which 'forces the listener to detach himself from his own present in order to arrive at a self which does not yet exist'. Such appears to be the effect, even if unintended, of many '*anti-romans*', meta-novels and experimental pieces of fiction. One of the noblest achievements so far is André Schwarz-Bart's *Le Dernier des justes* which won the Prix Goncourt in 1959. This attempt to imply the multitude in the individual, and *vice versa*, through an image of Auschwitz, and a Jewish succession of 'Just Men' from twelfth-century York to our own time, is both moving and lyrical—too resolutely lyrical, perhaps. A mock-deprecatory Yiddish humour enlivens and tempers the narrative: 'A few freight trains, a few engineers, a few chemists got the better of that old scapegoat, the Jewish people of Poland.' Ernie Levy, the last of the just men (if God does *not*, after all, exist), volunteers to go to Auschwitz and so gives the wheel its last turn. He thus, of course, as Gorz would say, defines himself.

It remains to be said that, alongside this fertile experimentation, standard types of novel survive by their own lights. Marcel Aymé and Gabriel Chevallier contrive adroit misalliances of the whimsically grotesque and the earthily commonplace. Roger Vailland, who edited *Laclos par lui-même* (1953), creates an old-fashioned lucid sensualist of his own in Don Cesare, the country nobleman in *La Loi* (1957), a kind of ritualistic detective story set in Italy. Françoise Mallet-Joris showed her insight into clashing personalities in *Le Rempart des béguines* (1951) and *La Chambre rouge* (1955), both of them—in Saint-Simon's words—'*tout serre, substantiel, au fait, au but*'. The latter novel prompts the thought that she writes best when cruelty is about; and *Les Mensonges* (1956) centres on an elderly brewer preyed upon, for what he has and for what he will bequeath, by a squabbling and callous family. The characterization stops carefully short of hyperbole; portraying humans yet suggesting also that their familial bond is lycanthropic. Georges Simenon has created his own mythology of the *quartier louche* in a prose style that shows a suspenseful, efficient lack of variety. Romain Gary—after the brittle, obtrusively corrupt vaudeville of *Les Couleurs du jour* (1952), set in the South of France—turned to African elephants for another, weirdly touching, attack on materialism in *Les Racines du ciel* (1956): Morel, after sustaining himself in a concentration camp with the thought of wild elephant herds, goes off to protect them.

But Gary is sometimes too preposterous (especially in trying to create Faustian heroes) and usually too disjointed (as if the novel were a shooting script first). The carefully machined products of Pierre Boulle (*Le Pont de la rivière Kwai*, 1958), Jean Hougron (*La Terre du barbare*, 1958), the Boileau-Narcejac combination (*L'Ingénieur aimait trop les chiffres*, 1958) and Michel Arnaud (*Le Salaire de la peur*, 1950) cannot compete with the work of Pierre Gascar, brilliant in its evocations of atmosphere and in suggesting claustrophobia (*Les Bêtes, Le Temps des morts*, 1954). Gascar's *Soleils* (1960) comprises four *récits* set, respectively, in Ethiopia, Spain, Italy and the Midi. The sun dominates the lives of the Sierra Nevada cliff-dwellers, the quarry-workers in the Italian labour-camp, the hunters in the Ethiopian forest and the blacksmith's son who (as if in Giono) takes off with the baker's wife. Gascar is at his best when he writes Norman Lewis reportage, at his worst when urging allegories at the expense of surfaces.

Sizeable projects abound, from Elsa Triolet's *L'Age de nylon* (1959) and Henri Troyat's *Les Semailles et les moissons* (1953–8) to Maurice Druon's lavish, sometimes ornately callous, historical series *Les Rois maudits* (1955–9), A. Soubiran's *Les Hommes en blanc* (1947–58) and Paul Vialar's *La Chasse aux hommes* (1952–3). Among individual novels of intrinsic or incidental interest the following should be named: Aragon's religious epic, *La Semaine sainte* (1958), Jean Dutourd's *Les Taxis de la Marne* (1956), André Dhôtel's *Le Pays où l'on n'arrive jamais* (1956), Roger Peyrefitte's Georges de Sarre novels—*Les Amabassades* (1951), *Les Amitiés particulières* (1944), *Les Amitiés singulières* (1949) and *Jeunes Proies* (1956), Raymond Queneau's *Zazie dans le métro* (1959)—which should be read in conjunction with *Exercices du style* (1947), Christiane Rochefort's *Le Repos du guerrier* (1958), Vercors's *Le Silence de la mer* (1944), Marguerite Yourcenar's *Memoires d'Hadrien* (1951), and, on Algeria and military service, Jean-Jacques Servan-Schreiber's *Lieutenant en Algérie* (1957)—between reportage and fiction, Micheline Maurel's account of a women's concentration-camp, *Un Camp très ordinaire* (1957) and Armand Lanoux's *Le Commandant Watrin* (1956).

A few ambitious but not always successful experiments with style merit note here. Francis Pollini's *La Nuit* (1960) deals with the brain-washing of American prisoners taken in Korea. One character, Marty, tries to remain independent of both Chinese and his fellows; and his difficult position is cleverly involved in a style that is a maze of recollections, actions, unidentified speeches and built-in parodies. Claire Sainte-Soline's *La Mort de Benjamin* (1957) shows how a dying man's need for the sister with whom he has quarrelled produces, between their reconciliation and his death, a sacrificial rebirth of spirit which initiates her spiritual death. A morbid and sombre novel, it is written in scrupulously reverberating prose and is an advance in subtlety over Mme Sainte-Soline's first novel, *Le Dimanche des rameaux* (1952), which explored dead lives' resonances in an abandoned house. Jean Cayrol specializes in mood, atmosphere and dream, all of which thickens up his style considerably without, however, clogging seemingly allegorical actions. *Le Démenagement* (1956) is his most articulate work so far. Just as articulate in its Falstaffian way is Alfred Kern's *Le Clown* (1957), in which Hans Schmetterling, the universal clown, takes over the mind of the narrator, a philosophizing polymath. The resulting mixture of exorcizing grotesquerie and satirical casuistry is breathtaking, but eventually—because the book goes on too long—wearisome. 'I find life,' shouts the incubus clown, 'unbearable and I perform in order to return all the shit I've taken.' Dada merges here into the nihilism of the *chosistes*. Learning is futile; it merely re-proves our essential ignorance of what matters.

So far the younger novelists have been, for the most part, remote from the kind of political interest voiced by Camus, Malraux, Sartre and Aragon, and (from the other wing) Céline and Pierre-Eugène Drieu La Rochelle (1893–1945). Drieu, ever unfixed in his beliefs, was claimed at different times as an adherent by Communism, surrealism and the Action Française. Essentially a dabbler, he tried Catholic mysticism as a salve for nihilism, but eventually came out for action and violence. He killed himself in 1945. His novels, from the semi-autobiographical *État-Civil* (1921) and *Le Jeune Européen* (1927) to *L'Homme couvert de femmes* (1925), *Le Feu follet* (1931) and *Gilles* (1939), exemplify a sense of futility which the *chosistes* display less frantically. The hero of *Gilles* finds fulfilment in fighting for Franco, whereas the *chosistes* fulfil themselves by cataloguing. Trifling with footling would be too harsh a description of *chosisme*, but compared even with the lurid monotony of Drieu it looks pale and out of touch with vital humanity. So too does their belief that man in general is man in private. But, for the time being, the need to experiment technically is also providing subject-matter that looks new as well as a pre-text for political opinionlessness. Some of what the *chosistes* are doing is exciting and intriguing; so too for a time is any enclosed garden. The most life-enhancing of the young novelists are not *chosistes* at all: these are Nathalie Sarraute ('we see how dan-gerous it is for writers to protect themselves from impure contacts'), Butor, Gorz and Schwarz-Bart. There are a few signs of something politically conscientious coming through: the common soldier's view of the North African war (like the view which Benjamin, Barbusse and Dorgelès gave of the First World War) emerges in *Le Dossier de Jean Muller*, the reflections of a young conscript eventually killed in ambush, and (in the April 1957 issue of *Esprit*) Robert Bonnaud's 'La Paix des Nementchas'. The anti-novel, so called, is in some ways as much anti-despotism as anti-tradition, and has something in common with the work of young novelists in Spain.

But, Article 30 of the Code de Procédure Criminelle and the Ordonnance of 13 February 1960 notwithstanding, and despite the seizure of books and the banning in France of such films as Jean-Luc Godard's *Le Petit Soldat* (in which Algerians torture French agents in Switzerland), the literature of protest continues. Maurice Maschino in *Le Refus* justifies his decision, after having been an elementary-school teacher in Morocco, not to join the army. Noel Favrelière's *Le Désert à l'aube* describes in lyrical, haunting prose how Favrelière, having done his national service in Algeria, was recalled as a paratroop sergeant. Put in charge of a condemned man due for execution the following day, he de-serted, taking the man with him. From then on he lived with the troops of the Algerian Liberation Army before going to Tunisia and America. This document, which reads like a novel, has much in common with the stories in Camus's *L'Exil et le royaume* and also, of course, with Camus's attitude to Algeria. At the opposite pole from the novels of Robbe-Grillet, it finds in the facts of the present Algerian horror the violence which Robbe-Grillet, for one, incorporates, although cryptically and abstractedly, into his own work. If we add the oblique to the direct, we find among French intellectuals a disquiet bound to predominate as discord goes on and literary experimentation begins to lose its glamour.

<h1 style="text-align:center">VII</h1>

So the French novel survives. It has already survived Symbolism, the arguing *fleuve*-novelists such as Rolland, Romains and du Gard, the cult of Gidean, Cocteauish thinness, and it is even surviving such theorists as André Gorz. Romantic influence is on the wane, and the exemplars now are not Bernanos, Céline, Giono and Malraux; not even Camus and Sartre, but Constant, Laclos, Sade, Rétif de la Bretonne and, above all, Stendhal and Radiguet. The dry and the laconic are in vogue. The *récit* survives, more muted and terse than ever: there is plenty of bit and snaffle but little horse. *Le Grand Dadais* (1958), by Bertrand Poirot-Delpech, and Marguerite Duras's *Moderato Cantabile* are typical. Then there is the picaresque tradition, re-fired by Giono and Aragon and taken up by Roger Nimier and Romain Gary, but much less acerb and satirical than the British version of the same thing. And Camus's absurd universe has been developed into the anti-metaphysical, anti-psychological *nouveau roman* which specializes in the inanimateness of the inanimate compared with man. The 'new novel' takes the robustness of the Americans and makes an unanalytical fetish of it: what counts is the robustness of the world of things, noted by a powerful lens slowly panning. The desert, for instance, in Claude Ollier's *La Mise-en-scène* (1958) becomes a minutely itemized counterpart to the main character's fluctuating suspicions as he travels across the North African sands.

In Claude Simon's *L'Herbe* (1958) the retrospections of the several characters are held together not by any narrative thread but by viscosity of style. Faulkner still influences the French novel, and it is his influence, if anything, which will keep it from degenerating into a gritty catalogue. Nathalie Sarraute, Simon Michel Butor and André Schwarz-Bart all owe a great deal to his bizarre example, as well as to Proust; and such less well-known novelists as Jean Cayrol, Jean Lagrolet, Robert Pinget, Kateb

Yacine, Françoise de Ligneris, Noelle Loriot, Jacques Howlett, Bernard Pingaud and Philippe Sollers take what life they have from him, and not from any theory evolved by botanists and engineers turned literateurs.

On the one hand, then, a stringency of careful lists; on the other, slow verbal lava, with, on both sides, narrative ranking low but character reappearing in a Stendhalian manner. Where the English novelists experiment little, dive elatedly into farce to escape the anger- or nostalgia-provoking face of modern Britain, and eschew metaphysics, the French experiment with new disciplines, still discovering the new liberties to be copied from Faulkner, yet discovering too the limits of art and, after the contrasting examples of Proust and Malraux, avoiding both psychology and metaphysics.

I think we can say that the English are less concerned with method and medium than the French, who above all are trying to keep the novel from being didactic. Durrell is more French than English; and Golding evokes Camus and Malraux, as does Greene. The English are more disposed to get to grips with the social pattern, and to make something sardonic or farcical out of it; the French have society much less in focus, and their eyes on the nature of man in general. The Americans, as I mean to show, keep anatomizing their society as well as reviewing the facts of human nature. The English novel still owes little to the American and even less to the French, from which it learned a great deal in the first decade of the century, and which still revives in such a Proustian novel as Richard Hughes's *The Fox in the Attic* (1962), the first volume of yet another projected panoptic design, to be called in a most un-English way 'The Human Predicament'.

The English novelist of today, stuck in a robust new provincialism, reminds us that, even by 1910, many of the best writers in English came from the periphery—Yeats, Synge, Joyce, Pound, Eliot, and that some of the most accomplished novelists writing in English are West Indians and South Africans. The outsiders are moving in. And, although the French novel is being given new exercises to do by writers trained in or influenced by other disciplines than the literary, the collapse of the French empire is beginning to find its way, through autobiography and documentary, into the work of the least timid writers. English and French contemporary practice coincide only to the extent that noncommittal picaresque does with society what the *chosistes* do with the world of objects. It is possible that the quest for new methods will lead to new subject-matter or *vice versa*; for many twentieth-century novelists have already treated the one as if it were the other, and simple definitions of 'the novel' have disappeared in the process.